LIGE OF THE BLACK WALNUT TREE

Growing Up Black in Southern Appalachia

by

Mary Othella Burnette

CONTENTS

FIRST LETTER TO ELIJAH

Route 1, Box 74

Black Mountain

North Carolina

December 8, 1941

Dear Cousin Elijah,

Sometimes, Cousin Elijah, when a member of the clan died very young, the old people stopped talking about them, except when they mentioned how many members were in a certain family. I don't have the date that you left us, but I know you must have been gone a very, very long time. No one other than Papa ever spoke of you. He would never let us forget. He always called you "Lige," and that's why your name is in the title of my book, Lige of the Black Walnut Tree.

The walnut tree was special to me. I played under its branches, but I never tried to climb that tree. It seems there was an unwritten law about protecting the Black Walnut Tree. Maybe it was passed down from another generation to mine. My brothers wouldn't climb it, either. The tree was much younger when you were a boy and the limbs, I guess, not so brittle.

A sturdy but old brown frame three room bungalow with a loft stood a few feet north of the tree. While that house lasted, the mantle above the fireplace held the photograph of a man who resembled your sister Rena, but I never knew who he was. In those days I took everything for granted, believing nothing would ever change. I didn't realize that only two members of the last generation of former slaves, my grandmother Mary and her uncle John were still living.

If only I had begun to ask questions and take notes back, then. I'm grateful for all that I do remember and some of it is included in the pages of this book.

What I don't know, I don't know, and I have acknowledged that. It is an awful deed to deceive members of a younger generation. For then they will believe nothing else even if it is shown to them in black and white. I have so many questions about my great grandparents' and their generation, but I've started too late. If only I had known what to ask when I was young. I wonder whether Aunt Martha ever talked about what it was like when she, Aunt Phoebe, Uncle Hardy, Uncle Sam and my grandfather Squire were slaves, and what they did when they heard they were free.

Grandpa Squire, a small man whom Papa said he could lift on the palm of his hand, told my mother that the slave master was not a brutal man. Working in the fields, Grandpa would tell the slave master when he felt sick and that man would give him a plug of tobacco and tell him to go and sit under a tree. After freedom, I heard, Aunt Phoebe got a job at a hotel where she earned ten dollars a month. With so little money to live on, she still managed to buy two acres of land that cost her two months' wages. Then when she lost her eyesight and couldn't work anymore, she went to live with Papa and Mama.

I imagine your mother got a job and bought the land the black walnut tree stood on, or maybe her husband, your father, James Stepp, helped her buy the land. In those days land inherited or purchased by a woman was hers alone and her husband couldn't lay claim to it. But for us, your land was Burnette land and the tree belonged to the clan. The Burnette's shared everything they owned. Your mother, Aunt Mattie, Uncle Hardy and Aunt Phoebe bought adjoining plots of land; Uncle Sam's lot was farther west on Cragmont Road. All of them stayed in Black Mountain as long as they lived. Grandpa Squire and Uncle George went to West Virginia to work in the coal mines and neither of them came back alive.

In the wonderful years of my childhood, my family was all of my relatives and many of the people of the neighborhood were like exteded family, too. If only I had realized that I was living in the last days of the old Black community and had kept a diary of what I saw and experienced. If only you or my father could have written a book for us. What a marvelous history we would have inherited.

I know there were only two Burnette-Stepp males of your generation. You, born before 1880, and Papa, born in 1881. Since I know so little about you, I have written mostly about Papa in my book. But your name will stand in the title, Lige of the Black Walnut Tree, because it really was your tree.

Sincerely,
Your cousin Othella

P.S. Yesterday was Sunday, December Seventh, 1941. Last night we were listening to the radio when President Franklin Delano Roosevelt announced the bombing of Pearl Harbor. Then he declared war on Japan and Germany. My schoolmates and I were so scared this morning when we went to school. One of our Stepp cousins, Edgar, asked the third-grade teacher whether the Germans were going to get us, and Mrs. Jones didn't say "No." I sure hope they can't find us in these mountains. Papa's going to be an air raid warden. When we have an air raid, the siren will go off uptown. Papa will take his lantern or flashlight and go around to warn the neighbors to turn off their lights. They will. Nobody will complain about having to obey any laws so America can win the war.

Old Black Walnut Tree at front of Mattie Burnette Stepp property on ragmont Road died after the last owner passed away. Huge daughter tree (left knotted trunk, roots exposed) sprang up and stands closer to the road.

Photo by Debora Hamilton Palmer

THE BLACK WALNUT TREE

O Marvelous Tree,
light of childhood memory,
pleasure of old age imagery, how majestically
you grow. Your lofty boughs spread softly o'er us then,
now pitifully bend on towards wood and field, once our own
land, just as when I was too young to understand how not it,
nor we, nor you would always be. Heartily you stretched those sturdy
limbs o'er precious soil we dearly loved, to cast your ripe and
verdant fruit, quickly turning golden brown to black, into our
gleeful hands. Our late apology, Majestic Tree, gorgeous still
but ever lonely. Never once did we, so often gathered at your
feet, look up to greet the tree, itself, to grasp your gnarled
and blemished waist, to clutch it to our own eager breasts.
When did we ever smile up, up into your tireless face, or utter
one grateful sound to you? How carelessly our childish feet
trampled o'er your mighty roots extended east to west, to
bravely press against impending signs of change. We were too young, too
blind, too sure of time to see. So many years you blessed
the grassy plain on which we played, a marked boundary
of the place, a space that stayed us by day, by night, where
silent walls once well-known witnessed death and birth,
a child born with suffocating veil upon its face who
lived and lives still. You so staid of old paternal grounds,
so oblivious to all changes found on paper deeds, on
Wills or purchased by new bill of sale: How long will
you stay strong, uplifting this same proud earth,
knowing ought of
whence or what awaits
it, or they, or us or
even what your own
fate another hundred
years hence may bring. Your
knotted trunk still straight,
your sable walnut heart ajar,
waits for all who pass along that gray
and golden artery, that road beneath your feet.

Your branches aging, reaching west and north and east, your heaviness sinking sturdily
against that well-travelled road below. Stand on, O Gallant Tree. Know you are not the first in
this place to grow. Watch! Live on and see your seeds spring forth and flourish on more distant
soil where never you intended them to sow

ACKNOWLEDGEMENTS

In *Lige of the Black Walnut Tree*, neither segregation,racial injustice, nor systemic racism occurs as a theme.

But these stories, mainly depicting life within a typical early 20th century African American family living in a unique mountain town that boasts of fewer than 9,000 residents today, do not shy away from the inevitable: For with few exceptions, the place where each story begins and ends is Black Mountain, North Carolina.

Ideally these stories may be viewed as a bouquet. In even the most gorgeous floral arrangement, the beauty of it is formed by what each sprig of foliage or baby breath contributes to the aster or rose. And even the loveliest rose bears a thorn.

This book, therefore, describes life as we lived it. And we lived it with the unfaltering hope for a better life in a country and under a government whose laws -- even while allowing and too often seemingly condoning the opposite, consistently promised equality, justice, and earned prosperity for all, regardless of race, creed or color.

My great grandparents and grandparents must have held on to that promise; if not, why would news of "the Surrender" have meant anything to them? Papa said the promise would come true, and I still believe what he said, and I have hope these stories come from my heart. But to all who have helped with this work, especially to my children who researched census records, saved and transferred files and photos during my several moves from state to state, and waited patiently for those files to rise into a real book, I say, 'Thank you.'

To Dr. Bernard Cooke who listened, asked questions and urged me to continue writing, Thank you.

To that highly diversified and welcoming reading group at Tarzana, Library, in the San Fernando Valley, I say sincerely, 'Your comments, and your concerns were helpful.' Thank you.

To the restaurant managers at Norm's who urged waitresses to keep the fresh coffee flowing while I sat writing long after y breakfast or lunch had been served, I'm grateful for your thoughtfulness. Thank you.

To those silent restaurant patrons who saw me writing and secretly asked for my check, I say 'Thank you for your kindness.

To Tara Lingeman who, like the old midwife character in my book, showed up when the time had arrived for this manuscript to be delivered, I can truthfully say, 'It would still be in gestation if not for your computer skills and agentive savvy. You have brought this work to life:' Thank you!

And to my daughter-in-law, Julie Gibney Logan who, like my childhood neighbor that regularly ran to town for the doctor, I say 'Thank you for telling Tara I needed help to deliver a work whose time had come.'

Orchids to all of you!

FOR MY CHILDREN

LIGE OF THE BLACK WALNUT TREE

For YOU, my children, Debora, Jill, George, Gordon, and Gregory

The past is an elusive ghost. YOU may visit the places
he's frequented, but YOU will not see him.
YOU may see the signs he's left behind, but YOU will be blind to their
meaning because you knew nothing of his existence
when he was more than a symbol of the past.
I was there.
That's why I have written this book for you.
Mom

PREFACE: STORIES OF THE
ORAL TRADITION

Part I. Prohibited Literacy & the African American Oral Tradition

Recently an herbalist in Asheville, NC, seeking information about my paternal grandmother, Mary Stepp Burnette Hayden, who was a native mountain midwife and herbalist, wondered why documentation of the lives of 18th and 19th century Black residents of the mountains was practically nonexistent.

Her contact at Swannanoa Valley Museum & History had referred her to a local newspaper article[1] that featured my grandmother's work and suggested that she call me for more
information.

I myself have wondered why so little has been written by us particularly; but the herbalist's question focused on the 18th and 19th centuries. My answer delves into two major conditions
directly affecting the lack of written sources of information produced by African Americans during the 1700s and 1800s. A third cause exists for the lack of information about Black mountaineers published by European Americans.

I am not a historian. But I had paternal great grandparents who were brought into the Swannanoa Valley as slaves during the late 1700s and early 1800s. They had children, my grandparents, who were born on slave plantations in the Black Mountain-North Fork area during the mid-1800s. And given what I have read about slavery in general, I can offer a logical reason for African Americans' not writing anything during that era. I will center this narrative around my grandmother who was the subject of the herbalist's question.

But putting last things first, generally non-African Americans who wrote about early mountain residents simply did not write about African Americans in general. This exclusion seems to have set the stage for defining a mountaineer only as a "hillbilly," a poor, uneducated, rural American of European descent. And this distorted characterization of a mountaineer has been extended by 20th century comic strips and other media. Not all mountaineers are hillbillies. Most likely, to support the warped regional propaganda, Black mountaineers simply could not exist, although we've been in the Southern Appalachians of Western North Carolina around three hundred years or more.

Like millions of other American slaves in many parts of the Deep South, my grandmother who came to be known as Aunt Mary Hayden, along with her older sister Margaret Stepp, and their mother Hannah Stepp, was not freed until after the Civil War ended, an event my paternal grandfather Squire Jones Burnette (1849 - 1914) remembered as "the Surrender". And I believe it is common knowledge that enslaved men, women, and children customarily were not permitted to learn to read or to write.

Until 1865, then, most Black people in the mountains were enslaved. Census records indicate that by 1880, at least 24 African American families had settled in the Black Mountain-North Fork area, and 15 of those 24 families were my blood relatives [see "A History of Black Mountain and It's People" (page 25)

[Appendix B footnote 2].

But even considering the new hardships facing my free fore parents, being released from the inhuman conditions of enslavement no doubt caused their spirits to rejoice. On the other hand, having to face a hostile unknown world of independence empty handed was not a cause for celebration.

I have never heard of any one of my fore-parents mentioning or participating in a freedom celebration. I have never heard of one at all. This is not to say they were not overjoyed to be free.

But whatever joy they had must have been mingled with the sadness of having left those plantations penniless and with only the hand-me-downs on their backs. In that state, they were hard pressed to lay hands on the basic necessities for survival.

They needed to find a place to live, to buy a piece of land and build a house on it as soon as they could, and then to make time-after a long day's work that paid, in one case, around two dollars a week—to raise crops of vegetables (often preserved by drying) in order to keep food on the table year round.

Faced with such tremendous challenge and granted their limited (if any) ability to read or write, they could hardly be expected to produce written accounts of their personal struggles, or of their service to the community which the midwife-herbalist faithfully gave. Even late 19th century Black residents had no leisure time or means to write and publish stories.

These freedmen had only slightly elevated their condition and status. Despite the miserable and disastrous conditions under which they were transported to these shores, our ancestors had not arrived here from Africa without survival skills; and that knowledge iron-forged into skills required on the plantation was passed down when possible from generation to generation through hands-on household duties or field labor.

In early childhood, my mother once said to me "Every one of the Burnette's (my grandfather and his siblings -- the last generation born into slavery) had a trade."

She didn't need to add, "And if you don't want to follow in their footsteps and work your fingers to the bone, scrimping and scraping to keep body and soul together, you'd better learn your trade in the schoolhouse."

I understood "schoolhouse" to mean 'Get a good education so you can earn enough money for you to live well.'

"Trade" meant, for example, a skill in carpentry, furniture making, blacksmithy, rock facing and brick laying, (all of which was passed down to my father); for women it meant cooking, baking, fine hand sewing, and doing laundry. These skills were in demand in hotels and in and around the nice homes in town. Freed men and women knew how to work, but they were not fairly rewarded for their labor.

At the same time, poor rural White families and Black families relied heavily on the knowledge of home-trained midwives and "herb doctors" who gathered, and cured native plants to make tonics, liniments, salves, and poultices to treat common ailments and ills. These life preserving occupations, midwifery and medicine making, were dominated by women like my grandmother and her mother who were often compensated by in-kind—not in cash, my grandmother said, and sometimes not at all.

Altogether Hannah Stepp (circa 1828 - 1897) and her younger daughter Mary Hayden (1858 - 1956) "caught babies" and treated the sick of poverty-stricken families in the Swannanoa Valley, regardless of race, for well over one hundred years. These women, along with other members of their race, did not lack the ability to communicate in whatever dialect or register of English they had learned on those plantations. They did not lack the ability to remember anything that was read to them, especially stories and verses from the Old Testament, (when they were allowed to go to church [2] nor would they forget what they had heard about members of their families, particularly of those who had passed on, whether those deaths occurred naturally or by tragic accident.

Part II. The Importance of Oral Tradition in Family History

While neither fatal accident nor murder was a stranger to the Burnettes, one of the oldest known family tragedies dating back to 1844 with its mysterious legend, involved a maternal great grandfather, Lonnie Mills, a slave trustee, who vanished while on his way to or from the home of his Cherokee spouse (another midwife) and their free Black children. That, I was told, happened when his youngest child, my grandfather, George Payne (1838 - 1927) was only six years old and another child (Lonnie Jr) was on the way.

Part III. Oral Tradition in Action

See Appendix B

Living concurrently under both vindictive racial oppression and within the buffered protection of close-knit community relations had taught my fore parents that a seemingly innocent word caught by the wrong ear and twisted by a malicious tongue could cause serious racial trouble, and that saying something negative about a neighbor could lead to unfavorable circumstances. A good neighbor was a valuable asset, especially as these families could not afford fire, burial, or health insurance. Offenses were to be carefully avoided. Consequently, my fore parents learned what was safe to repeat, how to say it, and whether to mention it at all during anyone's lifetime or afterwards. Often, they kept silent long after a real threat had passed. For that reason, much valuable family
history has literally been buried in silence. What was handed down to me as well as what I have observed has shaped my
personal knowledge of the African American oral tradition. That includes not only family history, but also other genres, such as fables, rhymes, songs, ghost stories, peculiar sayings and beliefs, all lending themselves to that style of reserving information without the use of paper and pen.

Hopefully for my children, for their children, their cousins and future generations, for others reading for pleasure, and for readers like the herbalist who was earnestly seeking information about native mountain African Americans of years past for educational purposes, the stories in this collection will be informative, interesting, and useful. For the oral tradition has a universal weakness: whatever is not written down is eventually forgotten and taken to the grave.

What an oral tradition narrator does by habit is to take a singular event and connect it to something of broader significance, to reveal its importance to life in general. A skillful reader does the same in comprehending, although he may not be inclined to associate oral tradition skills with literacy. Both literacy and oral tradition require comprehensive skill and critical thinking.

Over the years, by studying census records, consulting Cherokee historian in Oklahoma, and viewing documents retrieved from archives, I have been disappointed by the absence of truth in certain stories passed down to me. Still, I have learned that when I understood the period of history in which an event was said to have occurred, even a fictitious account of that event can be meaningful.

Part IV. Practical Use of Fable

As I pieced together what I could find and sized it up with what I already had, I came to realize that right behind the absence of fact stood a reasonable cause for the existence of fable. Sometimes when the situation demanded an explanation, when any reasonable story was better than dead silence, then a believable tale might be created to soothe the pain, to protect youthful ears and shield vulnerable minds from the harshness of truth.

A prime example of such fact-fable duality is the explanation given to my grandfather and his siblings when Great Grandpa Lonnie Mills vanished. His children were told "the Indians ambushed and killed him."

Over 90 years later, the same tale was repeated to me. I also heard of a later story that should have stopped the ambush tale cold in its tracks; but, strangely enough, it appeared to have had no effect on the fable and to have made a strange impression on the believer.

But what was easier--and safer--to live with? The truth with a predictably harmful confrontation with the real culprit, the slave master, who was protected by law, or a wrongful accusation cast upon an imaginary band of homeless Cherokees hiding out in the mountains to avoid the *Trail of Tears*, while delaying their inevitable capture and confinement to a reservation after their native lands had been confiscated.

This answer, too, is puzzling.

Part V. Use of Inspiration in Oral Tradition

An elderly White resident in Asheville, quite possibly a witness, let the cat out of the bag more than half a century after Great Grandpa Lonnie's disappearance.

"Your grandfather, a full-blooded African, was sold on the block," my mother mocked.

The woman had made that remark to my preteen-age mother as if it was absolutely normal, with no question of right or wrong, and therefore completely acceptable that a human being should be sold away from his family.

The statement had been made as if this immoral and injurious act of taking a husband and father with black skin away from his wife and children was really not different from that of selling a stallion away from its colt or vice versa. The justification was merely a natural condition of enslavement due to that man's accident of birth.

Being born in Africa and having black skin bore ample evidence of his moral guilt of an undeniable crime. Even without the determination of a jury or judge, that crime automatically deserved the life sentence of menial servitude recognized by laws conveniently created by the elite of a race of human beings whose skin lacked pigmentation. And by their favorable accident of birth, they believed themselves to be superior to other human beings considered to have been created in a lower state of humanness.

However, some of those others could -- if their skin was of a similar degree of non-pigmentation, eventually rise to a state of equality with their superior brothers; while the man with dark colored skin should be permanently subjected to bondage and equated with an item to be bought and sold for profit as the occasion arose.

I believe that woman's insensitive and chilling remark was so shocking to the child she spoke to that the youngster failed to see the African grandfather sold on the block with the grandfather who vanished and was said to have been killed by Indians.

That's how it sounded to me. It was as if the family man who vanished one night was completely different from the other one, the one systematically reduced to a piece of chattel that was casually sold off to fatten the slave master's pocket, or maybe to halt the creation of a large free Black family: free Black people were unwanted in a slave society.

How else could my mother have held onto the two contradictory stories without connecting the dots?

For oddly enough, from that moment (around 1904) until my mother drew her last breath more than eighty years later, that fact of the slave block sale stood right beside the ambush tale; yet the tale, with no bitterness towards the Cherokees that I could ever sense, stood firm. Moreover, it was never verbally disputed, not even after Great Grandpa Lonnie reappeared in the flesh.

Why? Well, with all of the older generations already somewhere on the other side of the grave, who is to say? But in 1844, who even dreamed that Great Grandpa Lonnie would ever come back, dead or alive?

We might ask, did he know what was going to happen to him? Is he the one who made up the tale about the Indian ambush and told his wife what to tell the children after he was gone? Again, who knows? Anyone who could have answered that question has passed on.

Even the Cherokee historian believed it and attempted to rationalize it. And I believed him because he, the expert, spoke from a cultural standpoint of which I was ignorant; but I accepted his justification for the murder: explaining that this Black man (albeit a slave), enjoyed a modicum of freedom, denied the true heroes of this land, and that he (moreover) was "cutting off the tribe".

I listened, knowing what I did about the social chaos created by the great upheaval of a nation that was split in two--part being marched off to Oklahoma, and the other part rounded up and confined to a reservation in Western North Carolina.

Hadn't members of three generations of Cherokees related to me by blood abandoned their tribal lands, given up their language, taken European names and identified with the races of their spouses, Black or White, to avoid being captured and removed? Great Grandma Sarah Payne surely had. And I have reason to suspect that her father, Joshua Payne, and Joshua's full-blood Cherokee father had done likewise. [See G.W. Payne's 1908 Deposition][3]

But that was before one of Lonnie Mills' great, great, great grandsons (John T. Bradley) discovered a post-bellum copy of the civil law certificate of marriage granted to Great Grandpa Lonnie Mills and Great Grandma Sarah Payne. And that certificate was only one bit of concrete evidence waiting to prove that Great Grandpa Lonnie had not been murdered by the Indians.

Not only had he returned and created written proof that he had remarried his faithful wife, he had also visited his children and had held a grandchild on his lap. And that grandchild (Latha Louise Payne Hamilton, circa 1881 -

1983) had lived to tell her grandchild (Virginia "Ginger" Clarke Garrett) about her great-great grandfather Lonnie's return, and that granddaughter (twice removed) told me what she had been told; and now--after 176 years, I, Lonnie's last surviving great granddaughter, am the one setting the story of his 1844 disappearance into writing.

So, while cautiously and earnestly seeking the facts of family history as we sift through ancestral records and attempt to evaluate what we have received through oral history, we must be careful not to "throw out the baby with the bathwater". Unwritten stories have guided and helped me to make sense of documented family history, which also is not without its flaws.

Part VI. Lige of the Black Walnut Tree

The stories collected in this work are about real people, many of whom are already forgotten — if they were ever known by current residents; and they lived in real places, some also unknown except to me and Wallace Lynch, my parents' oldest grandchild who remembers the land on which his mother, Juanita, grew up. What I know is often interwoven with facts and tales handed down by those who lived long before me. Most of my characters, however, were well known to me; and all accounts presented here are intended to depict the past as I saw it and lived it; that is, the life of a Black child growing up in the foothills of Southern Appalachian mountains.

In this place, the Great Depression left deep scars on the poor of both races until World War II created widespread employment with far better wages and increased many a meager family income through an allotment or some other military benefit.

See G.W. Payne's Deposition following the Preface

It is also the place where the Civil Rights Movement had not yet begun to loosen the grip of Jim Crow and segregation so tightly clamped around our necks. Yet, given that reality, race relations in my home town were considerably milder than those I had heard of in places far deeper South where it was not unusual to read about African Americans, particularly men, being intimidated and lynched.

Most of these stories depict life in my childhood communitywhich has undergone significant socioeconomic and racial change. Oldest members of the 24 original African American families have all died, often leaving their land to be purchased by developers and other individuals who have more money than the original settlers ever saw. The community I once lived in no longer exists, though the old roads are there and maybe one old house on the "Wilse", and Joanna Daugherty's home place remains.

Yet, my memories linger on and are captured in these stories about relatives I have only heard of and others I knew, as well as adorable old neighbors, church members, and teachers I cannot forget.

G.W. PAYNE'S DEPOSITION

Appl. #38405

George W. Payne being first duly sworn, deposes and says:

My name is George W. Payne. I claim Indian blood through my mother. I really don't know what tribe. When my mother told me she did not say what tribe. She said that her father was half Indian and her grandfather was a full Indian. My mother's mother was a white woman. I could not swear as to the tribe. I was born in 1838 in Rutherford Co., N. C. I never was a slave. My grandmother was a white woman, so my mother was a free woman, and therefore I was born free, according to the laws of N. C. and the laws of U. S. I filed an application here because I have been informed that there was no other tribe around where my grandfather came from. I claim through my mother and her father. He came from Halifax Co., Va. His name was Joshua Payne.

<u>George W. Payne</u>

Subscribed and sworn to before me this 18th day of July, 1908 at Asheville, N. C.

<u>Chas. H. Bradley</u>.
Ass't to Special Commissioner,
U. S. Court of Claims

MATERNAL GRANDFATHER

George W. Payne 1838-1927

Scottish Rites Master Mason 1897

George, the son of African slave trustee Lonnie Mills, and his siblings were never enslaved because of their mother Sarah Payne's Cherokee ancestry. George's siblings were Joshua II, Joseph, Thomas, William, Sarah II, and (youngest) Lonnie, Jr. Payne is an assumed surname, not of Cherokee origin.

31

MATERNAL GRANDMOTHER

Frances Freeman Payne 1849-1892

Frances was manumitted from slavery in infancy with her mother Sarah and older siblings, Alfred, Polly and Nancy (twins); younger brother James was born in 1850. After Sarah was freed, she assumed the surname Freeman and gave that last name to her children, rejecting the slave name Wright.

PATERNAL GRANDFATHER

Squire Jones Burnette 1849-1914

Independent Order of Oddfellows (1914 Baptismal Day), Oldest son of Esquire Alexander and Rosanna Burnette recalled being freed with parents and siblings, Phoebe, Hardy, Mattie, and Samuel at "the surrender" in April 1865, when Lee surrendered to Grant. Youngest brother George was born free. The Burnette plantation was located in North Fork/Black Mountain area

PATERNAL GRANDMOTHER

Mary E. Louisa Stepp Burnette Hayden 1858-1956

Mary Hayden remembered hearing the Emancipation Proclamation read at her mother Hannah Stepp's cabin door, Stepp Plantation, North Fork/ Black Mountain area, when she was five years old. Siblings were Margaret Stepp Littlefield, and Easter Stepp (born free). Hannah with Margaret and Mary were possibly not freed until the surrender in April 1865.

PROLOGUE

Less than three years after the Great Depression started, I was getting ready to be born in the foothills of Southern Appalachia, in a little old town known for its tourism.

Poor people working for five to seven dollars a week were hit hard by the depression. Local tubercular hospitals offered a few jobs. So did the hotels, particularly in summer when tourists from areas deeper South flocked to the mountains for relief from the hot weather. A few tourists owned summer cabins there. They needed help, but it was temporary.

For Black families it was a good thing that women living in town, the wives of doctors, lawyers, businessmen, and other women of means, needed help to do their cooking, housekeeping, washing and ironing. Those women gave jobs to domestic workers year-round.

Too often, the men in the hired helps' families-even highly skilled carpenters, brick masons, rock facers, mechanics and blacksmiths, along with ditch diggers and day laborers--did not have work, not until the WPA sent special programs to our town. And those projects were not permanent sources of work, either.

Like most rural residents in Black Mountain, even the poorest of Black families owned a little land. In spite of having no work, they would continue to send their children to school if they had shoes to wear. Coats could be passed down from child to child and other clothing could be made by hand. They would also continue to put food on their tables, if only they could get their hands on enough money to buy seeds and a bit of fertilizer for their favorite crops, corn, beans, tomatoes, onions, and a little okra, (pronounced as if the final vowel were I.)

But for a Black man like Papa, even owning a little land could be used as an excuse for denying employment.

Still, I was going to born. Fortunately for my family, my grandmother of seventy-three years was a seasoned midwife, having been trained by the old Stepp plantation midwife, her own mother. With that blessing, my parents had two fewer reasons to be concerned about my birth: 1) No doctor bill would follow: midwives, not medical doctors, delivered babies for poor families and 2) Granny Hayden knew just when to show up. Anyway, neither my family nor any other African American family we knew had a telephone.

Shortly after I was born, Granny said, I startled her and my father by opening my eyes, turning my head, and looking around the room. Apparently, that was not a behavior expected of a newborn.

In the fall of my sixth year, I went off to a segregated school where I received my first and only childhood vaccination, a shot in the upper left arm for smallpox. The scar is still with me, and so are the memories of that little four-room building made of river rock, with its three classrooms and three teachers for seven grades. One of those teachers was always the principal.

However, lacking in modern conveniences, inside restrooms and central heating, Clear View Grammar was a symbol of hope: education was the only means of escaping poverty, a way to prepare for service to the community. Through religion our community upheld the basic institution, the home. People lived as they wished but they understood the meaning of morality. Three other institutions were also functional, religious, and cultural: one Methodist and one Baptist chapel, both erected by the last generation of slaves, and a tiny school provided by the county. One other institution stood by the road. It was the home base of the Prince Hall Masons and Eastern Stars, with an upper floor reserved exclusively for secret society activities and a main floor used for special community affairs.

For me, as a child, school was very important. It was the way out and up. And

I loved learning. My first and second grade teacher was not like the motherly kindergarten teachers I had left behind. But she was instrumental in my learning an invaluable lesson. I describe that experience in "Miss Eula."

For Black teachers, being segregated meant not only being deprived of modern facilities, it also meant having to teach grade level subjects without adequate supplies, especially textbooks. But here's the advantage. Our teachers were not hampered by direct curricular supervision. As thoroughly dedicated workers, loyal to their calling, believing that education was a preparation for service to less fortunate others, our teachers used their academic freedom to introduce skills that were far beyond grade level. Consequently, my last elementary school teacher, a young man with no prior experience, being challenged to deliver all state required subjects to his 5th, 6th, and 7th grade students seated in the same room, started preparing us 5th graders for college.

Although he taught with a book, when he had one, in one hand and a leather strap in the other, I idolized him. It was not cruelty but caring he represented to me. A few male students left school and never returned. They found work in a local factory.

But I understood when my teacher said, in frustration, "You are Black, you have to get this!"

He said that one day while teaching English. My home language was South Midland Mountain. I didn't know its name back then, but I knew I didn't speak standard English. I didn't know any other way to speak. And I knew that what I heard spoken by people coming home to visit from "up North," places so many families fled to for work, well that language didn't sound right either. I understood why Mr. James taught English as a second language to native mountaineers. I'm grateful for that advantage, so grateful that I've devoted an entire chapter to "The Teacher Who Made a Difference."

In those days, the county didn't provide a dependable school bus for Black students. To prevent me from having to walk almost a mile to the main highway in rain, sleet or snow, to wait for a dilapidated school bus that might not show up, and if it did, to sit in an unheated vehicle that sometimes broke down miles from the middle school or high school sixteen miles away, my parents began sending me to live with relatives in other states. From their homes I could walk to school. These moves improved my attendance and enabled me to complete the courses I needed for college, but they undermined my sociocultural development. Every year I was a new student somewhere. Until my senior year in high school, I didn't get selected for a single school-wide activity. When family finances improved during World War II, I was able to attend a small private school for girls near home. I graduated with honors from Allen High and won a scholarship to Bennett College where I enrolled with the intention of becoming a premed student.

My best teacher and role model had been a premed student who had left school because he lacked the finances to complete his studies. He became a great teacher and helped many students.

I did well at Bennett, but more than one bad decision prevented me from continuing my education until I was older, wiser and much farther away. Living in Northern California, I realized that working as an insurance clerk was not what I wanted.

On my lunch break one day, I stopped by the campus of San Francisco State College. I took off my shoes and stepped on the grass. At that moment I decided to risk everything and go back to school full time. Taking all the grants and federal loans available and working part time, I finished my three remaining undergraduate years in two years, all the while remaining on the Dean's List. The following year I completed the necessary coursework for a master's degree in English, just in time to accept a teaching position in Washington, DC.

At the nation's first land grant, open admissions college, a school for the poor, envisioned by George Washington, signed into law by Abraham Lincoln,

I was in an ideal environment to develop my thesis study for the final paper, "Teaching Black Studies Through Language Arts."

Eventually I returned to California and was teaching part time at California State University, Los Angeles, when I saw an advertisement for high school teachers of English. For nearly twenty years, I taught regular and developmental English for the Los Angeles Unified School District. I was hired at a time when laws were becoming stricter, old teaching credentials were expiring, many veteran teachers were facing a new dilemma: pass the basic skills test or find work in another field; and state academic learning standards were rising higher and higher.

That was a great opportunity for academic development. Teachers willing to study and keep abreast of the new standards and methodologies received their regular salaries while attending unlimited hours of relevant seminars and workshops. Substitute teachers were paid to maintain our classes and to follow our lesson plans. It was also a time to prepare for the community service which Clear View, my little elementary school in the mountains had taught me to seek.

Early one morning after I retired from teaching, I was awakened by the realization that I was an elderly member of a vanishing society, the Southern Appalachian African American who stood between the remnants of that last generation of slaves and my children's generation. They had the right to know about the worlds their great grandparents and grandparents lived in, and they should be able to hear it from someone who had firsthand knowledge about those eras. I knew of only one book narrated by a Black mountaineer, and it dealt with assistance to coal miners in West Virginia.

As often happened during visits with one of my medical doctor's, we found time to talk about my family history. On one occasion, the doctor said, "Do you know how incredible it is (for me) to know someone who has actually known a slave," I hadn't thought about it. But her remark may well have ignited the spark that urged me to write this book.

I realized that my own children could not imagine what my life had been like. They had been born in a different time. Yes, my three oldest children went to a segregated elementary school, the last one in our hometown. But their modern building was equipped with running hot and cold water, with toilets not only for girls and boys, but also separate toilets for faculty and central heating; and their school had a cafeteria with a steam table, and an auditorium with a stage for school-wide functions.

My school had been a four-room building with three classrooms and a fourth room, called the cloakroom. It had coat hooks on the north wall; on the west wall, a single drinking faucet was attached to a wide basin below a small dirty window. I seem to remember a cold-water faucet for hand washing but no fixtures for soap or paper towels. On the south wall a door opened to a coal cellar that supplied our tall potbelly classroom heaters, managed by our teachers. We entered that room from the door on the east, and girls were never sent to the cellar for coal.

My children did not face the indignity of riding segregated buses, of having to pay the same fare as White passengers but being forced by Jim Crow law to sit on the rear seats even when seats near the front were empty. Those busses were still in existence, but my children did not know life without private transportation. I did.

It seemed that when the system began to awaken, to realize that segregation had failed to deliver its promise of separate but equal facilities, the Civil Rights Movement was breaking down the door.

I had lived in both worlds.

CHAPTER 1: ONE SUNDAY AT LAKE TOMAHAWK

Burnette Family at Lake Tomahawk 1934

Left to Right: Irene, Charles, Juanita, Blanche (Juanita), Marjorie, Papa, Mary Lee Boyd (Lorenzo), Wallace, Othella, Garland Alfred

Same day
Mary Othella Burnette (bottom left) with sad face after
being told she could not dip her hands in the lake.

It would have been a normal Sunday, I guess. But for some reason, every last one of my brothers and sisters was home, even the ones that didn't live there no more: Lorenzo [wife, Mary Lee], Juanita [husband, Blanch], and Marjorie who lived way off up in New York where her own mother was.

Papa never worked on Sunday unless he was doing some blacksmithing for somebody or puttering as he called it around our land. Mama worked on Sunday because that family in town, whose last name kinda rhymed with Puzzle, wanted her to cook dinner for them. And we didn't go to church that Sunday--not even Irene, and I think she needed to be there to sing in the choir.

Something was different about this Sunday.

I was three years old. I didn't understand much about anything except what

I saw and what I wanted. But I would listen when I heard the grown folks talking about different things, and if my head just packed it all away, then when
something would happen, I could maybe reach back and pull up something I
had heard and the two things would match up just right.

Now if Papa and Mama just plain didn't want me to know what they wanted
to talk about, they wouldn't whisper, but Mama would say words in what she
called Tut. Mama was better at it than Papa was, but he acted like he understood what she was saying.

I heard it so much, I started to pick up a word here and there. I found out
Dud O Nun Tut meant Don't. That meant Somebody was not doing something
or wouldn't do something he was supposed to do. But my mother could talk
it so fast, I couldn't do much with what she was saying.

I heard Papa and Mama talking about a "PWA" and a big man named Frank N
Rooster-felt (Roosevelt) that was doing good things for the people in our town.
And he had made a PWA to pay men to build a lake not far from where we
lived but closer to town.

I heard Papa needed a regular job and had asked for work, but the man over
that PWA in town wouldn't hire him because he owned land. It wasn't a lot of
land, but it was more than most people in our neighborhood had except for
Mr. Lank. But the land wasn't giving Papa any money.

Mama said she went right to that woman she worked for and told on that
man who didn't seem to have much sense. Then the woman [WPA chair-
person)] went straight to that hiring man and said, "You either put that man
to work or feed his family."

We always had food anyway, but that hiring man listened to her.

Papa got the job and all of us got dressed up to go see the lake. They called
it Lake Tomahawk. Tomahawk was the same name Granny Hayden called the
little ax she used to hack bark off the trees for medicine. Granny was a herb
doctor and she delivered babies, too.

Well, somebody that Sunday had a camera - Lorenzo, I guess, and he was gonna help Papa take pictures at the lake. We took the short cut. Still It was a pretty long walk. Everything was going pretty good until I saw all that water, and I just wanted to stick my hands in it and make splashes like I did in the stream that run across our land. But Papa wouldn't let me.

"No, hon, you don't do that here."

I started crying. I was so mad I couldn't stop crying to straighten up my face for the next picture. Papa snapped it anyway.

Papa must have been thinking way ahead when he sold the land, he got from his Aunt Phoebe. She was born a Burnette, but she married a man with a last name that sounded like ham-biscuit (Hambisco). I guess that man went away. So, Aunt Phoebe fixed it so he couldn't touch one clod of dirt she owned if he ever did come back. She made Papa the owner of her land and Papa took the money he got from selling it and bought more land at the foot of Mount Allen where a little branch would run from one side of the place to the other.

I guess Papa had heard that his children wouldn't be going to swim in town.

Even I knew that Black people--White people called us "Colored," but Papa always said "Black"--did not go into town for anything much except to work, to see a doctor sometimes, or to buy something, and maybe to go to the station and watch the trains go by.

They had a movie theater up town, too, but none of us ever went to it. I don't think they would've let us in, anyway. Papa said places up town sold food, but Black people had to go to the back door to buy a sandwich.

Mama said, "Hmf! I wouldn't eat, then."

We could go to the drugstore and we didn't have to go to the back door, but we couldn't sit down in the store to eat our ice cream. The tables and chairs were for White customers, just like at the eating places.

Papa would always take time to explain things so, we could understand. I found out that if somebody had passed by and seen me, a "colored child" play-ing in that lake water and reported it, Papa could have lost his job for being too uppity or breaking a law.

That must have been my first clobbering from what they called Jim Crow. He's the one that made Black people go to the back of the bus and ride in the train coaches up close to the engine where all the smoke comes out. That's the only way we could sit up in front of White people.

But I just wanted to touch that ol' water in the lake, an couldn't even do that Years later I walked and drove past that lake many imes, and I never went close to the water. But I always admired it because Papa had helped to build it.

One time after I had moved far away, I came back for a Fourth of July family get-to-gether. I walked over to that lake alone and took my own picture of it.

It was 1996. By then the whole area had become a beautiful place with trees and flowers, ducks swimming on the lake, and a paved walk that went all the way around it.

I saw how pretty it was and thought about that sad day back in 934. Things had changed, but I still wanted to touch that once forbidden water. And now I could do it!

I walked around that lake until I found a place where I could get down to the water without slipping in. I bent over to scoop up a hand full of water and stepped back. Right at the edge, in that shallow, still water, I saw mosquito larvae wiggling around. I was shocked.

I felt disgusted. Was that what I had cried about 62 years ago when I was three years old? Was that what I had come all the way from the San Fernando Valley to see? Some mosquitos? I wasn't dipping my hands in that water. I just walked away. I don't

remember ever going back again. But Somehow, I'd like to go. I'd still like to have the satisfaction of touching that water.

At least, I know I can if I could get there.

49

Lake Tomahawk 1996 Black Mountain, N.C.
Photo by M.O. Burnette

CHAPTER 2: MORNING IN THE MEADOW

Decked out for a normal sunny day, wildflowers greeted us along the path.
Sentries of common meadow daisies, dressed in ragged skirts of green and wearing
white collars about their golden faces guarded the delicate Queen Anne's flowers,
their own lacy white heads dangling at the end of fuzzy green necks, as pink nosed
milkweed stood tall in the background, all damp and sparkling with beads of dew.
So much peace and beauty! I could not have imagined what lurked ahead, buried in
the black meadow soil.

We are in the meadow that morning. I'm not old enough to go to school, so
I tag along behind him. Papa has the hoe, chopping here and there. And I'm
watching, for there's nothing Papa doesn't ' know. He's explained to me that
the holly bush at the edge of our front yard will never have red berries at
Christmas time because it's a male tree.

I feel sad, but that's the way it is if Papa says so. He knows all about trees. He
knows how to protect the budding peach tree from frost and knows exactly
when our newest apple tree will bear (fruit). He knows all about the seasons
and soil, knows which seeds to plant or when to gather their crops by the sign
of the moon, knows which seeds not to sow on the dark of the moon, when
to rob the bee hives of honey, when to hunt certain animals, and that certain
small animals ain't fit to eat during months spelled without "R's" [pro-
nounced /ar-rahs/] in their names; he knows how deep our neighbors 'wells
are and how to clean the well water of the falling stones and dirt; he knows
which critters to avoid during Dog Days; knows that the hatefulest thing on
earth is a snake and tells us they're absolutely the meanest when molting,
shedding their old scaly hides. I can't follow Papa around the farm for long

without learning something else I had better not forget.

We haven't been in the meadow long before he sees a clump of crabgrass, chops at it with his hoe and the blade sinks deep into the soft earth, sinks all the way up to the wooden part of the handle. Papa jerks the hoe handle forward, bringing up a large clump of black, rich dirt. He bumps the hoe blade against the ground, like he's in a hurry to get it cleaned off, scraping away the remaining moist grains of soil with the sole of his right shoe, then he slowly raises his height to its full five foot-nine inches, and grasping the hoe with both hands, he waits. He's dead still, and he's not saying a word.

The ugliest snake I've ever seen is wiggling its way out of that hole opened by the hoe. Papa is between the snake and me. I'm not afraid, but Papa's keeping quiet and not moving. I'm supposed to keep quiet, too. But what on earth is he waiting for? Why, give mama that hoe and she'd be hacking that critter to pieces soon as ever it stuck its sneaky head out of that hole; then she'd tell us what kind of snake it was, and mimic its hiss or puff, if it had made a sound.

"Papa" (circa 1909)
Garland Alfred Andrew Burnette

1881 – 1954

Papa waits. The snake comes out, turns its head towards Papa and starts to stretch out, stretching, stretching, and stretching out right in front of him. Papa waits. I don't understand, but I can count the rows of round white spots going up and down that serpent's back. A strange looking creature it is, its shiny black skin powdered with dust, making it almost the same color as the soil.

The minute it's stretched its full length and is as straight and stiff as Papa's razor strap, the blade of that hoe rises and falls so fast I don't see it move. But I hear the solid blow, "Whack!"

I don't look at the snake; don't want to see its twisted body trying to talk to its severed head. I watch Papa. He's just standing there, looking down, and nodding his head. Somehow, I know just what is going through papa's head. If that snake had been a human being, another man, Papa would have said, "I know you're hanging around here. But just stay out of my sight and don't come here trying to fight me. This is my land." Papa, clutching the hoe handle with his left hand, turns to me, shaking the finger of his right hand and saying, "Now, you see, before a snake can strike you, he has to get into a coil. But now before he can do that, he's got to straighten hisself."

Then with a final nod of his head, looking down at me, Papa adds, "And that's when you strike."

CHAPTER 3: BRIEF TREASURES
Part 1: Stars Sing a Sad Song

Miss Lena

The homes of Mrs. Alice Daugherty Carson and Mr. Winston Carson was lo-cated just a few feet from Mrs. Daugherty's two-story frame house. And Mrs.

Lena Daugherty and her husband Mr. Julius Whitesides had built their house right on top of the hill, not a good stone's throw from the edge of the woods that continued up to the mountain above and into the mountains beyond. While the Daughertys were like extended family to us, I remember Miss Lena as absolutely one of the kindest human beings I have ever known. I cannot imagine a harsh word coming from her mouth nor a scowl to mar her pleasant face.

Miss Lena was an Eastern Star, and though she frequently came to visit my mother, I cannot forget the special visit she made one afternoon. She came all dressed in white, she and another woman whose face with its name has left me, if I ever knew it at all. They wanted Papa to play for them a song they apparently planned to sing later on. If a note was flat or didn't belong in the song, Miss Lena knew that Papa would know and would help them to get it right.

I watched and listened as Papa took his guitar down from the wall to accompany them, and they began to sing. I had never heard the song before nor have I heard it since; but as understanding came with age, I reasoned that it contained some coded message that had something to do with the Underground Railroad, and that they might be planning to use it to symbolize an upcoming event at their meeting.

Verse: Good morning, Bolder Pilgrim,
Pray tell me what's your name?
My name is Bolder Pilgrim
And I'm traveling to the same.
Chorus: And it was joy, joy,
Joy in heaven with the angels,
And it was joy, joy
All around the throne of God.

I reasoned, 'What could a *bolder pilgrim* be other than a slave who had dared to make his pilgrimage to freedom by means of the Underground Railroad? And who could the person greeting him be, other than a designated agent of that system? And how would that traveler have known how to answer except he had been a trusted passenger on that railroad?'

And the chorus was joyfully repeated by all three of them.

Part 2: A Stranger Sings Shamefully

It was one of those intolerably warm summer days. But two huge black cherry trees in full foliage shaded the front of our house. Looking east, a narrow sandy road wrapped itself around a broad patch of trees, mostly oaks, and led to the houses on the hill to the north.

At the foot of the hill, another wagon road turned westward and led right to our front doorsteps. Up to the point where that road branched left, a row of wild bushes, little more than shoulder high, stood like sentinels between the west side of the road and our apple and cherry tree orchard.

Except in winter, nobody could see the road from our front porch, but in summer, if the approaching visitor was tall enough, I could measure his gait along the road.

Neighbors and other local folk heading up the hill moved slowly, as if conserving energy for the steep climb ahead.

From where I sat on the porch floor, my head barely rising above the windowsill, I could watch Mama and look to see if anybody was coming along the road.

And sometimes it would happen. One time it was a Black man I had never seen before, walking with a guitar and playing the blues. But he went on up the hill to Mr. Winston's house.

Mama had ironing to do, and she had brought out the ironing board and set it up next to the bannisters pretty close to where an electric light hung down on a long black cord attached to the ceiling. That made it easy for her to remove the bulb, twist an outlet gadget into the socket and plug in the iron's cord. Busy at the ironing board, Mama's face hung down. Something was bothering her.

I had seen that look before when my oldest brother was away and hadn't been heard from. Sometimes he'd send a pretty postcard mailed from wherever he'd hopped off a boxcar of some   moving freight train.

   And he was often away. Rinky's business was hoboing from state to state. And he was pretty good at it.

   One time he got all the way to Fresno, California and back, after spending some time with Aunt Latha and her family.

   Rinky was always neat as a pin. He'd get dressed up in a suit one day, pull on a pair of big baggy overalls, and off he'd go, saying othing to anybody. And for weeks we'd never know where he was (or had been) until one of those postcards would show up in our mailbox way across the hill. But it had been a good while since we'd received one.

   I don't know who saw it first, me or Mama. But clearly visible above the bushes, a brown derby hat on the head of a light-skinned man had just turned the corner and was moving along the Sandroad.

   Looking through the bushes, I couldn't really tell if he was Black or White. But he wasn't dragging his heels. The man was moving along, walking fast, as if he had some business to take care of. 'Could it be my rail-riding brother?'

   About the same time as I saw him, Mama threw both hands up in the air, screamed, and that iron hit the floor, Ka-BLAM!

   The next thing I knew that burial insurance collector was right in our front yard, walking towards the porch.

   He looked at Mama, grinning sheepishly and starting singing, [Melody of Battle Hymn of the Republic]

"Pass around the bottle and we'll all have a drink,

Pass around the bottle... "

Mama hung her head again! She had mistaken a stranger for Rinky, and the stranger had misjudged her joyous scream as the antics of a woman who had been hitting the bottle too heavy--a drunken woman in broad daylight.

What an awful disgrace in that time! Mama's joy was shattered. The disappointment was crushing! Sadness returned but was momentarily over-shadowed! temporarily swallowed up! smothered in shame!

CHAPTER 4: PRECIOUS SPRING WATER FOR PAPA

"Mama" (circa 1918)

Hattie Payne Burnette

1892 - 1986

There wasn't a water spigot anywhere on the place, but by the time I was five years old I guess, our house had been wired for electricity. On the front porch, we would need a light at night, especially if company came because the front porch in summer was an extended living room, night, or day. That's where the grown folks sat and talked about family, named and counted off how many children some aunt, uncle or cousin had and which way they all went when they got grown. We children were expected to listen, remember, and make sure we never met up with and married our kin, and had a crazy child. But It was too costly to add a light we didn't need. Besides, the back porch was not used much after dark anyway....

At dusk my two youngest brothers and I have to come in from play. We like to listen to mystery stories on the radio, especially the one from some weird-sounding place way out in California, called San Felipe Otis Obappo, or something like that. Mama listens with us but seems to enjoy wrecking our imagination. She keeps on telling us that the sound of trotting horses is not real, just somebody drumming on a table with his fingers; and the sound of gravel crunching under footsteps is not real, just somebody rattling paper. I wish she wouldn't'do that. Anyway, we are trying to enjoy the story when I hear Papa calling me.

"Come here, hon." My dad always has nickname for me. Kuda is his favorite, but hon will do.

I get right up, leave the living room and go through the kitchen to the back porch. From the kitchen, a little ray of light filters through the screen door, falls towards the center of the porch floor and drops off the edge onto the back yard. Papa is leaning across the banisters, facing the woods beyond the sweet potato patch. He's got a flashlight in his left hand and a pistol in is right. Beyond the yard, the night is pitch black, so black you couldn't see the palm of your hand in front of your face.

And I'm thinking, 'Papa's getting ready to do sound practice. Maybe he just wants me to witness how good he is at sounding out a target in the dark. And there's a plenty of them--hoot owls, whip-poor-wills, frogs, crickets. But the birds are awfully quiet tonight.'

'What is it, Papa?'

He straightens up, pushing his weight up from the banister by his elbows, turns around, and hands me a little gallon bucket. The tin pail glows in the dark. "Here hon," he says, as if this is something I do every time the sunlight drapes her skirts about her ankles and skips over the farthest hill and not a single star dares to show its face, not even the Big Dipper.

" I want you to take this little bucket and go, bring Dad a cool drink of water."

My heart sinks. 'Ooooh God. 'I want to yell and cry 'I can't do this! It's too dark! 'But Mama will come running and accuse Papa of doing an awful thing to send a little child out in the dark. Papa may give in for my sake, but then they'll be mad at each other—Mama'll be mad because it makes no sense to her for Papa to want to send me for water in the dark, and Papa'll be mad 'cause he gave in and didn't send me. Besides, Mama will swear that Papa's clean gone and lost his mind for sending me for water while my two brothers sit in the living room listening to the radio.

I don't say a word. I just take the pail from Papa's hand and turn towards the steps at the north end of the porch.

Somehow, I know Papa is testing me. I know he wants to see if he's raising a coward. Papa's already in his fifties and he's always saying how he hopes he lives 'till I get grown. Yeah. He just wants to see if I've got enough starch in my spine to stand on my own two feet when I'm 21, and not lean on some no-account man.

That's important to papa. He's said so. He says that women who lean on men and don't have money to take care of their own self can get mistreated. An' he's seen a lot of women in his day that couldn't. I don't believe it's the water Papa wants that bad. I just feel that Papa thinks he's doing something for my own good. But, anyhow, I'm scared. I was never out in pitch blackness before by myself. I clutch the little wire handle of the bucket 'til it feels wet and slippery. My heart is racing, too.

As I mope through the back yard and go past where Papa is standing and the light from the kitchen fades away, Papa, again leans over the banister, looks down at me and with all the confidence in the world says, "And daddy will stand right here and nothing will bother you." Leaving the paling light behind and stepping into sudden darkness, I can't see a cuss'ed thing.

I'm thinking, 'Oh yeah, Papa. You are on the back porch, you've got the flashlight, you've got the gun, I'm out here in the dark with all the frogs and lizards and snakes and other night creepers, and nothing will bother me.'

At the same time, I'm plotting my path through the dark. Papa wants a cool drink of water. No mountain man in his right mind drinks from a branch. Somewhere upstream something could fall in the water and die, and you'd never know it. So, I have to go to the spring.

I'm getting near the south edge of the back yard. Soon I scoot down a bank onto a narrow path leading through a cornfield on the left and another sweet potato patch on my right. The path is steep. If it's not hard enough to try to keep my footing with no light, the chuckle headed corn stalks march right up to the edge of the path, reach out, and swipe me across the face. I hold up my left arm to push the long leaves away. The blades are soft to touch, but sharp at the edge. My face and arm sting.

Deep inside the fields, the katydids screech, crickets chirp, and frogs are croaking, too. That gets on my nerves. I think 'I don't know what you have so much to sing about. It's scary out here.' I have to keep to the path.

If I go too far to the right, I can get my feet tangled in the sweet potato vines and fall down. Coming down the hill seems like a long stretch, but pretty soon I'm on flat ground. Flat ground won't last long. It'll soon take a sharp dip down to the water.

If it was daytime, I could just arch my toes and slide down the bank. But I can't see, and nobody's ever built a bridge here, just big flat rocks across a shallow stream. I don't want to fall in the branch like Papa's Aunt Phoebe did years before I was born. But she was old, and blind, and couldn't do no better.

I stop to listen. The water ripples and pushes its way between the rocks. I don't want to step in the water, maybe even get my foot wedged between the rocks. If I listen to the running water, maybe I can tell where it bumps up against a stone and gurgles and where it goes past with its mouth shut. I get 'cross the branch. A little meadow rises up on the other side. As I near the heavy cluster of poplar trees, willow trees, and sarvis bushes loaded with fox grape vines draped over the path, the night gets darker.

Everything is silent. I imagine the water moccasins telling each other.
"Don't' go crawling around now, somebody's coming."

How many times have I seen them pulling their sneaky heads back into their holes or heard them go flip-up into the branch during the daytime when I was getting close to the water.

Once past the grapevines, I have to turn right and go down three wide blue slate stone steps. On the solid stone floor below, the spring will be on my right. If I go too far left, I'll surely fall into the spring box. That's where water from the spring trickles under the stone floor and wells up in a solid long box cut out of the rock floor. The trees overhead, the stone floor, and the icy water make it the coolest place on the farm. Even in summer, the water's so cold we can chill watermelons, milk, and butter in the springbox.

It's cool and damp down here.' I sniff the sweet smell of rotting leaves in the woods sheltering the spring.

At some time after Papa bought this land, years before I was born, he built a well around a tiny geyser that bubbled up right out of the ground. The thick arbor of trees he planted around it, or the trees left there by the Indians before the soldiers drove them way off to Oklahoma, kept the sunlight away from the water even on the hottest summer day.

And Papa took a big stone from the side of the hill near the spring, made it into a great rectangle and set it in the earth beside the steps. On a hot day, anybody taking a break from his fieldwork could sit right there under the trees and enjoy the cold spring water.

And Papa had boxed in the spring. From the same quarry, he took a big wide stone for the spring cover, with three walls of stone holding it up. From the stone landing in front, the mouth of the spring was wide enough for anybody to dip up water in a bucket that held two or three gallons.

One time, right next to the spring cover, I had seen a snake in a hole, shying away from me, sliding backwards. This spot was surely the darkest hole any human was ever in. I think about the time Papa went to get water when he was a little boy. He saw a black bear up in a tree at the water hole. I don't know if Papa got back to the house with the water or the bucket.

But I had the nerve to get this far. I'm not going back without the water. I ease up to the mouth of the spring, bend over real quick and dip the little pail into the water as fast as I can. My right hand goes down into the icy water. The bucket fills with a soft gull-up and it's heavy, too.

I'm not thinking about my feet now. I'm not afraid, I have the water, and dark as it is, the whole path comes clear. I turn and run with the bucket, up the stone steps, across the meadow, down to the stream, over the flagstones, up the bank, up through the fields, up, up the hill and back across the yard. I don't stop 'til I get clear to the porch.

And, sure enough, he's standing right there with the flashlight and the gun. I feel so good when I hand Papa a full bucket of cold spring water.

I can't remember seeing him take a drink of that water. I don't even remember hearing him say "Thank you." I don't care whether he did or not. I know I won, passed my test, and I'm so glad I didn't let Papa down.

CHAPTER 5: MY EARLY SCHOOL DAYS

Literally speaking, my first formal schooling started in a little wooden church on a hill above Flat Creek in Brookside. My second formal school, Clear View, the school known publicly as the Black Mountain Grammar School for Colored Children, sat alone in an open field where the grass that once grew must have taken its worst beating from older generations of students. They had played football or softball games after school and even had their own song, as sung for me by my brother.

Clear View's gonna shine tonight, Clear View's gonna shine.
Clear View's gonna shine tonight, all down the line.
Clear View's gonna shine tonight, Clear View's gonna shine:
When the sun goes down and the moon comes up,
Clear View's gonna shine.

That's how I came to know the name of my school, for it was too modest to display its name in public. And I spell Clear View as I do because I am probably the first person to write that name and to publish it in a book.

Even before 1937, from my kindergarten days, I had come to know Clear View from the inside out. That connection started when our elected driver, one of the fewer than I could count on five fingers Black men in our community who owned an automobile, Mr. Charlie Brown, Baptist Church deacon and World War I veteran, picked us up from kindergarten at the little wooden church on the hillside in Brookside and dropped me off to sit in stone silence in one of the rear seats of my sister Rena's classroom until Clear View dismissed for the day. That's where I first realized that grade school was serious business.

One afternoon, I saw Mr. Blair take a switch to a group of girls for passing a note in class. Rena was one of them, but unlike her classmates who cringed and cried, Rena just puffed up like a frog and took the blows without wincing. I was proud of Rena and hoped I could one day be like she was. Except for the misconduct, Mama would have been proud of her, too. Rena, (named Irene), was born under the sign of Taurus the Bull, and Mama always said she was as strong as an ox; but it was her refusing to cry in public that Mama would have loved hearing about. Of course, I could not tell that part without revealing the other part, too. So, I kept my sister's secret from my mother, but now I'm telling it to you.

Brookside Kindergarten 1934-5

(Author attended in 1936)

Courtesy of Swannanoa Valley Museum and History Center

From Brookside came schoolmates from families surnamed Baxter, Daugherty, Dixon, Flacks, Forney, Gardener, Lawton, Leonard, (Helen and Creola), Long, (my cousins on the Payne side), James, the older brother, and Nathaniel who became our self-appointed monitor when stepped out of the room. And when we became too noisy for him, he would say to the rest of us in a strong, clear voice "Aw, be kriet [quiet]."

Other families were named Lytle, Nabors, Pertiller, Rutherford, Stepp (the name originating from the same plantation but not related by blood to my grandmother Mary), Strickland, and Young.

On Black Mountain side, homes were relatively far apart and opportunities for sleepovers were rare. Thanks to a Sunday-after-church invitation from (Mrs. Bessie-Fourney), I enjoyed two rare experiences: I rode the Brookside bus to school one Monday morning after I had spent the night with Jessie and her younger sister, Betty. During my seven ears at Clear View, that was the only time I ever had the privilege of spending the night at a schoolmate's house and riding a bus to school.

From Swannanoa came the Boyds, the shy, chubby Arnold and his strong sister Roberta, one of my playmates at school. I also remember Davis, and the Dillinghams, the Montgomerys, John, my classmate from first grade, John's little sister, and Annabel Lytle.

From Ridgecrest came the Conleys, one of whom was Peggy, and the Greenlees. The Greenlees: Johanna, James, and Dorothy had graduated, but Elizabeth, Erlene, Fannie, and Margaret were there; and Ralph, Precious, and Pansy would come later. I will never forget how good-humored Erlene heckled me when I returned to my seat after having tried to practice looking up from the page I read in the Bible.

"Um-huh," said Erlene with a big grin, "Lost your place, didn't you?" Not a question, but a fact. From the High-Top Colony community, came the Lytles, Keters, Mooreheads, Stepp (Bll's) and Daughertys (grandchildren of Anne Daugherty, midwife.)

And from the old Cragmont community, Clear View received Browns, two generations of Burnettes and Canadys or Kennedys, Fortunes, Hoopers, Graggs, Carsons, and Groces, new resident   Daniels, Daughertys (Tom's & Charley's), Fortunes (Ethel's and Mary's), Hamiltons, Hardys, Harper, Hoopers, Jones (Rosalie),

Inabinets, Littlefields, Lynches (Selina's & Juanita's), Perkinses (Irene's), Pertillers, Rutherfords (Norah's), Stepps (Arthur's Eddie's & Lester's), Wells (Louise & Betty Faye), Whittingtons, and my neighbors, Earnest, Johnny, Helen, and Howard.

Fortunately, not all came at once, but in their time, they surely passed through Clear View's doors. And, if I have failed to name a family from any area, it is the aging of an already old mind that's to blame and not an intended act of unkindness towards any one of you.

On its west side, Clear View looked at Fortune Street through six all transomed windows. The height and width of the windows insured that any two of them would provide ample daylight for each classroom. While our teachers and we could clearly see what went on outside, the angle of the building and its distance from the road made it inconvenient for passersby to visibly trespass on the sanctity of our classrooms.

Within that safe distance of a few yards behind the church, Clear View nestled right down in an open treeless field that still boasted of an occasional tuft of wild grass. Beneath its concrete window ledges, a straggling of scrub bushes lingered next to the building, defying time and absence of any attention whatsoever but appearing to thrive by their closeness to the wall. The grounds, front and back, west, east, north and south had been worn smooth by running, skipping, rope jumping, ball playing, ring-gaming and secretively dancing feet of generations of elementary school children making the best of their noontime recesses without a single piece of recreational equipment. By the time somebody uptown paid Papa to install a slide at the north end of the building, my classmates and I had grown a bit too big to use it.

But Clear View's walls were straight and strong, built of concrete studded with river rock. Rocks, of different hues, faced and stacked close together to give the outward appearance of a solid rock wall, boldly stuck out of the cement and looked for all the world like a big caramel candy bar that had been rolled in peanuts, just like one of my favorites. And most candy bars would have been my favorites because money was too scarce to buy one very often.

The last separate - and obviously unequal - school for Negro children in Black Mountain, Clear View preceded Carver Elementary. Carver, named in honor of George Washington Carver [1864-1943], a man who had worked with Booker T. Washington [1856 – 1915]. Carver, also segregated, was a modern flat roofed, red brick building, graced with restrooms, a cafeteria, and an auditorium with a real stage. No member of my generation or those before me experienced such luxuries in our makeshift schools. But the two schools did have something in common. Where Clear View's largest photograph had been a drab commercial reproduction of President George Washington, the largest portrait at Carver was a colorful painting of George Washington Carver, created by Cousin Jesse, youngest child of Uncle John who was my grandmother Mary's paternal uncle. Cousin Jesse painted that portrait with a vibrant true blue for Mr. Carver's suit and a deep copper brown for his expressive facial features. Both the painter, a well-educated man of many talents and interests, and his painting have left their mark on my memory.

On the cautiously chosen windowless east side of Clear View, a long high wooden porch clung to the building. The porch, centered along that side, starting near the first door at the north end and stopped just beyond the last door at the south end, spanning almost the entire length of the building. At each end of the porch, a sturdy set of wide thick wooden steps allowed us to ascend to and descend from my classrooms. A physical handicap made it impossible to use the steps, and one child in our community, received no formal education at all. The tall pillars beneath the porch raised it high enough to shelter many-a-rainy day marble-shooting contest, one of the favorite games for boys.

On that side, our kindly but cautious teachers used the elevation of the porch to monitor our activities on the grounds, much like wardens in a prison watch tower. And at that height above our play area, we could quickly spot any teacher who ventured out of a classroom unannounced. On that side only, we held our ring games. One that needed to be hidden from the windows and from the road was a circle formed to shield older girls who vigorously and skillfully demonstrated the *Charleston*, or later, the *Jitterbug*.

Forming a circle, each one of us, tall or short, could get a good view of the dancers, and see the steps of the dances we hoped to learn and secretly practice one day. These circles would quickly break up whenever a teacher appeared on that platform that overlooked a flat, red clay terrace. The terrace ran about fifty feet farther towards the east and stopped suddenly at the ledge of a steep hill above a grassy meadow that had been willed, I was told, to the Baptist church. That meadow, we also heard, was destined to become our future playground. We could stand at the ledge and dream of a playground down below with slides and swings and maybe even a swimming pool. But that dream never materialized; and the meadow site of Papa's uncle Sam Burnette's old homestead, well beyond our teachers' view from the porch, was positively off limits for girls or boys forever.

Possibly intended for the location of the building, but for some reason abandoned, that little red clay playground, mostly for girls, lay between paths to the two outhouses, one on the northeast and way down the hill for boys and male teachers, and one on the southeast and not so far down the hill for girls and female eachers. Then, on the southeast side of Clear View lay a shallow patch of dense woods where older boys sometimes played or gave one nother the unwanted gift of a birthday spanking, but more importantly where a marvelous tree, the Black Gum, grew: It's fibrous twigs were used for toothbrushes by native mountain adults; but for the teachers, those trees provided supplies of long limber switches, plentiful in fall, winter or spring, and far safer to use than the wooden ruler, or the wooden paddle that broke as one little offender lying belly down across the teacher' lap kicked so violently at the paddle that it broke, sending a piece of the wood flying at the side of her face, and nicking at the corner of her right eye. The gentle Black Gum switch would wrap around the shoulder and sting like the dickens, but it wouldn't break.

My last teacher, coming from Delaware, lost no time learning about the benefits of that tree and where to find it. He would send a group of older boys into the woods each Monday morning for fresh "limbs." I got a taste of the Black Gum one day when I joined in the loud giggling as the tallest boy in the room pinned a donkey tail to the teacher's coattail. Mr. James, sensing ridicule in our cackling and undoubtedly having felt a jiggle at the back of his coat, calmly laid his chalk in the tray below the blackboard, turned around without lifting his eyes to search for the culprit, raised his eyebrows, pressed his lips together and selected a long slender switch from the nearest corner. Then he began marching up and down the aisles. Heads down, backs exposed, and each of us would get a solid whack across the shoulders.

That year, my seat was next to the windows. I don't know why I wanted to watch as the children on the east side of the room took their punishment. Maybe I was comparing the event to my sister Rena's day of reckoning in Mr. Blair's room years before.

As I peeked from under my right arm, I couldn't help seeing that Mr. James kept pressing his lips together as he gave us our share of the Black Gum; and whenever he made that "I mean business" gesture, the short, curled goatee below the center of his lower lip stuck out, as if pointing a finger at the one he was about to strike.

School days, school days,
Dear old golden rule days,
Reading and 'riting and 'rithmetic,
Taught to the tune of a hickory stick...

Only one time would I ever question his wisdom. One day, two or three boys were passing a note in class. Mr. James took the note and called the boy it was addressed to, to come to the front of the room for his punishment. Later, I was shocked to learn that my name had been written at the bottom of the note. William was as innocent as I was, but he got punished. I never saw the contents of that note so I couldn't understand the teacher's reasoning. But it surely caused "bad blood" between William and me.

Yet, in spite of his love for the old black gum switch, I adored Mr. James. No other teacher had tried so hard to teach us so much and for so practical a reason so plainly spoken in so few words:

"You have to learn this; you're Black."

I understood Mr. James. He was a man with very black skin. He had been through it, forged his way through the system we would have to face, a system that — if not by intent, had the potential to prevent Black children from becoming prepared to compete in a White dominated society. And in spite of Mr. James's education, the same system oppressed him, forced him to walk on eggs in the classroom lest anything he said should be misconstrued and relayed to the wrong ears up town, and thence to the Board of Education. And despite his superior education, he knew that his monthly teacher's salary was roughly equivalent to that of a barely literate cook at the tubercular sanitarium and definitely inferior to that of any White teacher who might be far less qualified than he.

Yet, he was trying to help us, and nothing tried his patience more than seeing us trifling away our time in the classroom. Now I had betrayed him. I had giggled with the rest of the class. The switch stung my back, but I was too ashamed to cry.

It didn't matter who started it: we were to understand that education was serious. The classroom was no place for pranks and he, of all people, was not to be played with. The donkey-tail prank never returned.

He must have heard about the misfortunate fourth grader whose kicks broke

Mrs. Jones's wooden paddle and sent a fragment of it into the side of her face and frighteningly close to the corner of her eye. Mrs. Jones also became a wonderful switch wielding teacher, but she was always very kind. It was she, with her gentle manner, who first made me aware of the difference between Black English and school English in one easy lesson, leaving me with no negative feeling towards the language I spoke at home, in the community and on the school ground. Mrs. Jones was my third and fourth grade teacher. Then came Mr. James for the fifth, sixth, and seventh grades.

Mr. James, being forewarned, I suppose, before taking his switch to us, made certain that our heads were on our desks, face down and encircled in our arms. Perhaps not having to look into our faces made it easier for him to punish the children he loved so dearly. For me, it was better not to know exactly when that one lick, just one, was coming.

Now our school, standing in the wake of Mills Chapel Baptist Church, could allow no dancing. But on the east side of Clear View, we shielded the dancers with our circle of bodies. And even from the vantage point of their watch station, given the confusion of the rapidly scattering ring, no teacher would be able to tell who the ring leaders of the dance session had been. Of course, the teachers knew who the leaders would be, but it was part of the game they also played of upholding the rule of what we allow is not always what we may condone.

Good Baptists didn't engage in social dancing, and our teachers could not afford to be accused of allowing on a public school round an activity that offended local religious tradition. That kind of leniency would surely damage their image as trustees of the school and harm their relationships with church leaders. Our teachers were wise: they needed the church sanctuary for our school plays. More than that, they needed the good will of the church members, our parents, who supported them without question in discipline through which some of their high academic standards would one day be glorified, if not through us, then hopefully through our children or grandchildren.

But other ring games we played freely, such as London Bridge is Falling Down. The literate phrase "fallen down" was not part of our mountain vocabulary. What's more, the phrase "is falling served as a clue to what was going to happen to a child passing under the bridge, sooner or later. Two girls would stand about two feet apart, facing each other, arms held high and palms touching, imitating a drawbridge raised for a passing ship. The rest of us would walk swiftly in single file beneath the arc of those upraised hands, singing, London Bridge is falling down, falling down, falling down,

…, my fair lady.

The second verse warned:

Catch the last one that comes through last, comes through last, comes through last …, my fair lady.

On the signal of the third verse, the raised arms would fall, entrapping a child pretending surprise, as the group sang,

You're the one who stole my wife, stole my wife, stole my wife, …, my fair lady.

Caught between the strong arms of the falling bridge, the thief might be rocked back and forth to the verse of,

Take the key and lock him up etc.

This version of London Bridge was certainly more fun than trying to build up a fallen bridge with inconceivable gold and silver or even iron bars, as the traditional versions suggested. Besides, we had a different concept of the use of iron bars, though lawbreaking and jail were rare events in our small community. In fact, arrests were as rare as keys to the front or back doors of our homes which were seldom locked

Ring Around a Rosie

At the end of one brief verse, down we fell, knowing nothing of what our simple words signified, neither the massive scourge deaths (falling down), nor (posies) the flowers brought for the dead, nor the ashes, not the ashes of the dead but of their belongings believed to have held the seeds of the Black Plague. In our age of innocence, Ring Around a Rosie was just another variation of our play time.

Now, on either side of the building, all play and games ended with the loud clanging of the schoolmarm's hand bell with its carved and polished black handle. Miss Murray was the principal, a tall, stout woman with defiant gray hairs sprouting about the forehead and temples and her otherwise black, pressed hair, pulled back smoothly and coiled into a tight bun at the back of her neck. One look from her through squinting eyes above spectacles resting on her nose would remind us that Clear View was no place for nonsense, and how fortunate we were to be here at this plateau of learning for which most of our fore parents had not dared to desire for themselves, though they dearly sought it for us. But one time she did smile when an older girl, Geraldine Canady, sneaked up

behind her and planted an admiring kiss squarely on her left cheek.

Miss Murray, whose name was Mrs. Peggy Murray Goldsmith, an admirable older teacher who understood rural mountain people and their ways, was the only other woman I ever knew who was as strict as Papa's cousin Isabella Burnette White. Cousin Isabella, who never had to remind us that she wanted to be called Aunt Bell, was a born-in-the-mountains and dyed-in-the-wool third generation descendant of one of the oldest Black families to enter the hills.

I recall Miss Murray's sturdy frame and her matter of fact "Here, honey." She bent over the railing of the porch to poke a note at me as I left the classroom one afternoon. "Take this to your mama."

As usual, the note politely announced to "Dear Mrs. Burnette" the date of the next PTA meeting. Miss Murray did not need to tell Mama that she and the other teachers who carpooled from Asheville could not make the 32-mile round trip and get back to school in time for PTA. She did not need to remind

Mama that not a single Black person owned a sandwich shop that could be found near the school and that they would not be seated at any sandwich shop or restaurant uptown.

Miss Murray wanted to ask Mama if she and the other teachers might come over for dinner. Miss Murray knew that neither Papa nor Mama would be coming to the meeting. For what? Most of the time, at least at school, their children were going to do as they were told and they would learn whatever they were supposed to learn, practically all the time. Mama already knew that.

And Mama would prepare her fresh from the yard chicken, purify it in salt water, then wash, drain and drop the pieces into a brown bag of seasoned flour and deep fry them in bacon grease until each piece was crispy brown; and she would make rich brown gravy from the drippings of the last pieces of fried chicken. And the teachers would scoop that gravy into hollowed mounds of creamy rich mashed potato made with real butter and whole milk; and they would sop the remaining gravy with Mama's made from scratch, flaky hot biscuits. Mama, also born in the mountains, but farther away from the foothills of Little Allen, would never initiate an invitation to the teachers but, if asked, she would graciously prepare that special southern fried chicken meal for them. Miss Murray knew that. And it amused Mama to watch one of the newer teachers bouncing out of her chair to reach across the table for another biscuit or two. They would go to that PTA meeting well fed. Miss Murray knew that, too.

Like squirrels, we ran from every direction at the sound of the bell, older children towards the south end of the wooden porch to form two lines at the foot of the steps: the fifth, sixth, and seventh grade girls and boys on the outside; the third and fourth graders next to the wall; first and second graders, towards the north end of the building, boys on the outside, girls next to the wall. And there we stood, waiting like robots for the teachers' signal to ascend the steps and enter our lofty classrooms.

That signal was merely a precursor to the rigidity we would face once inside Clear View's walls. Not only did our teachers have us file into the classroom in an orderly fashion, they also demanded a period of absolute silence after we entered the room. So, the first command we heard after we were in our seats was "Heads down." And after what was probably only ten minutes but seemed like an eternity, we heard "Heads up." Now it was time for lessons to begin. In the classroom, naturally, the light had to come over our left shoulder, never over the right. No doubt that was in the mind of the people who designed Clear View, who planted its tall windows in its west side, who securely bolted down into the floor the wrought iron feet of every old inkwell oaken desktop, every one facing north in each room. Students could be moved, not the seats they occupied. Students had to be molded to fit the society they

were supposed to live in, to rise above the constraints Of racism, and to be somebody that Black people could look up to, somebody that White people could respect.

Those bolted to the floor seats must have symbolized the whole system of racism and segregation, back to back in vertical rows and just so many inches apart horizontally. They would not be moved so long as our little no-name consolidated county school stood in an open field facing the big road towards the sunset.

The county paid three certified Black teachers to educate seven grades of Black students. Therefore, the rooms had to be large enough to accommodate at least two grades of fifteen to twenty children in each class.

CHAPTER 6: THE BIBLE AND MR. BOB

And he went up from thence unto Beth-el; and as he was going up by the way, there came forth little children out of the city , and mocked him and said unto him, Go up, thou bald head; go up, thou bald head.

And he turned back and looked on them and cursed them in the name of the Lord. And there came forth two she bears out of the wood, and tare forty and two children of them. [(KJV) 2Ki. 2 : 23 – 24.]

Around 1938, it's summertime in Southern Appalachia. My youngest brother and I make fun of an old man who was not born in the Swannanoa Valley and a lesson from the Bible is brought home to us.

From time to time, they warned us: "And the children made fun of Elisha and the bears came out of the woods and ate them up. And so, you must never make fun of an old person."

School is out and my youngest brother, Wallace, and I are playing near the Black Walnut Tree in Cousin Irene's front yard. We wouldn't have seen Mr. Bob that day if we had stayed home instead of coming to our married sister, Irene's house. At home, we could have played in the meadow and dug gray pottery clay from the south bank where the branch turned due east and ran right across the foot of the big meadow. We could have followed the stream north, then west to play in the clear shallow pool above the stone footbridge. Right there in that water, we would often find soft gray creatures that came from goodness knows where, for that stream started in on the mountain to the west of us, where the water bubbled up right beneath the leaves, ran out of the woods and crossed our land from west to east. We called those critters crawfish.

They had little beady black eyes and we could poke sticks at their dark whip-like whiskers and watch them tuck their see-through tail fins and back away to the center of that narrow crystal-clear stream.

For my brother and me, that little branch was the wonder of our playgrounds. The branch flowed out of the woods onto the west side of the farm and wound its way from west to south to east, crossed the property line under the fence and disappeared back into the woods of the adjoining farm. Somewhere along the way, we would always find that flood waters of a summer past had gouged a great chunk of earth away from a field or carved a deeper bed for a little pool. There we could build a dam for a swimming hole, as we often did after Papa left for work.

It's strange how that sharp break between smooth concrete and hard dirt seems to point like a finger right at that house. And while I knew that the White family living there was as poor as mine, maybe even worse off, their house marked the dividing line between the Black and White neighborhoods. Poor as they were, the pavement had come to their door and stopped. The rest of Cragmont Road, the part that went past the property owned by Black families, was not paved. And that break in the pavement sent a message that even a child could understand it said that White people were supposed to have a smoother life than Black people. And other such messages came to taunt us.

I would always feel slighted when I looked at that line and I'd think, 'The pavement stops here; my people live over there. Why won't they pave the road where Colored people live?'

If I really needed to ask that question, the answer would be the same as if I asked why our school had only three classrooms and no indoor toilets, and why each of our three teachers had two or three grades of students in the same room and never enough textbooks. Usually, the few books our teachers did get were used, worn and torn, from the big brick schools in town, and some are even marked DISCARD.

Of course, the road in front of Cousin Irene's house was dirt, but it was wide and smooth, kind of like life in our community where everybody knew everybody else and grown people looked after everybody's children. In that road, here and there a big river rock pushed one side up through the hard soil like a half peanut in a chocolate bar. Like the hard parts of life in a Black neighborhood where we felt accepted and nobody looked down at anybody else, and the rocks were just part of the road.

Some days we could see strangers walking by and sometimes even a long string of black cars comes by, going to the cemetery where they buried White people.

One time when I was a lot younger, Grandma Mary Elizabeth and I stood under the walnut tree and watched a White funeral procession go by. Granny was born in 1858 and she knew all the old families, Black or White. As the cars passed, Granny said, "Well, there goes poor old So-and-so's body," as if she knew it was his time to go. Granny knew the man's name, too. She never owned a radio or a telephone, and she didn't read the newspaper, but she always knew.

Even at five, I understood that watching a funeral procession wasn't no time to be disrespectful and go asking questions. I had never been to a White person's funeral, but I had been to many a Black one. Besides seeing which member of the family "took it the hardest," and which ones acted like they had just come to the funeral because they were expected to be there, Black people were always eager to see the expression that man or woman was wearing in that coffin—not what they were dressed in, just the face. They wanted to see a peaceful look, not a face drawn and twisted in signs of pain, sorrow, or sadness. That wouldn't be a good sign. It would mean the person died unhappy and might come back to set things straight.

But Granny hadn't mentioned the dead person's head, just the body. 'Why?' I wanted to ask. Granny would surely have scolded me for "asking a fool question." I was used to hearing about somebody who had died, but it was always, "Mr. So and So" or " Ms. So and So died," and we would hear the person called by name and nobody would talk about a body.

Granny doesn't have the patience to explain things the way Papa does. And I forget to ask him before I'm old enough to understand that White people are buried with their heads on just like Black people are.

Now from the road where Wallace and I are watching, a narrow foot path comes right up a steep bank held up by a single tree, the Black Walnut Tree. Then the path cuts right smack through the grass like a crooked part in some-body's hair and comes on up to the front steps.

The three-room bungalow with attic, built for my great Aunt Mattie Burnette Stepp sometime after she was freed from slavery, looked every bit of its age. The back of the house squats right flat down on the ground. But under the front porch, it rares up on tall brick pillars. The steps coming down from the porch are steep like the bank at the edge of the yard.

If a paint brush has ever touched the heavy brown siding of that house, I can't see any signs of it. Whether it's from weather or old age or both, the dark brown of the house is the same dark brown of walnut stain. Cousin Irene comes home from work on Sundays and at other times, unless the house is rented out, it just sets there facing the road, like a big brown bunt tail dog, watching, its mouth open, its tongue hanging out, just watching.

I sure don't see anybody on the road today. Still pointing, Wat turns to me. "There he comes!" he says.

'Who?'

'Mr. Bob'

'Where?'

'Righ teah."

Oh. Well, it's a public road. Anybody coming from town and going to one of the homes below the school ground has to pass along this road unless he knows the paths over the top of the hill above us. I bet Mr. Bob don't know any short cuts. 'You know where Mr. Bob lives, Wat.'

Now the old fellow has passed the mailboxes at the corner of Aunt Phoebe's old place, where Brooks Road spills into Cragmont. He's coming from the direction of town, but I can't see that he's bought anything. At least, he's not carrying a grocery bag or anything else in his hands. Some people just like to walk, I guess, even when they don't have to. Papa calls it taking a constitution, like he does some Sunday afternoons, and sometimes takes me with him.

Wat stops pointing in the direction of Mr. Bob and lowers his voice. "Now when he gits righ' teah," he motions towards that part of the yard where another narrow path angles upwards from the road through a patch of honey-suckle vines, "We gonna say, 'Da na, Maggie, patch ma BBDs!" [There now, Maggie, patch my BBDs.]

I don't ask 'Why?' When you are the youngest, you just get in the habit of doing what anybody older tells you to do, I guess. Mr. Bob, maybe in his eighties, is not really one of our old people, though he is old. But he's not old like our old people or like Grandma Mary Elizabeth. Heck! Mr. Bob wasn't even born here. And if he had been, he was not born into one of the old settler families. I have known that for as long as I could remember. But I also know that none of our people would allow Mr. Bob to go hungry or to sleep without a roof over his head.

Nearly everybody in our community is dirt poor, but nobody is homeless and starving. In town, there's no soup kitchen waiting for long lines of hungry people, either. We sometimes see such pictures in a newspaper that Mama brings home from work, or we hear about it on the radio.

Mr. Bob doesn't talk like our people do, either. I talked   mountain English all the time until I started to Clear View Grammar and my teachers kept tellin' me to speak the King's English, tellin 'me there's no such word as this and no such word as that when I don't know any other way to say a word I have been saying ever since I learned to talk.

It's like that day at school when we've finished our lessons. Mrs. Jones has put down her leather strap, she's sitting at her desk, and we are having quiet time. I go to the bookshelf next to the piano, take down a faded blue book and turn to a story about The Big Blue Balloon. I'm sitting at my desk, reading along, when suddenly I see a strange word: I try to pronounce it and it just doesn't sound right. B-u-r-s-t. Whoever heard of such a word as that? Had to be a mistake.

I raise my hand and Mrs. Jones motions me up to her desk. I open the book wide, jabbing my forefinger at the page. 'Mrs. Jones, they's a mistake in this book.'

"Where honey, show me." I put my finger on the word, 'Righ' teah.'

"Well, what is it? What's wrong?"

"See, it's spelled b-u-r-s-t. It's s'posed to be b-u-s-t-e-d, bus-ted,' I anxiously pronounce.

Mrs.Jones doesn't smile, doesn't even raise her voice, and in her calm minister's wife voice, says "No, honey. There's no such word as busted."

I go back to my seat behind a desktop with the empty-ink well hole on one side and the nailed down black wrought iron legs below. 'Another one of them no-such-words.'

At home there most certainly is such a word and all of us students know about it. It means when something blows apart, a soap bubble, a dress that you outgrow and have busted out of…. But I understand. Mrs. Jones knows we don't speak school English at home, and she wants me to learn so that I can get a good job someday. So, I won't say busted around her no more.

Just like all the other children, I keep on speaking mountain English at home and on the school ground because we don't know any other way to speak. And we keep on believing that our mountain way of speaking is better than the way Black people from farther South speak. We absolutely hate the way Black people speak after they go off up North and stay a while. Mama says they're just puttin' on airs, with their sharp Yeses and Hi's. In the South, we say Yeah and Hey. And to any grown person, don't matter whether they are Black or White, we children always have to say "Yes, Ma'm, Yes Sir" and "No, M'am, No Sir."

In our way of talking, they's just no polite way to say just plain "Yes" to anybody. Anyhow, the proper-talkin 'been-up-North-and-come-back-to-show-offs, they don't come back better educated than when they left home. Same old faces, same old didn't-go-on-to-school bodies up North where they have so much better school buildings and better chances than we have, and the mouth spoutin 'off proper talk like we don't know who they are.

Mama says, "Makes me sick at my stomach." But in mountain English, our the sounds like tuh or duh; Mr. Bob's the is dee. Well, I'm thinking about what I'm supposed to say to him. I'm wondering, 'What difference will it make if we just repeat what we've heard our older brother, Garland, "Brud," say about Mr. Bob behind our parents' back? Out of earshot, Brud makes fun of almost every-body, and nothing ever happens to him.'

Mr. Bob is getting pretty close to right there. I haven't noticed that Wat, Ol' We Gonna Say, is nowhere near right there. He is ten years old; I'm seven and I don't understand what he's up to.

Mr. Bob is almost there. He's wearing his full-dress three-piece suit, shirt and tie, and a round brim hat—just like the one Jiggs wears in the funny papers. [Maggie and Jiggs is the name of the comic strip. Maggie, the wife, likes opera. Jiggs hates it.] And just like Jiggs, Mr. Bob wears white leather spats over his dress shoes, and he carries a walking cane, too. Maybe except for our preachers and Mr. Faust, who owns the little candy store on the west side of Cousin Irene's property, most Black men we know usually wear rough work clothes and Brogans during the week. But Mr. Bob dresses better than any other man I've ever seen.

We hear that Mr. Bob and his wife have come here from farther South. Maybe he did come to work in one of the T.B. hospitals; but he is too old, he walks too slow to have a job now.

When Mr. Bob gets right below where I can stand and look down on the crown of his little round hat, I blurt out 'Da na Maggie, patch ma BBDs.'

I turn to look for We Gonna Say, and he is standing way up by the side of Cousin Irene's house. If the old man had any idea of trying to climb that bank to shake his stick at us, We Gonna Say could have a good head start up the hill towards home. Besides, Wat can run faster than I can.

Standing there by myself, I start to think about what I've done. Mr. Bob wouldn't have paid any attention to us if I hadn't opened my big mouth. And I could've said 'Patch ma underwear,' but BBDs was easier to say real fast. It didn't matter that I didn't know the meaning of a single one of those letters, the first B, the second one or the D. I knew they meant underwear, long underwear like mountain people, men, women and children, wore in winter. And we had no way of knowing whether Mr. Bob wore long johns, too. The man was always dressed up and with his spats covering the space between the cuffs of his pants and the tops of his shoes. We couldn't even see his socks, much less the legs of his underwear.

What's more, I know that we have no business telling an old man that his long johns are so raggedy his wife needs to patch them. And I sure have made bad matters worse, calling his wife, a grown woman, by her first name.

Without saying a word, Mr. Bob shoots a look of shock and anger up at me. I feel it as much as if he'd said, Oh if I was your papa for just five minutes, you'd never say nothing like that to me again. For that minute, I can see the whites of his eyes. But just as quick, he turns his head and goes on his way, his head held high like I've done nothing more than poured water on a duck's back.

Well, it was done. We thought it was over with. We don't see any more of Mr. Bob the rest of that week. But Sunday comes and Mama takes Wallace and me to church.

Mills Chapel Baptist Church circa 1933

Courtesy of Swannanoa Valley Museum and History Center
Mr. Lank stands in the back row, 5th from left.

Mills Chapel Baptist is a pretty church. Its walls are strong and straight and it's painted white, just like a little country church you might see on a Christmas card: it's got a steeple and a bell that's rung for services and for funerals, one chime for each year of the person's life. The back door at the rear leads to the choir box. At the front, another side door on the east side of the vestibule goes out where two or three cars are parked. In front, facing the Big Road, two tall doors open wide to make it easy for men to carry a casket out and across the road to the cemetery that surrounds the

Methodist church right across the road. The family walks behind those men and the women closest to the dead person wear black and cover their faces with veils. But I can still see when they have been crying. Their eyelids look red and swollen.

On regular Sundays, church service starts with the old common meter hymns and with Deacon Dave doing the lining. In 1938, our church can't put even one songbook on every bench, and the people have to be told what the words of the song are so they can all sing the same thing at the same time. Papa's Uncle Sam, born in 1858, must have known the church wouldn't have any hymn books when he built those solid oak pews with no book racks nearly seventy years ago.

But if we do have one hymnbook, it's going to be in Mr. Dave's hands because he's the one who can do the most with it. Most of the time I don't think he even needs it. So, why's he using it? Is it because some of the old people want to make sure he's saying the right word? Is it because some of the old people can't read even if they had a book? My mother can read, and I can.

I wonder how long he's been doing that—reading the words t the congregation, one line at a time, lining the hymn.

He looks, to me, about seven feet tall; he has a great big body and it seems to be just full of songs, church songs, and he knows all the words to every one of them. On top of that, he has a great big voice, not a beautiful voice, but it's strong and he can lead the congregation and the choir, too. Pretty often, he gets happy and stomps his right foot, and I feel the church building tremble. He acts like he enjoys reading the words of the songs, and the people act like they expect it, though I'm pretty sure they've all learned the words by this time.

Common meter is slow and mournful, like a chant, and it sounds like you are in awful trouble. If I stretch my imagination, I can see a group of field workers, heads bowed and backs bent, men and women with their hoes, and I can hear the blades chopping into the hard ground at the same time, Cuh-cuh-WHACK-up, at the end of each line of the song. In our church, it was as if the grown people were rejoicing over their freedom from slavery while, at the same time, looking back, feeling sorry for their parents who had been born into slavery. And some of them had missed it by only a few years. Papa's cousin Isabella, Aunt Bell, born in 1876 -- she's one of them.

The singing is sad, but it's beautiful. Everybody sings the same line—no alto, no tenor, baritone or bass like we hear from the choir. Just the same old lead voices. But a woman with a high pitched voice can sing above the rest, she can twist the melody into a lilt or a warble as she pleases, but she has to get back in time with the other singers before the next line comes. I can hear Aunt Bell's Voice. She's the oldest Burnette living, and she'll sing any way she wants to in the church built mostly by children of freed slaves, her own generation.

And even if the song is not really a common meter hymn, it gets sung that way when the church meeting first starts. In our Baptist church, mostly only members of my father's generation know how to sing like that.

Any song in common meter has the same melody. It's the way of singing a song—any church song, except for the spirituals that we sing in major and minor keys—songs about Pharaoh, Moses, and the Jordan river, but the common meter songs are almost always sung in minor keys, very slow and lonesome sounding melodies.

Mr. Dave starts the lining at the beginning of the service. All of us stand and he reads a line to us, "Amazing Grace, how sweet the sound, that saved a wretch like me." As soon as Mr. Dave says the last word, the people start singing.

"A-a-uh-a- Ma-zin' Gra-a-ace, how-ow-ow su-wee-eet the sou-uh und…."

On the piano at home, I can pick out the traditional melody of Amazing Grace on the black keys—just using the black keys, but that doesn't work for common meter. And playing the melody on the black keys doesn't work for some of the spirituals either.

Listening to the congregation, that song in common meter reminds me of soft cotton white clouds that hang over our mountain during summer vacation and sometimes drift down in wispy white curtains over the highway on the Old Fort Mountain. But it's sad, maybe like a blue-gray storm cloud, too. The song rises up above me, above the pews, pushes against the walls and lifts up to the ceiling with all the voices around me, male and female, joining in. Then it drifts down to wait for the next line, like the lull between a crack of lightning and the thunder that comes after. And then, just like a sudden thunderstorm that can come out of nowhere on a summer day, a big boom comes from Mr. Dave, That saved a wretch like me. And while the last note of that line hangs all around us, like a raindrop clinging to the tip of a leaf on a black cherry tree, Mr. Dave belts out another line, "I once was lost but now I'm found, was blind but now I see."

The next line of that lonesome sounding chanting continues until all the verses he likes have been sung. And because I don't know how to sing along with the old people, the song seems to take forever. Then when the singing changes to regular church hymns, sometimes I sit on the bench and try to shove the song along faster in my head. I want it to move along the way I've heard it at home where I've been listening from the time I was born to the clipping movement of tones Papa makes when he plays the guitar or the country fiddle and stomps out the timing with his heel.

Still, they sing the Christian hymns enough like they are in the book for anybody to recognize them. But the old people have their own way of singing those songs, too. It seems to me it's hard for them to go from common meter to the strict book rhythm of the choir singing that always starts with a do-sol-sol-do-do-mi-do and in the right pitch.

One song almost gets me in trouble. It starts with that line The consecrated cross I'd bear, Til death shall set me free. I nudge Mama and try to get her to look at me. I whisper, 'Mama!'

Without looking back at me, Mama shakes her head and puckers her lips in "Shhhhhhhh."

I can feel Papa's Cousin Isabella looking at me out of the corner of her eyes. I stop trying to get Mama's attention, but I know what she told me. Crammed in between Mama's shushing me and Aunt Bell's rolling her eyes at me, all I can do is think. They can't hear that, so I think about what Mama said about that song, about when she was a little girl in Shiloh, her hometown, and she used to go with Grandpa Payne to their Methodist church. Mama hadn't learned to read yet,

When the congregation started singing that line about the consecrated cross I'd bear, Mama chimed in with "The constipated cross-eyed bear...." Thank goodness nobody heard the pastor's daughter saying such words right in church, and on Sunday, too.

Now our choir has to have its turn. When Mr. Dave faces them and swings his right arm, they all rise from their seats behind the pulpit. Not many of the congregation know shape notes and the choir kind of shows off by singing a few lines using the names of the notes instead of the words of the song.

I know what the choir's hymnbook looks like because I've seen shape notes at home. Besides, my older sister Rena has a beautiful voice, and Papa has taught her to read shape notes; so, she started helping Mr. Dave with the choir when she was just thirteen years old. But she had to get baptized first. Rena sings solo, so she stands on the front row looking kind of pitiful, eyes rolled up towards heaven like she thinks somebody up there can hear her. Maybe they can.

The symbols in the choir's song book mostly look like little black pyramids turned different ways, one upright (Do), one sideways (Fa), one upside-down (Ti), one like a half moon (Re), one shaped like a diamond (Mi) and one like a square box (La). Only one of them looks like a real note of music (Sol), but they're all connected to stems pointing up or down and sometimes the notes are white. The choir members can't read real music either, but once they get the pitch from Mr. Dave, they know which tone every one of those symbols has. Deacon Dave pitches the song to give them the right key: "Do-sol-sol-do-do-mi-do." The congregation settles down for the show. Some don't even own a good radio, and they love any kind of entertainment.

Church goes on and on, and oh those big heavy benches that Papa's Uncle Sam built for this church are getting so-oo-oo hard. I'm sandwiched between Mama and Papa's cousin Isabella. Aunt Bell has told me what she'll do for me if I don't act good in church. She's the oldest of Papa's cousins on his father's side, older than Papa or Mama. I know she will whip me and neither Mama nor Papa will say one word. Aunt Bell looks at me out of the corner of her eyes. Aunt Bell has really black skin with some white spots on her hands where she got scalded a long time ago, and her eyes look scary white, especially when she's threatening me.

Aunt Bell must have taken her skin color after her dad, Papa's uncle Hardy. Mama said one Sunday, long before I was born, a White man came to church to speak and he talked about how Black people looked like a flower garden with all the different skin colors. Then he looked over and saw Uncle Hardy, and said "And there's one way over there that's blue black," and he gave Uncle Hardy fifty cents—probably more than he could earn on any day with his horse and his wagon.

They say Aunt Bell really knows how to make children straighten up, and some of the children's own mothers bring them to Aunt Bell to be raised right. They leave them with her a few hours in the daytime. At her house, Aunt Bell treats all children alike, kin or no kin.

Mama told me when my oldest sister was a baby, she used to grab the table-cloth and pull it off the table. Everything on the table would come with the cloth. My sister must have liked hearing things fall on the floor, and that's why she kept on messing with the tablecloths. One day she forgot and did that at Aunt Bell's house, and Aunt Bell slapped her little hand. Nita was just eighteen months old, but she never yanked another cloth off anybody else's table, Mama said.

But in church, I sit with the women and I'm the one that catches it.

Next comes the preaching with some shouting and jo-ree hopping. Another one of Papa's first cousins, Nora, says that's what her husband calls the special church dance that two or three women do when they get happy. One of them lives far away, New Jersey or New York, and she's not always here, just when she comes to visit and stays with Cousin Lizzie.

I look up at Mama to see how she's taking it. Mama was raised African Methodist Episcopal Zion, and they are quieter in church than the Baptists.

Two of the dancing women are kind of skinny and they like to dress in black. When they dance, they look like dark shadows, holding their bodies in straight lines, hands folded and their feet moving fast. The dance steps look like the Charleston mixed up with a Scottish fling and an Irish jig. Age makes no difference when the preaching and the singing hit those women and the feeling touches their toes. Their shoe heels striking the wooden floor make an awful noise and I can see dust rising from the floorboards. I love the singing, but I don't like loud noises and shouting. It scares me. At school, our teachers won't allow us to dance, not even during recess, but these women can dance in the church on Sunday. Grown people have so many rules for us, and some of them don't make one bit of sense.

I can tell that Mama's not taking the noise any better that I am. She just knows how to put up with it better. I move over closer to Mama. Papa's cousin Isabella, Aunt Bell (she makes me call her "Aunt Bell," and says "Cousin Bell" don't sound right), rolls her eyes at me.

Now the Burnette's and the other died-in-the-wool Baptists don't dance in church, but two of Papa's first cousins on the Stepp side do, and the pastor's sister, Miss Elena, does.

The poor preacher catches it, but not in the same way I do. The congregation and Mr. Dave in front, Mr. Dave and the choir behind him, and the A-men-ers on both sides, men on the east side of the church, women on the west side. Finally, the preacher gets up from his armchair, walks towards the pulpit stand that holds the big church Bible and starts to read:

By the rivers of Babylon, we sat down, and there we wept as we remembered Zion. They bade us sing.... How can we sing our sweet songs in a strange land?

Looking up from the Bible, he says "But folks, I tell you we have to sing. The people sitting by that river, they remembered where they'd come from. We don't, and singing is all they allowed us to hold on to from wherever we did come from. So, we have to sing."

"Amen! Amen! It's one of the head deacons. I know that voice, too, and sometimes it says, "Amant!

A song rises from somewhere. I shall not, I shall not be moved. I shall not, I shall not be moved. Just like a tree that's planted by the water, I shall not be moved. (My brother Charles sings that song at home.) And another verse starts, "On my way to Glory, I shall not be moved...."

The preaching goes on. "That's right. We'll stay right here. Even if it means we have to wander in the wilderness for another forty years, a-leaning on the Lord."

The preacher has mentioned the word wilderness. We have a song about that, and they sing,

Tell me, How did you feel when you come out the wilderness, come out the wilderness, come out the wilderness. Tell me, How did you feel when you come out the wilderness, a-leanin' on the Lord?

The verses continue.

Did your soul feel happy....?
Did you feel like shoutin'....?
With the chorus,
I'm a-leanin' on the Lord,
I'm a leanin' on the Lo-o-ord,
I'm a-leanin' on the Lord,
Who died on Calvary.

And more preaching, "Brothers and sisters, let's stay right on the path; let's just
keep on looking towards the promised land, that land flowing with milk and
honey. Didn't my Lord deliver Daniel? Then, why not every man?"

"Hallelujah!" comes from one of the dancing women.

One dancer drops her chin down towards her chest, shakes her head from
side to side like she's trying hard to understand, and shoots an arm straight up
in the air, fist clenched "Glory, glory, glory!"

Papa's cousin Lizzie, sitting near the dancers, takes out a white handkerchief
and wipes a tear from the corner of her eye. You couldn't'pay her to stamp her
foot, or yell out in church, or
anywhere else.

Sounds to me like the preacher talks in riddles and the people help him by
singing in riddles, too. We gonna stay here and look
towards another land flowing with milk and honey.

"Good grief! We've had our own honeybees. You have to scoop the honey out of the hive.

Now Papa always does everything by the sign of the moon. New moon means maybe you can plant something; another phase of the moon means you can cure something; then there's the dark of the moon. One-time Papa told Mama not to go messing with the honeybees because the moon wasn't right. Mama, born Some thirty miles away, tries not to act like mountain folk sometime, and she hates any kind of what she calls fogyism. Well, she went anyway to rob the hives, and the bees covered her. I don't know if Mama's mind changed about going by the moon, but I don't think we had any honeybees after that.

And the dumbest child at school knows that milk comes from cows, and you don't get it from the river. So where is this land that's flowing with milk and honey?'

And before I can figure that out, another song starts. It's about some river, too, maybe recalling the Bible's account of slavery in the Land of Egypt—
"Lord, I ain't comin' back no more; lord, I ain't comin' back no more. I'm gonna sit down on the bank of the river, lord, I ain't comin' back no more."

Next, a dancer's heel drums against the floor, *Pamp-a-pam! Pamp-a-pam!*

Lord, I ain't comin' back no mor-oo-ore. [Pamp-a-pam! Pamp-a-pam!]

'They won't drag this one out til it falls apart.'

Well, I'm gonna sed-down on the banks of the river. Lord, I ain't comin' ba-ack no more. [Pamp-a-pam-pam-pam!]

One dancer goes back to her seat while the heel of her shoe raps the floor, Tap-tap-tap-tap! Tap-tap! and she moans "Lord, lord, lord, lord."

"Amen! Amen!" says a deacon.

An upright piano stands silent near a window behind the women's Amen pews because nobody can play it well enough to keep up with all that singing. And the people and the choir don't really need it anyway.

I sit, listen, soak it all up and I'm thinking, too. These strange people the pastor and the old people love so much to sing about, these people who sat by rivers and cried and wandered in a wilderness somewhere, who are they? Where are they? Do they know about us? They wrote all those books in the Old Testament, and we don't even have enough song books to go around.' In Sunday school, we have little leaflets with pictures of Jesus on them. I like to hear about the strange people of the Old Testament, and I like the leaflets, too. But I don't feel too good when I think about the two bears tearing up all those children that made fun of the old man and got cursed by him.

I can't see if the old man's in church, and Aunt Bell will really get me if I turn clear round to look back for him. If Mr. Bob is here, maybe he's forgot about me. I hope he has.

Well, we did get through Sunday school; church is almost over, and nothing's happened to Wat and me. Finally, the preacher stops preaching, the women stop dancing, the shouting and singing stop, too, and everybody gets quiet. Up in the pulpit, the preacher stands straight and wipes away the beads of sweat still popping out on his forehead. His right arm, with an open hand, is stretched out towards the congregation. He squeezes his eyes shut like he's trying hard to remember the words he says every Sunday. Now his voice is calm and soft like he's talking to little children,

trying to get them to go to sleep at night, and he says,

"Now may the grace of God rest, rule, and abide with you all henceforth and forever more."

Anybody would wonder, "Does he expect to ever see us again?" 'Anyways, when he opens his eyes, church will be over,' I'm hoping. But I know we have to sing one more time.

Blest be the tie that binds,
Our hearts in Christian love,
The fellowship of kindred minds,

Is like to that above.

It's over. Nobody owns a telephone, so the grown people always gather outside to exchange greetings, and maybe talk about what happened at work that week. Some of the people they work for ask for an awful lot for the little money they pay. Our people can groan and cry about that in church. Outside, the women stay close to the church, the men move farther away and huddle in their little groups.

My mother has been talking to Mrs. Ollie Daugherty, another woman I know. I go to school with Edie and Willie Belle, her two youngest girls. They live right down the road from the church, and Mama says Mrs. Ollie is part Indian, too, like Mama is, but I don't think it's Cherokee like Mama is.

I notice that Mama seems to enjoy talking to women who are not old family in this part of the mountains. She says she and Miss Ollie are outsiders, too. Today they stand in the courtyard where little gravel stones make a long, wide platform that's held together by a rectangle of cement curbing. Each corner of the courtyard is marked by a big round dark green boxwood. The waxy teardrop leaves fairly sparkle in the sunlight that afternoon.

My brother Wat stands way over at one corner, right beside one of the bushes, staring at Mama as if he wants to jump behind the bush or under it. I keep close to Mama, waiting. I want to go home. Oh Lord! Here he comes. Mr. Bob is a dumpy, short man with a large stomach pushing his vest way out in front. From the men's side of the outdoor gathering, he comes ambling up to the courtyard and, lifting his little round hat by the front tip of its brim, he speaks to my mother. Then, with a round, sad face that's wider than his hat, he bows politely. But his politeness can't hide his hurt feelings, not from me. I feel kind of sorry for him, sorry for what I've done, and sorry for what's going to happen next. Mr. Bob doesn't look at me but says,

" Mz. Bun-et, could I have a word wif you, Ma'm?"

Now Mr. Bob doesn't know my mother well enough to call her Mz. with her first name. No matter how well grown people know one another, they always start with Mr. or Ms. But to use that title with the first name means the person is closer to the family than if they use Mr. or Ms. with the last name.

People of our community might even be close cousins, as many of them are, but they call one another Mr. and Mz. or Miss, particularly in the presence of children. I s'pose we say Mr. Bob to the old man just to make him feel more welcome to the community.

I know what his word is, and it's going to sound awfully bad to Mama, especially if Mr. Bob tells exactly what I said, calling his wife by her first name and talking about his underwear. My heart is beating so hard I hope Mama can't hear it.

To Mr. Bob's question, poor Mama, not knowing what to expect, just puts on a Sunday smile with a wonder-why wrinkle on her forehead and says, "Why, certainly, Mr. Bob." I stay close to Mama.

With that, Mr. Bob turns towards my brother, points his walking cane at him, and says, "Dem two lil' chillum, righ' deah, made fun o' me." What he meant was, "That little boy over there behind the bush, and the little girl who was up on the bank when I passed along the road, made fun of me."

Funny how he knows Wallace put me up to blabbing about his raggedy underwear, because Wallace didn't say it.'

And that was all he needed to say. He didn't call our names; he probably didn't even know our names like any of our old people did. But "Them two little children right there" belonged to Mama. And as much as Mama may have wanted to disown us right then and there, she couldn't. Not a single person at Mills Chapel Baptist Church would say they didn't know Wat and me as well as they knew everybody else.

Poor Mama is disgraced. Now she has to put up a good front and try to make the old man feel better. Papa always says, "Pacify a baby, humor a fool."

Maybe Mr. Bob doesn't understand our mountain ways, but Mr. Bob is neither baby, nor fool. So, Mama has to do something to pacify him. After all, he will forever be a stranger among us, and it's her own flesh and blood that's vexed him. Loud and clear, just in case anybody else has heard the old man complain about her young'uns, and the youngest ones at that, Mama ups and says,

"An' Mr. Bob, if it ever happens again, you just take a stick to 'em yourself."

I'm thinking, 'Surely she don't mean that big heavy brown walking stick?

Except by marriage, Mama was an outsider, too. But not the same way Mr. Bob was. Mama at least was married to an old settler family favorite of the community. And Mama was mountain born and raised, too. Hmf! If we had been growing up in Shiloh, Mama's hometown, Papa would have been the outsider. But here she is, raising this stranger to the level of, well, something like a member of the family or a close neighbor that could whip us if they ever felt we needed it. What a way to end a nice day at church, charged and found guilty right in the church courtyard, and not even one question asked! The old man was not to be further aggravated by Mama's probing into who said what and when it was said, and whether he had provoked us in any way. If the old man said we did it, we'd done it. Thank goodness, he didn't even have to repeat what we—I—said about his raggedy underwear and his wife having to mend them. Just saying the famous words, "Them two little children made fun o 'me" was enough. We had violated an old rule that dated back to Bible times in the days of Elisha.

It was as if Mr. Bob had just read the words right out of the Bible about the old man and the forty-two children that made fun of him and the bears that tare them, and was reminding Mama of how serious it was.

After we got home, Papa heard about how we made fun of Mr. Bob, and how it made Mama feel so ashamed to hear about it right in the churchyard. Then my brother and I got the taring we'd earned. But old Mr. Bob, after that day in the courtyard, he never so much as scowled at us. And we never made fun of him again, bears or no bears.

CHAPTER 7: PORTRAIT OF AN ANCIENT LAUNDRY WOMAN

On that stretch of road coming up the hill from Old U.S. 70, curving due north at the corner of the front yard of the gray

two-story frame Fortune home, and not far from the original Mills Chapel Church building that was moved in the 1950s to the west side of that road, a new frame house had been built. Its roof was rather flat and that feature with the oblong shape of the house reminded me of Noah's Ark. That's where Miss Emmaline,

wonderfully African, old Miss Emmaline lived. To people on our side of Mt. Allen, Old Miss Emma was neither kith nor kin, but to me, she had a strange way of being special. She was a symbol of what they said we had been, Africans; but nobody seemed to care about what that was like. Our paths led in opposite directions: Miss Emma would never know the inside of a classroom. I would never know the life of a laundry woman. But I looked up to her.

It's around 1938. I'm seven years old, but I can tell that Miss Emma's not much looked up to on our side of the mountain. Hardly anybody ever mentions her name, except for one time, just once to say how stern she is. Her husband has pneumonia and he must be feverish at times. Miss Emmaline, they say, sits at his bedside with a little stick in her hand. When the old man pokes one foot from under the quilts piled on to keep him warm, Miss Emmaline taps that foot with her stick and that foot quickly disappears beneath the covers.

What else could she do? In that time, no poor Black man was going to the hospital, no matter how sick he was. He couldn't even be sure that they would take a Black man in.

And even if they did, where was the money coming from to pay the bills? I thought Miss Emmaline was just trying to keep him warm, trying to help him get well.

When he died, Mama took me to his funeral. Would he have looked so peaceful if Miss Emmaline had been cruel to him?

I didn't think so. But that's how the grown people talked. People thronged to funerals for three reasons that I knew of. One, naturally, was to show respect for the dead and his family; another was to see which member or members of the family would "take it the hardest." If nobody shed a tear or cried out in grief, they would say that funeral was "a mighty dry one," and that was sure to arouse suspicions of how the family got along with the dead when he was alive. Certainly, a sorrowful look on the face of the deceased meant that all was not well in that family. That was the third reason, to get that last look at the face of the corpse.

An old superstition told them an unhappy face could mean the spirit of the deceased might return to haunt the family. A calm facial expression meant the person had died in peace.

Well, whatever they thought of Miss Emmaline and her husband, I knew she could do something that not another blessed woman in the whole bloomin' community would even try.

Coming down Kennedy Road, high above the Big Road on my way to Clear View Grammar School on Monday mornings, I would see her. From below the hill, the image of her sturdy frame would always rise above me. She was a stout woman who appeared to nearly six feet tall or more. Her round cold black face turned towards the early morning sun, her body a straight figure moving slowly, most of her wirey, graying hair tucked under a faded bandana, Miss Emmaline was headed for town. By the time our paths met, she had already come nearly half a mile over the same road I would take in the opposite direction. I had about that far to go to get to school. Miss Emmaline still had a good country mile ahead of her.

As if every muscle of her back had been starched and pressed without a wrinkle, she walked tall and straight, her head held high. Never looking to the right or to the left, she kept to the south side of the road where fewer trees had been felled for a house to be built here or there. The shade would be kind to her body, kind to the tedious burdens she bore.

On top of her head, towards the forehead, rested a huge wicker basket of freshly done laundry protected by a pale pink cotton cloth neatly tucked in around the edges. Two smaller baskets, also covered, snuggled into the pyramids of her sleeved arms bent at the elbow on each side. With palms turned outwards, the backs of her huge hands rested against the sides of an ample waistline as her fingers curled upwards, revealing the black outside and tan inside of those great organs that earned bread for her and her blood kin, her niece, the wife of a man who wanted to be a preacher, and their children.

Everything about her was important to me. To get a closer look, and maybe because I longed for recognition from this remarkable human being, I would come skipping down the hill towards the Big Road, as Cragmont was known. When I got close enough, I would eagerly call out to her, 'Mornin' Miss Emma.'

But Miss Emmaline, staring intently ahead, would move only her lips to utter an almost inaudible response, less a greeting than a grunt that always puzzled me. Yet I was certain Miss Emmaline meant no harm. While her lack of recognition always disappointed me, I could never blame Miss Emmaline for ignoring me—or for anything else, for that matter.

I was growing up in a community wherein Black people on one hand striving to escape their visual kinship to Africa, tried to adopt a style of dressing that came from Europe, and at the same time, clung to a way of cooking, socializing and talking that was solely ours. It was a three-sided culture that we children learned to accept without question. We got used to the scornful expression of "Comin' in here wid your nappy head, lookin' like a African" and "Comin' in here tryin' to act White on me (pretending that you don't know how poor we are)," also a rebuke, and one even worse than the other; for any kind of pretense was seen as a mark of shallow character, a sign that the offender could not be trusted.

Submerged within but not crushed between those two conflicting concepts, I had no proof that Africa was evil; and that vacuum of the absence of truth I filled by imagination.

One of the last bits of graceful Africanness left in our village, Miss Emma was my only symbol of the goodness, the greatness left behind when our fore parents were torn from the shores of West Africa, driven aboard waiting slave ships and stored in tight quarters, sailing to slave markets in the Americas and in Europe. Much more goodness must have been left behind, I firmly believed, though with that belief I was surely in the minority. Yet, Miss Emma was my affirmation that Africa had been a good place to live, that the people, too, were good. For that reason, she could do no wrong.

Among other women from any part of our community, I never saw one who would put even a soft bundle on her head and walk for any distance at all. Miss Emmaline could walk up and down hill for a mile and more, carrying the bundles of wash she must have labored over from Monday 'till Friday, probably doing most of the ironing on the weekend. I hadn't been inside her house; but I knew that she, like most everybody else, most Black people I knew well, had no running water, no washing machine, and maybe two heavy smoothing irons to be heated on top of a wood-burning cook stove that had to be scrubbed to clear away any soot, or a bit of charcoal that could leave smudges on a spanking white starched shirt that some doctor, lawyer (we did have two doctors and one lawyer) or business man would wear the next week. I barely recall seeing Miss Emma in church one time other than at her husband's funeral. She just wasn't there on Sundays.

The weekly sighting of powerful Old Miss Emmaline always reminded me that, in spite of ages gone by and oceans of distances separating us from Africa, we in our isolated mountain community were culturally connected to that continent yet.

Mama said that Papa's Aunt Phoebe had done laundry until she lost her eyesight. She had been a slave, too, and was even older than Miss Emmaline. She had a strange way of speaking English, Mama said. Other than that, nobody connected her with Africa. *Could she have carried laundry on her head like Miss Emmaline?*

To me Miss Emmaline was the proud symbol of the past we heard nothing about at school, the past too many Black people of my childhood would rather not be reminded of at all.

Remembering a picture I had seen in a book Papa brought home one day, a rare gift from somebody in town, I could imagine seeing Miss Emmaline in her native African village, returning home from her farm, a basket of vegetables balanced on her head, a bundle of firewood tucked under each arm. She must have been working for her own family and had the freedom to go visit a neighbor. Miss Emma had no time to visit. Slavery had ended when my grandfather was 16 years old, Mama said, but Miss Emma still worked for White people.

The difference was that she got paid a little money for her work, just a little. In the picture, the African woman carrying sweetmeats" on her head to a sick neighbor's hut wore a bandana like Miss Emmaline. *Was the hair under that bandana kinky like Miss Emma's?*

In my hometown, by the mid-1930s "straightening" or "pressing" hair had become more popular than with the previous generation of women, two of whom—both of Papa's first cousins on the Burnette side—Cousin Isabella and Cousin Rena, had wrapped the locks of their hair in strips of silk stocking as I'm sure their more African mothers, Aunt Harriet and Aunt Mattie and their grandmother Rosanna Burnette had done.

Along with the newer inventions for smoothing out tight curly hair had come common expressions for hair texture that included "good hair" and "bad" or "nappy hair." *Bad hair* described tresses that could be made more appealing only by applying great dabs of gooey hair pomade and pressing them with hot combs. *Good hair* could easily be styled without the use of hot irons.

What's more, with the exception of my father, I knew of no one who dared to use the word "black" to describe the color of anybody's skin. So, we heard "dark complected," and its opposite, "light complected," neither of which applied to the color of my own skin. I was somehow grateful for one of those term's having replaced two outdated ways of describing people of lighter skin colors: those terms being "yellow" and "high yellow," with *yellow* pronounced as "yalla."

At the age of four I would be given a shocking reason to fear using the word "black" for dark skin color. It must have been late fall or winter; for the in-law who stopped by our house that Sunday after church was dressed not only in black suit, but also in black overcoat and black hat, all in black, the favorite color of *Sunday-go-to-meetin'* clothing for adults. His skin, too, was black; and I was so impressed by this admirable unity of color that I walked right up to him, looked up, called his name, and chirped, 'Dewey, you're black all *over*.'

The man looked down at me, his eyes twinkling with amusement. But before he could thank me for my compliment—as I thought he was fixing to do, Mama whisked me out of that kitchen and turned me across her knee. The surprise of that reaction all but numbed the pain, but what really stunned me was the realization that my own mother's opinion of black skin was so different from Papa's and mine.

Papa must have been out in the fields somewhere that Sunday. Papa believed that preachers, especially uneducated ones, should go out and earn their living like other Black men did. He used to say that some of them had just looked up in the sky and seen the letters G. P., believing they meant Go Preach; but Papa said they meant Go Plow. So instead of going to church on Sundays, Papa had the judicious habit of going to the fields to step off the acreage of some section of his land. He didn't have very big feet and he probably under-stepped the actual measure of an acre or two before he got it right.

Point is: he would keep accurate track of each Sunday's tally and if that count had changed at the next stepping off, he would just pull up the surveyor's stake and put it right back where it was at the last count. He had learned that from his Uncle Hardy, his dad's older brother. Uncle Hardy, too, had been a slave, but he wasn't afraid to try to protect the land he'd been able to get his hands on after he was free.

In our town, no Ku Klux Klan paraded through town and threatened Black people for standing up for what was right. Black people did bow to laws of segregation, one-sided as they were. For us, as Papa explained, the good laws were still hiding in the books somewhere; so Black people bided their time, waiting for better days to come. But, in other ways, like refusing to drink the water a "COLORED" water fountain rising out of a white porcelain basin encrusted with dirt and spattered with hardened brown tobacco stains, they held their heads high.

Only White people lived up town, but out where we lived, Black owned property adjoined White owned property; and fudging a few inches of a Colored man's land now and then was commonplace. That's what Mama told me. And whoever told her, Papa's aunt Phoebe I guess, had said that one time the foot-stepping and the stake-shifting got so mixed up that Papa's uncle Hardy had to send for the surveyor to come back and reset the corners of his property lines. When the surveyor's chain dropped right were Uncle Hardy expected it to, he looked straight at his squelching neighbor and stammered in his heavy West African accent,

"Den, den, you see whar de chain fall?" [*Now then, you see where the chain falls?*]

Being so much younger than my mother, Dewey could say nothing that Sunday, but later told my sister that my mother shouldn't have spanked me. And when he got the chance, he told us about the days when he had played at the home of a little White child way back in the hills on the Blue Ridge side of our community. That youngster was around Dewey's age, and neither of the boys had shoes. They apparently played well together and at no time had the other child ever noticed his playmate's black face, hands and feet. But one day as they were playing, the other child suddenly looked down at Dewey's feet and motioned him towards the rain barrel at the corner of the house.

"C'mon over hyer," said the child, "'n lemme wash ye feet. Ye feet's got mud on 'em."

Dewey paused, waiting for us to figure out how humiliating it must have been for him to explain that his skin was clean, but its color wasn't going to scour.

More than the portrayal of childhood innocence, this story points up the undeniable record of an ancient scorn of skin color that is black. Who knows how many ages had passed before Solomon himself would say, "I am black but comely…"? And again, "Look not upon me because I am black, because the sun hath looked upon me: my mother's children were angry with me; they made me the keeper of the vineyards; but mine own vineyard have I not kept"?

[KJV, *Song of Solomon* 1: 5 - 6]

We weren't keeping our vineyards too well either. At any time in our community I myself could hear, as if the logic were indisputable, "He is dark, but he's good looking." It was as if some unwritten commandment had declared that comeliness and blackness, the twain, should never meet.

We children, too, adopted the language of scorn; and lurking deep within our home language, that scorn followed us to school. Not one of us would speak disdainfully of dark skin in our teacher's presence because his own skin color was a deep rich black. But the teacher had big ears and one day he said to us:

"Students, in the King's English, there is no such word as com-plect'-ed; and if you have enough hair to cover your scalp, you *have* good hair."

At school, hair grooming always got more attention than going over our lessons before the school day began. Braiding hair in different styles was ritually practiced before the teacher arrived each day. I didn't need my classmates' help with homework, but I envied their hair-dressing skills. So after school, having no "head of hair" other than my own on which to develop that art, I would go out under the fruit trees at home, find a few tufts of tall, tough orchard grass and practice my braiding there. That's how I learned.

But in spite of the teacher's comment, the notion of "good hair and bad hair" stayed right on with us. And I would guess that the whole industry of hair products, treatments, processing, and hair styles for African Americans could have grown out of these tainted ideas and borrowed opinions of black skin and kinky hair -- those physical features our fore parents brought with them from West Africa.

At home, being around Papa, I was conditioned to respect and love whatever was left of my African heritage. After Grandpa Squire and Grandma Mary Elizabeth divorced, Papa was exposed to more Africanness than he ever would have known with his mother, who was more Native-American and Scotch-Irish than African. Grandpa Squire Jones Burnette and his youngest brother, George, were away in the coal mines of West Virginia, so Papa's rare philosophy of self-worth must have come through the influence of his grandparents, Squire Alexander and Rosanna Burnette, and through their oldest daughter Phoebe and their younger son Samuel--all former slaves. From childhood, Papa and his sister Margaret had the unusual advantage of being brought up in a family of two generations that had stayed close together right through slavery. What's more, those two generations had held on to their black skin color, their wooly hair, broad noses and full lips along with more than a spoon full of their African culture that flavored a whole chunk of our behavior at home and in church, so I heard. But I didn't hear a lot that I could put my finger on.

Early in life, Papa had told me that all of our people were supposed to be black. And he said the Black man was in no wise inferior to any other man except in the "hand that had been dealt him." What Papa meant was, through the coincidence of his brutish captivity, his unwilling and inhuman means of migration from Africa, and the demeaning consequences he had inherited upon his arrival here, the Black man had been forced to take the back seat to citizenship: and that seat was designed to ensure that he would never arrive at the forefront of prosperity along with Americans from other countries, particularly those hailing from Europe.

Papa would speak vaguely sometimes about the disadvantages Black people faced as being the result of losing a war. Then, I would imagine he had heard that from his father's people and I would get visions of a more warlike tribe of West Africans having the weapons to overpower the tribe of my ancestors, of capturing and selling them to European or American slavers who coffered them in irons and marched them off to a waiting ship. Sometimes, what I'd heard got mixed up with what I knew and the little I'd read and, altogether, it made sense.

But Papa did say that one day, in spite of all odds against him, the Black man would rise. And he didn't say the Negro or the Colored man, but the Black man, would rise. Papa was using the word *Black* back in the 1930s, and I understood that *Black* meant a person of African descent, regardless of the color of his skin.

Getting an education was one way to rise. But somehow the concept of a more European-like appearance became immediately desirable and with or without education our people developed a color cast system that can best be described by this saying, "If you are white you are right, if you are brown stick around, if you are black, get back: get way back."

In our community of many colors, in spite of what any one of us believed, we were one people, regardless of skin color. While I knew nothing of the practice of people of very black skin discriminating against people with very light colored skin, I did hear of brown bag parties where the host tacked a brown paper bag beside the front door. Nobody whose skin color was darker than the color of that bag would be allowed to enter that house.

It's no wonder that one of my elementary school teachers who seemed to be well ahead of her time gave her students a special poem to recite as part of our school-closing activity. As I write these lines, a few candid words of those verses I learned at Clear View come back to me.

So eager to please our teacher, our parents and all the other grown folks, we third graders stood in the church sanctuary one evening and repeated these words, understanding at the time little of the value they held. We had memorized all of several stanzas, but only the chorus, the punch line of that comical but wise piece of advice, returns today. It went like this.

So, honey, don't you be whut you ain't,
Jes' you be whut you am,
Cas' ef a man am whut he isn't,
Den he isn't whut he am.
'N if a man am whut he isn't,
Den he aint wuff a d—n.
Author unknown

We couldn't't repeat that last word in the Mills Chapel Baptist Church sanctuary, so the teacher taught us just to clear our throats, saying "Ah-hem."

The people got it, the last word, that is; and they roared with laughter at the comical language, so different from our own mountain speaking in "broken" English.

It all comes clear to me now. It comes clear to me why the sight of Miss Emmaline left its mark on my childish mind. Miss Emmaline wearing a long, spotless but worn, pale blue cotton dress, the hem stopping slightly above her shoe tops as her raised arms hugged those two smaller baskets and caused her dress to lift a bit more and show the thick hem of a homemade petticoat, clean but dulled with age.

Knowing well that dirt road leading out of the Black community, the dirt stopping where the paved section started to pass through White owned property west of town, I can still see Miss Emmaline steadily bearing the burdens of her weekly labor for which she may have received two dollars and a half for the big basket and fifty cents for each smaller one. I still remember her bearing that load with the skill she had learned from her slave mother, maybe, or her grandmother, walking a winding country road alone, oblivious to what anyone might think of her who looked so much like a pure peasant woman from the backwoods of her once native land. It's clear to me why the sight of her more than seventy-five years ago inspired me then and why visions of her have remained with me through all these years.

Miss Emmaline flawlessly lived those lines other grown-ups thought were so comical, lines we children diligently learned but mindlessly spoke:

"Honey, don't you be what you ain't,

Jes' you be what you am

Case, ef a man am whut he isn't,

Den he ain't whut he am,

N, ef a man am what he isn't,

Den he ain't wuf a damn.

Miss Emmaline was not ashamed of who she was. And she was the best of what *her time* would allow her to be.

CHAPTER 8: MISS EULA

Clear View Grammer School (Circa 1934)

Courtesy of Swannanoa Valley Museam and History Center

First grade was different from kindergarten where Miss Sophia sang spirituals to us, Miss Beatrice helped Miss Sophia and Miss Eugenia to fix hot lunches for us; and they all made us as comfortable as they could so we could take a nap on those hard wooden church benches at noontime. I went off to public school thinking all other Black teachers would be kind and helpful. I learned better soon enough.

My kindergarten teachers were mountain women: Miss Beatrice was my mother's cousin, and the others had lived in the mountains long enough to act like mountain people. But Miss Eula was a lowlander, better educated than most of our people; and even in first grade I could tell that she looked down her nose at us.

In two years, I remember two things she taught us. We didn't have any readers, but one day she read the story of Robinson Crusoe to us. It didn't make a lot of sense to hear about a group of Black men chasing another one named Friday so they could eat him. I guess that was her way of telling us something about Africa and slavery. We didn't need to learn about slavery from a book. My grandmother remembered hearing a man read the Emancipation Proclamation to Great Grandma Hannah and Granny's older sister Margaret when Granny was just five years old. It seemed that our teachers were afraid to teach us anything about that history of our race, but they hinted at it in songs and stories. I guess that was better than doing nothing to enlighten us about the past.

The other thing she taught us was to sing all three verses of the Negro National Anthem, "Lift Ev'ry Voice and Sing." That was good. At every important meeting at church or school, we had to stand and sing every word of that song. It was or song and every school child was expected to know it—one verse about our *gloomy* past, one about the present, t*he stony road we trod*, and one, a prayer, about the future we hoped for—"*Where the bright gleam of our bright star is cast.*" I loved that song.

And there are a few other things Miss Eula did that I will Never forget. Now I've always loved nursery rhymes—still do. But I wondered why it was so important for every single child to take part in an activity from which I learned absolutely nothing. I had been running, jumping and climbing trees for as long as I could remember. Now comes *Jack, be nimble, Jack, be quick; Jack, jump over the candlestick*. Why was it so all-fired important for me to jump over a candlestick not more than seven inches tall? It looked like something I had seen in the Bible or somewhere, with the metal circle at the back to make it easier to carry. I jumped when my turn came. Most of the other children did, too.

But one child was quieter than the rest of us. He and his twin brother had the names of those Biblical twin brothers who fought over some land after the older one agreed to give up his birthright for a bowl of pea soup. That quiet little boy had the name of the one that made the soup. His brother had the name of the one that ate the soup. Our own precious twins were the youngest of a large family of neighbors mixed with Black Hawk Indian and African. Except for the wavy lock that swooped over his left eye, Jake's hair—unlike his brother's-- was as black and as straight as a crow's feathers and as shiny as a raven's. He was such a shy little boy, not one a real teacher would ever try to force to do anything, not with his whole classroom looking on. But we just had to play that silly game.

Well, I have to give Miss Eula credit. She was young. She didn't have any books to give us so that we could look at the pictures and learn to read the nursery rhymes. She was doing the best she could with what she had to work with. And being young and on her first job, probably, she still had to teach two grades in the same room. She was lucky she got the two lowest grades and didn't have to teach three. Our school had seven grades and just three teachers including the principal.

One bright spring morning, Miss Eula brought an old-fashioned candlestick to school and set it on the floor in the front of the room—good thing she didn't bring the candle too and light it. We lined up behind the candlestick. Then the teacher would say *"Jack, be nimble, Jack, be quick, Jack, jump over the candlestick!"*

When she said "candlestick," the child standing right behind it was supposed to jump over it. We had jumped, one by one, and nobody had tripped over that thing. Then came little Jake's turn. The teacher said the word, but Jake just stood there, looking down. She said it again, and Jake didn't move. I started to wonder what was wrong. It seemed such an easy thing to do. But I was me and he was Jake. The teacher continued to coax, adding "*Jump, Jake, jump!*"

That lock of hair didn't move, but his face turned a bit ashy, and he stood like a statue, refusing to budge. The teacher wouldn't give up. "*Jump, Jake, jump!*" Now, that child's body didn't move but something else did. The wooden floors in the classroom had recently been oiled to keep the dust from stifling us when the floors were swept. I looked down and saw a puddle of water rising on top of that oily floor. That's when the game ended and, I guess, one of that little boy's big sisters took him home for a change of clothes.

I think that's the only nursery rhyme I learned that year. But I will never forget looking back at little Jake and staring at that large puddle of water on the floor where he had been standing. That's when I understood Jake's fear and shared his embarrassment. Miss Eula had a way of pushing everything to the limit.

On cold winter mornings, she would make us line up, a row of girls behind of boys, or the other way around. Then she would go to the little light oak colored piano near the door and start playing a march. Around, around, and around the room we marched until Miss Eula figured we had worked up a good sweat. Then she would jump up off the piano bench, spread her arms and block the line. We had to stop. Next, she would go up and down the line stretching open the collars of our shirts and sweaters so she could poke her nose inside.

Now, at home, none of us had a bathroom or even a cold water faucet in the house and none of our parents was going to make a child take a bath before going off to school in the snow with the pores of our skin wide open to suck in the cold air and catch galloping consumption like so many of our neighbors had done and died within six weeks in decades past, Mama had said.

But we were little children and we didn't stink. The classroom wreaked of cold sandwiches, peanut butter and jelly, scrambled eggs, bologna, and sometimes the smell of leftover meatloaf from a Sunday dinner. Except for the peanut butter and jelly, it was all crammed between pieces of soggy white bread swabbed with relish or mayonnaise. Papa said "light bread" wasn't fit to eat and called it "wasps' nest"; and Mama used the bread she baked in his lunches. But nobody dared come to school with a sandwich made from good brown whole grain wheat bread baked in his own mama's oven. Even when we raised wheat, Mama would buy "light bread" for our lunches. And all the different scents got mixed up with the odor of dust rising from the wooden floor we had trampled over and the scent of white chalk dust that we fanned out of the chalk trays under the blackboards as we marched by. It was the way school smelled. But that wasn't good enough for Miss Eula.

One day she stopped the march, stood on tip toes to stick her nose into Johnny's shirt collar and sniffed. Johnny was always the tallest boy in class, and he didn't stink. Miss Eula must not have liked what she smelled because she made an awful face and told us to sit down. Then she went to her desk and started writing something. A few days later she read to the class what she had written to Johnny's grandmother, a mountain woman whose mother had been a slave. Miss Eula's note said "Please give Johnny a bath."

Johnny's grandmother wrote right back, and Miss Eula read that too, with Johnny sitting right there listening: "Johnny hain't no rose and hit's too cold to take a bath."

Nobody giggled. I just stared at the teacher. Johnny's great grandmother and my father's mother had once lived on the same plantation. I felt bad for Johnny and his family, and I thought the teacher got as good as she sent.

But that's not the worst of it. The other problem was she didn't spend much of her time trying to teach us anything like the kindergarten teachers had done. Miss Eula spent a lot of her time sitting at her desk next to the window, and with never a spot or wrinkle on her skirt or blouse, looking as Mama would say, *like she had just stepped out of a band box*—whatever that was. Her short black hair was straightened and plastered down to her head so that not one strand ever moved, not even when she jumped up from the piano to sniff into our clothes.

I could tell that I was one of the children Miss Eula liked the least. But at home I never repeated the unkind things she said or did to us. If I had, my mother would have marched over the hill to give her a piece of her mind. The teacher's dad owned the candy store and my dad ran an account there. It wasn't that. I wasn't betraying my family for a piece of candy. Fact was, Miss Eula was not mountain bred and born and nothing she said or did really amounted to much in my book.

Well, we are not at home. We are here because Papa and Mama can't afford to pay somebody to watch after us, and they don't like to leave us home by ourselves every day, either. So here we are, like an old T-Model Ford out of gas and two flat tires in front, too.

A grassy plot with just a little space between the front steps and the high bank above the road. Not much playing can be done in such a shallow yard. Besides a couple of scrubby apple trees at the edge of the garden on the west side of the house and the big black cherry tree near the backdoor, we have no trees to climb. Of course, the black walnut tree stands in the front yard, but nobody ever climbs the Black Walnut Tree in Cousin Irene's front yard. Maybe some unwritten law was handed down by older siblings, maybe the tree was too old to bear the weight of even young children; there must have been a good reason. Maybe it was because the limbs didn't spread out to make seats for us like the big black cherry tree in our front yard or the biggest apple tree on our place, the Pippin tree that stretched out one giant arm for my swing and dropped twenty-ounce apples that woke me up when they fell to the ground in the middle of the night. Maybe it was that the black walnut tree held its arms up towards the sky like it was praying. Whatever it was, we didn't climb that tree.

We can't play Annie-over. The roof on Cousin Irene's old house is too high for us to throw the ball over; and anyway, we forgot to bring the ball.

It doesn't take us long to get tired of chasing each other around the yard, so we just sit near the bottom of the front steps and watch the big road that runs along the south edge of Cousin Irene's property. Maybe somebody we know will come by and wave at us or maybe just anybody....

On the other side of the road, Ms. Polly's old grey empty house is falling down, both sides of the roof caved in with eaves sticking up like the wings of a big crow getting ready to fly away. Long time ago, she took her two sons and a daughter and went off up North somewhers. I wonder why they never came back.

I sit there, hunched over, elbows on my knees, face cupped in hands and mumble, 'Wish we'd stayed home today, don't you?'

Wat doesn't answer. That means, "Yeah."

Suddenly Wat jumps up and points east towards the house at the top of the hill on the big road. The house with the wide angled roof always reminds me of a big "A" that's lost its middle bar and is crumpling down like two sides of a giant pyramid going flat at the peak. I can see the roof through the apple trees and the overgrown hedge bushes clustering around it. I pass that house every time I go to Grandma Mary Elizabeth's. She lives a little piece back from the south side of the big road in one of Cousin Nora's houses.

But the house Wat's pointing at now sets right off to the north side of that road where the pavement stops. Then the road keeps on coming this way without pavement, right through the Cragmont section of the Black neighborhood.

Speaking of books, there's another thing I will always remember. In our first and second grade classroom, a tall bookshelf stood near the piano. Miss Eula would sit at her desk doing nothing and give us "free time." That meant we could go to the bookshelf, select a book and read all the way through it. If she ever helped us to learn to read anything, my four great grandmothers did; and I never met any one of them, living or dead. No, Miss Eula just sat there, looking all prim and proper and angry. Since she didn't care for mountain people, she must not be happy about having to teach their children, I reasoned.

That woman did so little that we started teaching ourselves to read and write in our free time. We had that much sense.

One day I had a raggedy, old, thick hardback book on my desk. The cloth cover was faded and thin, but I could tell it had once been blue. I was trying to read a story when I saw David go up to the teacher's desk to be tested. All we had to do was to raise our hand and say, "I have finished this book." Miss Eula would call us up to her desk, take the book, leaf through it and point a clean painted fingernail towards one word. If we could say the word, then we could select another book. David lucked out and passed his test, and I watched him heading towards the shelves for another book. I wanted to keep up with him, so I raised my hand to be tested.

When I got to the teacher's desk, she rolled her eyes at me and turned to a page I hadn't tried to read. On top of that, she pointed to a word that didn't even look like a word to me. It looked like a set of blocks: two short ones, two tall ones in the middle and two more short ones. I didn't know the word.

"Miller!" she scolded.

I stared at the word, dumbfounded. In my village, I had seen a real miller many times. He's the one who ground our home grown corm for Mama's sliders of hot cornbread for dinner, and he ground our dark brown grains of wheat for Mama's naturally sweet biscuits that we had for breakfast with real butter, homemade molasses, fresh milk from the cow and scrambled eggs that came from the henhouse.

But I had never seen that word in a book, and I was trying her patience.

"MILL-ER!"

So that's what those funny-looking letters spelled. The teacher got so mad because I had tried to fool her, she called me a liar and sent me back to my seat with that same old book. I felt a little embarrassed and kind of dumb because I didn't know how to say a word, I knew more about than the teacher did. Her dad didn't grow corn and wheat that had to be ground by the miller. She never had to walk nearly a mile carrying a bag of shelled corn or a bag of threshed wheat so that her mother could bake bread. My brother and I did. All she knew was the word in a book. As for the rest of it, it didn't matter a fig. She was no mountain woman.

At the end of second grade she put me to another test for the school closing program. Just me. I, not any other child in her room, had to stand before an audience of parents, cousins and neighbors to repeat her six handwritten pages from memory. When I showed the paper to mama, she grunted and said, "Is the teacher crazy?"

I guess if mama thought the teacher was crazy and she helped me to learn something a crazy teacher asked for, that would make her look a little crazy, too. She didn't see it the way I did: The teacher was trying to make me look stupid and my mother thought the teacher was crazy. Maybe she was, but that all meant that I couldn't look for any help from either of them. Mama didn't help me, but she did go out and buy me a beautiful navy blue dress with a flared taffeta skirt and a velveteen bodice, Mary Janes--black patent leather slippers, and navy blue socks with pink roses embroidered around the tops. Now I really had no excuse. I couldn't let this low lander teacher make a fool of me and my family in front of the whole community.

Before I entered third grade, I learned that she wouldn't be teaching any-more because she couldn't meet the new state laws for teachers. Miss Eula had just finished high school and taken a teacher training course, I heard.

What do they say? "What goes around comes around." But the coming around was bitter and sad. Miss Eula's teaching career was over. Yet, I can't forget the three things she did teach me. The first two were the story of Rob-inson Crusoe and Lift Ev'ry Voice and Sing. I'm glad she taught us that song.

All three verses would e sung at any important meeting in our community for years to come.

Well, the third thing she didn't teach me but she's the cause of my learning it. I had plenty of reason to believe Miss Mae Eula didn't believe I could learn that six page recitation about two boats racing to the shore in a storm with the sky turning dark, with thunder booming, lightning flashing and the waves rising and threatening to sink both boats. If I couldn't learn it, then I would have been left out of the school closing activities and that would have been a disgrace to my parents. Every child had to have a part. And if a child had problems learning a speaking part, the teacher would find something for that child to do, maybe just helping to create the sound effects for one of the songs, or maybe just drawing the curtains—the spanking white bed sheets draped over a wire strung in front of the choir box behind the pulpit. Those parts were usually given to boys. We didn't need any sound effects; I was a girl and I wasn't tall enough to draw the curtains.

Miss Mae Eula was planning it so that my parents couldn't blame her if I was left out. She had offered me a part thinking I would be too dumb to learn it. What else did they expect her to do? And if I couldn't learn it, well that would have been an embarrassment to my parents—not as bad as being left out altogether, but not good either to stand up before the whole community and stumble and blunder through a speech.

And in my second-grade brain, there was no way either one of those what-ifs was gonna happen.

I don't know where it came from, but the thought came into my head.

Write that speech. Write every word of it and read and recite it on your way to and from school.

I listened to that little voice in my head. I sat down and copied all six pages. Then I had it. I didn't miss a word as I stood at the edge of the pulpit in Mills Chapel Baptist Church that summer evening and recited every word Miss Eula had put on those six pages. I still remember the proud gleam on Papa's forehead as he sat in one of the pews at the back of the church that night. So many people were sitting in front of him, I could just barely see the top of his head. But he was there, and I wasn't going to make him ashamed. Those pages held more than words; they held a story and I understood the story. One boat kept going through the storm and won the prize. It was all about not giving up when you are faced with a problem. Once I understood that, it was easy to remember the words. And I thank Miss Mae Eula for forcing me to teach myself how to learn something that looked like it was going to be awfully hard to remember. I never forgot that lesson.

CHAPTER 9: THE DARKEST NIGHT

Thomas Chapel Cornerstone 1922 Historical Monument

It was late October. No longer warm in the mountains, but not yet cold. My youngest brother and I had been allowed to go to the Baptist Young People's Union meeting that was held at our church on Sunday evenings. In 1939 our neighborhood roads and paths were safe, even for young children, even at night.

Every wild animal, the black bear that once raided village cornfields, the stealthy catamount that had stalked my grandmother as she walked home late at night after delivering another youngun on a far distant hillside, the fleet-footed deer and even the conniving fox, all had retreated farther back into their a safer habitat.

Bear meat was a delicacy for the old native mountaineer, either gender of which knew how to use s firearm. But a few men were not just great marksmen they had learned by necessity to hit the spot where a growl or screech came from in pitch darkness.

What's more, not a single dwelling yet stood among the soft blue peaks towering above our tiny town. Animals had their places and we had ours The night was strangely silent. Yet a few frogs croaked to tell us summer still lingered around, and crickets chirped to tell us the first cold of winter was on its way.

"Just six weeks away," as the old folk would say.

So, it must have been early fall. I was around eight years old and my brother Wallace was eleven, --- going on thirteen. We had been allowed to attend a Baptist Young People's Union program alone at our Church (we called it "B.Y.P.U"), and the program had lasted longer than usual.

Leaving the church, I looked back at the round frosted globe of light craning its neck over the wide white double doors. During my few years, I had seen any number of mountain moons rise up and do a better job of pushing back the heavy shadows of nightfall; but that globe did what it could to get us started home. It was casting a misty yellow glow over the hilltop of Cragmont Road and sending a flicker of light across the stained brown weathered doors of Old Thomas Chapel African Methodist Episcopal Zion Church that faced Mills Chapel Baptist from across the road.

Thomas Chapel didn't hold regular Sunday evening programs for young people. Beyond its closed doors that night, the church was veiled in darkness. The cemetery surrounding Thomas Chapel also was shrouded in deeper hues of night, the thickest shadows falling on the east side that lay farthest from its only neighbor, Mills Chapel. Our road home led right past that section of the old burying ground, a precious piece of soil proudly purchased in 1897, by former slaves and their children. As the road ran downhill, passed a patch of woods on the right and blocked our view of the church with its soft light, the darkness of that night gathered thickly about my brother and me.

Knowing that the roads in our community were safe even at night, Wallace and I chatted as we walked past the lower part of the cemetery. By the late 1930s, few people had been laid to rest in that area; and we didn't know them so well as those on the west side, a plot that we children would not hesitate to stroll through in the day time whenever we got the chance; for it was a time to read names and dates on tombstones--where there were tombstones, and to stand silently beside a grave marked by a nameless native stone, a grave we'd been told held the remains of one of our close kin. A visit to the cemetery was kind of like going to a museum—if there had been such a thing. It was a time to bond more closely with relatives we had heard about but would never meet.

The oldest family graves were on the west side, and if the spirits of the east side had anything against my brother and me, there would surely be enough kindred spirits to take up for us—at least one Stepp, Great Grandma Hannah, and a whole party of Burnettes—just about all of Papa's people, except for his mother's father who was properly buried in the White cemetery, and Papa's uncle George Burnette hadn't been buried there because he was murdered in West Virginia and never got back home. Most likely Papa's paternal grand-parents were buried there, and certainly his other uncles, his aunts, and his father, whose three-pronged iron headstone with the three iron rings sym-bolized Grandpa's membership in the Odd Fellows, a marker Papa had made in his blacksmith shop in 1914. Yes, Grandpa Burnette was there. Then there was Papa's younger sister, Ada; a first cousin, Elijah (half Burnette-half Stepp, as Papa himself was), and a younger Burnette cousin, Aunt Bell's only child, Robert, a teenager who had been murdered in cold blood. They were all there.

Tonight we could at least act like we were not afraid and show off the same kind of bravery we pretended to have in a game we and the neighboring chil-dren, usually John and Helen, played well into the dusks of summer evenings at the edge of the woods near our homes. One child, the elected bear, would hide in the woods while the rest of us skipped about the road singing "Ain't no bears out tonight: Papa killed them all last night." Eventually the bear would leap from behind a tree, catch one of us, that child would become the next bear, and the game would go on until we heard calls from across our orchard and from the hillside above to come in for the night.

Not being able to see each other in the darkness that Sunday night, Wallace and I talked. When I could tell by the evenness of the road that the hill and the cemetery lay a little ways behind us, I knew we should be passing by that mysterious two-story, dark brown frame building where a fierce Billy goat guarded those quarters used for membership meetings by the Prince Hall Masons and Eastern Stars.

Well, if such an animal did exist, we had never seen it. Strange animal it would be that stayed indoors all the time and never came outside to graze as our own goats did. We chatted. Wallace would say something; I would answer. I would say something; Wallace would answer. It was my turn now. 'Wallace, wonder why everybody's gone to bed so early.'

In the silence I was caught up in answering my own question. I knew that people used electricity sparingly. Most Black families had been able to wire their houses only three or four years earlier, and they certainly couldn't afford to "leave lights burning," wasting electricity when it wasn't needed. Grown women, domestic workers, earned less than five dollars a week; men, less than seven—even for skilled labor. But what excuse did the town have for not stringing a light on a pole along the road every quarter mile or so? Not a single light pole stood along any public road anywhere in the Black community. Well, that was the answer.

But Wallace hadn't answered me. I stopped, called his name, questioning, 'Wallace?' Then I stretched out my arms as I did when we played *Blind Man's Buff* and groped around in the darkness. But I wasn't playing, and I was staying close to safe ground, keeping my bearings on a road where a deep ditch lay between me and the old masonic building that housed the mysterious Billy goat. Wallace was gone. I was dumbfounded. If he had run away, I would have heard his footsteps. If he was tiptoeing away, I could catch up with him. One thing for sure: I was alone now on a dark road and with other roads, hills and ridges a good way to the north between home and me.

I held my right hand close to my face to test the darkness. I could see nothing, neither my hand nor anything of the road ahead of me. What's more, not one of the three neighbors, neither those in the two Daugherty homes nor the Faust family, both fairly close to the road, had left a porch light on.

I stood still, wondering what to do. *What if…, what if I went back to the church? But what if I got there and saw that everybody had left and that light was off, too? Well, at least I hadn't had to come this far by myself.*

I didn't want to go back up that hill past the cemetery alone, and nobody who could take me home would be passing by in a car that night. I hadn't seen Deacon Brown in the church before I left. And Mr. Faust never came to church at night.

After any church meeting was over, nobody was either Baptist or Methodist any longer—just another neighbor. Pastor Williams was Methodist, and he lived north of the Masonic Hall, up towards the foot of the mountain. But he already had nine in the family to find beds for. Just the same, he might send his two older boys, James and Thomas, to see me home.

Uh-huh, …. Wagon roads had too many gullies and ruts in them. I never had walked that road to their house in the daytime, and I wasn't about to try it in pitch blackness.

I thought about the masonic hall over to my left—not about that silly old Billy goat tale, but about that bright summer Sunday afternoon months ago, coming down that same hill from church with my mother, with Cousin Lizzie and a few other women, when we had to stop for a scene never witnessed before nor since.

A group of young men had gathered right in front of the hall to gamble. They must have got into an argument, a fight broke out, and by the time our church

130

group met up with the gamblers, one of them was coming across the road right in front of us. He wasn't running he was actually sailing through the air. From some childish fantasy came the vision of a man doing a somersault in mid-air. What I was certain of is that his body *wasn't touching the ground no-where* until it landed. And it landed, I guess, where it was meant to go, into the front yard of the little red tar paper house right across the road from the hall. That's where he lived, and he lived after he landed, thank goodness.

I was so startled by what I saw that I failed to recognize the fist that sent that other gambler flying home. But Cousin Lizzie had spotted it right away; and quicker than Mama or any other woman could say, "Lord, Lizzie, look!" Cousin Lizzie had rushed at that crowd of sinners like an old "banty" (bantam) hen, had singled out one of them and was staring up into his knife-scarred face: "Haven't I told you to stop fighting? I've taught you to do better than this! Aren't you ashamed of yourself?"

She was mountain born and bred, too, but didn't speak mountain English. We never said, "Haven't I...." For us, it was "Ain't I "this and "Ain't you" that. And here she was—even at a time when you would expect her to forget her proper English, saying "Haven't I and aren't you...."

Cousin Irene Stepp Underwood

Cousin Lizzie, who worked for the richest family we had ever heard of, was genuinely refined in her manners, and I had never seen her get all riled up like some of the other women did when they got angry or excited.

She never once yelled at the man. She didn't even raise her voice, but she did land several hard slaps on his back, high up on his back, just like she was trying to help a naughty little boy who had defiantly swallowed something that might choke him to death. And wouldn't you have thought that strapping hulk of a nephew whose name rhymed with Roy, the name of his more docile brother, wouldn't you have expected him, being shamed to death, getting scolded right in front of those other tough men, wouldn't you think he might have at least tried to shoo his old aunty away? He didn't. That big good-looking man, dressed in a light grey suit, white shirt and pretty necktie, just like he had meant to come to church but fell into temptation along the way and got sidetracked by a dice game. He just dropped his fists and bowed his head --

just like somebody getting ready to pray. He wouldn't' even look up at his Aunt Lizzie.

And I'm thinking 'His silence shows less remorse for gambling and fighting on Sunday than reverence for this wonderful aunt who has mothered his brother and him ever since their real mother passed away.' To me, who had never seen a doctrine book, who understood little of the religion we were supposed to be following and even less of repentance, that act of respect for Cousin Lizzie showed the gambler's good side. And I was also thinking, 'In spite of that ugly scar on his cheek, he's still a mighty handsome man, that fighting Cousin Foy Lytle.'

In the presence of Mama, Cousin Lizzie and the other church women, the rest of the gamblers fell silent, too. But that was another time, another Sunday. It was nighttime now, and I was alone. I wished Mama was with me. Mama wouldn't be afraid of the dark.

The head of the other Daugherty family in the bigger house near the red tarpaper bungalow was Miss Callie, a kind older woman. She used to live in Cousin Irene's old house; and one

evening when Papa went there to do some carpentry work, he took me with him. Miss Callie was preparing her dinner and as was customary, she set a place for me, too. Even as guests of the old families, children were not invited to the table with the option of saying "No, thank you," especially when they knew it was time for you to eat. They were just politely told "Sit down and eat your vi'tals."

Miss Callie *helped my plate* and to my surprise gave me a cup of black coffee. I don't recollect what she had cooked, but it tasted good, the coffee had been sweetened, and I didn't bother to tell her that I wasn't allowed to have coffee at home. I well knew that Papa had said it wasn't good for children to drink coffee any time of day, especially in the evening. What they actually said to us was "Drinking coffee will make you black." Well, Papa had said that we were supposed to be black anyway. To me, being black was not a bad thing. So, what difference did that make? Nobody gave us coffee at home. I'm guessing it was just too expensive to give to children who shouldn't have it anyway. But kind old Miss Callie gave me sweetened black coffee because, I reckon, she didn't have milk or hot chocolate to offer me. That's what children were supposed to drink with their meals.

Maybe Miss Callie was asleep now. I wouldn't disturb her. Could just have to rely on my mind and my feet to find the way, the way being more than half a mile ahead. I knew the way like the back of my hand, and I had to get home. I could do it even if I couldn't see how to get there.

Just past the front of Mr. Faust's candy store, I would have to go a few feet beyond a scrubby green apple tree that shaded a single unpainted wooden bench where we sat in summer and cooled off with a bottle of cherry, orange, or grape "sody-water." To the right of the store and at the center of their gated lawn stood a pretty green and white house with tall round columns on the front porch. That's where the first and second grade teacher lived.

No way would I bother her tonight or any other time. She would probably scowl at me the way she did at school. She wasn't a bad woman. She just didn't like mountain people and wasn't happy about having to teach their children. She would be sure to tell everybody how I was out at night by myself and how awful that was.

But right beyond that tree and next to the other corner marked by one or two mailboxes, I would have to turn left and take the road up a steep hill. I was used to that road I took to school. It was a wagon road, too, but a car could make it if it had a strong motor and the driver was skillful enough to keep both front wheels out of a ditch. Off to the right of the road uphill would be Papa's Cousin Irene's spooky brown house with the black walnut tree in the front yard. I could have been on her porch in seconds. But it sure didn't occur to me to go there and listen to all of her questioning—if she was home. On Sunday evenings, she usually went back to her job where she lived-in all week.

After church on Sundays, she used to give me a nickel to spend at the candy store where she spent much of her Sunday afternoons with her cousin, Aunt Bell, Papa's other first cousin. But one Sunday right after I had finished a cone of vanilla ice cream and ordered a cold strawberry drink and Cousin Irene had just said "Now, O-O-O-zell [that's not my name, but that's how she pronounced it], O-zell, don't waste your money," some of my schoolmates, the Daniels girls, came by and called to me. I forgot all about that cousin watching to see if I could be trusted with her money, sat that half full bottle of red drink on a table and rushed out the door. Never again, during the rest of her life, did Cousin Irene ever give me another red cent.

"Willfully waste, woefully want!" That's what we heard all the time. And we children didn't think about saving money because there was hardly any to save; and the little we got our hands on we wanted to enjoy.

Lord bless that Cousin Irene. She had never learned to pronounce my middle name. Nobody else in our community ever pronounced my full middle name either, but they got more of it right than poor Cousin Rena did, and she stuttered, too. I could imagine her saying, *O-O-O Ozell! What on earth are you doing out here at night by yourself? Where are you coming from? Does your mama and papa know where you are?*

Both of Papa's first cousins were as strict as an old schoolmarm. I didn't want to be scolded on top of all the other stuff I had to worry about that night. I wasn't even halfway home yet.

And while she was scolding me, wouldn't she blame Papa and Mama, too, for letting me go to church at night with no more than an eleven-year-old brother to see me home? Maybe she didn't know that when Wallace and I were much younger and Mama needed fresh corn meal, we went farther than the church to take our sack of shelled corn to Mr. Taylor's mill. We were small and the way was pretty long for two children aged eight and five, so Papa wouldn't let us carry more than a peck of shelled corn at a time. After the corn was ground, the miller would take a small portion for his labor; and with part of the meal gone, the load was lighter coming home. I always enjoyed helping Wallace take the corn to the mill for Mama's homemade cornbread. But that was in the daytime.

Well, it didn't look good. Not that I was in any danger. If there was any danger, we wouldn't have been allowed to go to church that night in the first place. But it was shameful for me. Here I was, a little eight-year-old girl, out in the dark alone, Mama and Papa were at home, my brother was God knows where; and for my own concocted reasons, I didn't want to go and rouse up the neighbors.

Climbing the hill, I was thinking about what had just happened near the edge of the cemetery. 'Why had Wallace disappeared? Had he slipped off and left me on purpose? Was he trying to get even for something I had done, and forgotten about? Had he gone back to the church to walk home with some girl? Which girl? How could he dare to run off and leave me to face Papa? Maybe he was creeping along behind to get a good laugh on me? He sure was getting sneaky.'

I had heard the old folk speak about teenage boys who had started "to smell themselves." Maybe Wallace was already "starting to smell hisself" enough to want to chase after girls. Maybe that's why he'd run off and left me. But whatever it was, I still had to get home.

I passed right by Cousin Irene's place. The first house at the top of the hill was where the Canady family lived—a big family of ten, counting two of the grandchildren living there since their mother passed away. The youngest son, Howard, was in the fourth or fifth grade. If he saw me, he would surely walk me home, or at least a piece way. He was a nice boy, and once before he had walked me clear home from B.Y.P.U. But I remember that program had ended way before sundown. I had never been in an awful fix like this before. Anyway, Howard's whole house was dark.

How could I just walk up to somebody's door at night, wake them up, explain that my brother had run off and left me, and admit that I was scared to go home by myself? Why, people would be talking for weeks.

I didn't want them to go blaming my parents and I didn't need their pity. I knew the way home.

Hmph! Hadn't my grandmother walked through the mountains alone at night when Papa was a baby? Grandpa was away in the coal mines, and Grandma, barely 20 years old, would have to go way back in the hills to deliver a baby and then try to get home without getting mauled or killed? Many a time, she had told me how she had to run from wild animals. Back in the 1880s, not many houses had been built in the hills, and they were not only few, but far between.

As soon as she heard the scream of a catymount (catamount--cat-of-the-mountain), Granny said, she would start running and untying her apron strings. She'd let that apron fall to the ground, run a ways and throw down a bonnet, next a shawl, maybe even a petticoat, leaving her hard-to-come-by clothing strewn along the path for some stalking wildcat to stop and tear to shreds so she could stay ahead of that varmint.

But that was nearly sixty years ago. What did I have to be afraid of? The wild animals had all gone farther back into the mountains. If the yard dogs had been tied up that night and no snakes were crawling around, I'd be all right.

Below the Canady house I had to turn onto a rutty footpath that angled off to the right, still heading towards the top of the hill where Papa's cousin Isabella's house stood. If it was daytime, Aunt Bell would be standing on her screened-in front porch with her face pressed against the wire mesh, so she'd be sure to see anybody coming from any direction. I wouldn't get past her keen eyes. But Aunt Bell, born way back in 1878, was the oldest living Burnette, older than Cousin Irene or my father and my real Aunt Margaret, and probably asleep by now. She was calmer and more levelheaded than that other cousin back down the hill. And though I knew Aunt Bell would punish me if she thought I needed it, she had never once lived up to a single promise to whip me for squirming around when I got tired of sitting through a long church ser-vice with all the preaching, praying, singing and shouting. But I couldn't wake her up for no good reason.

Just past the last apple tree below Aunt Bell's house, I had to turn sharp left and go through the backyard of the old Brooks place, land that had belonged to my family before I was born. *Why did Papa have to go and sell that house? I could be home now.* One of the darkest places would be that narrow path going between their barn and the high red clay bank at the edge of the field to my left. Out in the open I would pass their pigpen—couldn't miss that! And in just a few yards, I would be passing through the rickety old cattle gate to set foot on my own land.

A few feet inside the gate, on the left, a tall round shadow loomed up in front of me, black and still. Whew! That would be our biggest "chinkypin" (chinquapin) bush. I had been walking fast, being careful not to make any noise. Now that I was on my own land, I could run. Between that gate and my house, no dogs would be waking up to bark at me. I started to run, counting the
landmarks planted in my mind, right and left; and knowingly I leapt into the air here and there to avoid a sharp rock that could injure a foot or cause me to stumble and fall. In my head, I knew where every stone was.

I could have walked that ledge blindfolded. The east side wound along the upper ridge at the bottom of two hills. The higher one, being reclaimed by the woods, was a wide circle of small yellow pines and huckleberry (blueberry) bushes at the very top. It sloped down into a great swatch of an old cornfield just above me on the left. On the north side of that hill was a green pasture that Wallace and I would climb to the top in summer and then roll down to the edge of the wagon road below. The lower hill below the ledge on my right was another broad stretch of idle fields Wallace and I played in from spring to fall, whenever we got tired of the meadows and the stream.

In those fields, we would sometimes come across flint stone arrowheads left by some poor Cherokee hunter more than a hundred years before, when he had been forced to leave this land behind. At other times, we'd find little bunches of yellow-green ground cherries, sweeter than yellow or red tree cherries, or Maypod vines with dark green leaves. And hiding under the leaves we'd always find gourds, the same color as the leaves, soft and sweet inside, plants that had sprung up from old seeds or roots deep in the ground. But whatever the wild berry or fruit we discovered, if Wallace swore to me it wasn't poison, I wouldn't hesitate to eat it.

Wallace had been around that farm a whole three years before I was born, and from the top of that hill on the west, crested by woods that ran all the way from the west to the foot of Mount Allen on the north, and to the edge of the Sand Road on the east, I trusted his common sense about what was good to eat. That's not to say I believed everything he told me, or that we didn't have our squabbles.

One day he made me so mad that I went straight to Papa to let him know that I hated that brother and wished he would die. Well, that's what I said right then.

Papa had been digging a drainage ditch along the north side of the house and he was working right beside the front porch steps. I didn't tell him what Wallace had done; I just wanted to let him know. I was mad as a wet hen, and it would be good if Wallace would just up and die and I wouldn't have to be bothered with him no more.

Papa always had a saying, "Pacify a baby, but humor a fool." At first, he acted like he was in sympathy with me. But he didn't stop shoveling dirt, didn't say anything. And since he hadn't stopped to "chewder" me, hadn't scolded or said, "Shame on you!" I read his silence as "Yes, I know just how you feel."

Well, I wasn't a baby. What was Papa thinking? He didn't even look at me but set his right foot on top of that shovel, appeared to be deep in thought and pushed the shovel hard into the ground. That raspy, scraping noise the metal shovel head made against the gritty soil made me wonder what he was getting ready to say. He must have been thinking of something I knew nothing about, and he wasn't about to explain now. Why had he pushed so hard on the shovel? What did that mean? It made me think of somebody starting to dig a grave. Then, still looking down at his shovel, he said "Yes, and one day you will wish you could just see him."

I had been too busy thinking about myself to remember that poor Papa never had a brother, or that Aunt Margaret was the only one of his two sisters still living. Cousin Lige, the first cousin on the Burnette side had died and Cousin Ben Littlefield, the favorite cousin on his Stepp side, the only one still living, had moved way off up to Ohio. And except for Aunt Margaret's two boys, Harry and Floyd, the rest of Papa's close male relatives had all died off, too.

I was in no position to question Papa's wisdom, so I thought *Well, maybe one day when we are really old, Wallace and me, maybe in our thirties or forties, but sure as you're born certain, not today.*

Wallace was so sure of Papa's fairness that he hadn't even bothered to follow me out to the porch to hear what I was going to tell. Papa's silence was telling me that my problem was not my brother; it was my temper I'd have to learn how to deal with. I hadn't been able to name one thing Wallace had done wrong.

Finally, Papa spoke calmly, the way he always did when he was giving us a lesson:

"Be ye very angry, and sin not; let not the sun go down upon your wrath."

(Ephesians 4:26 [AV])

Well, I didn't know how to do that, --let go of my anger; but if Papa was quoting from the Bible, I couldn't question that, either. I never forgot what he said about wishing I could see Wallace one day, though I had my doubts. Little did I know that Papa's words would come true so soon. Here I was only *eight* years old and already I'd been wishing I could see Wallace on that dark road.

Along the foot of the high ridge, I was running past yellow hedge roses near the chinquapin bush, past a thicket of maple saplings on the right and the crochety white flowers, called *Ladies Lace* (Queen Anne's Lace), making a frilly white collar for the neck of the bank on the other side. Without stopping for a second, I ran on past the lone dogwood tree above the spring arbor, and past the sugar cane mill about two yards below me on the right where we would be making molasses pretty soon. That tall shadow below me would be the chimney of the fireplace for cooking the sugar cane juice.

After the stalks of cane had been crushed and the juice caught in a large vessel, it had to be poured into a six-foot long metal tray carried by four handles, two at each end, about two feet apart. The tray would be placed over the long fireplace and the juice stirred with homemade giant size ladles as it simmered over the coals, thickened and turned a dark reddish brown. Then it was molasses.

On I ran, past another chinquapin bush and the little sassafras tree standing beside it. That's the one half-Indian Granny Hayden hacked away at, with a small ax she wielded with one hand and called "my tomahawk."

Early in the mornings before sun up, I could hear "Whack! Whack!" Granny needed that bark for her herb teas, and the bark and roots of that tree turned dark red when boiled and tasted just like root beer.

Now I was close enough home to be heard if I called out. Mountain people would be quick to answer a call from somebody in trouble, especially at night.

But why hadn't I kept to the big road leading to my grandmother's house? Why hadn't I even thought of going there? I couldn't count the nights I had spent with Granny. She had made herb teas and salves and "caught babies" until she was nearly eighty, but she would get up the next morning, fix our breakfast, tidy up the house, and then we would go sit out on the porch where she would tell me stories.

Remembering what had happened near the east end of the cemetery that awful night, I wonder whether the ghost of poor Cousin Robert was teasing Wallace and me, confusing and

separating us on that dark road to get back at Papa because he didn't get a chance to avenge his cousin's senseless and untimely death.

Unlike Granny Hayden who didn't try to hide her annoyance when a "fool question" was asked or when somebody made a wild prediction, Papa would say—as if it didn't concern him one bit, "Maybe so, maybe not."

It was a strange set of circumstances to think about, a creepy experience I myself was going through that Sunday night; and I have never understood it. But is there anyone who has not heard of weird happenings in and about old cemeteries in the Deep South of yesterday?

Now that the trees and bushes were behind me, the path I had taken along the ledge of the hill widened into another wagon road. Coming down the hill from the north boundary of our land, that road crossed the stream, came up a steep rise and turned west to run along the foot of the high pasture. Over to the left, the stream ran along right beside a little meadow where Wallace and I played now and then with a crawfish (crayfish) that came from somewhere. That stream, we knew, came from a spring that gurgled up through the leaves on the hillside to the west, but we didn't wonder then where the crawfish had come from.

On the other side, to the right, the stream ran under a wide stone bridge, and flowed into the best place to dam up the stream for our summer swimming hole. I could slow down now and catch my breath. I didn't have to run any more. I was safe. As the mountain folk would say "Why, any fool knows that ghosts and haunts won't cross over a stream."

The only shadows now would be from the fruit trees--apples, cherries, and peaches to the right and more apples to the left of the path.

Through the trees in the distance behind me, I'd glimpsed a welcome sight, a faint light filtering through the south window of the bedroom next to the front porch. That light had to be coming from the living room, and it meant Papa was waiting up for us, probably smoking his pipe, and maybe now and then checking an old pocket watch that kept railroad time.

So many mornings I'd noticed him looking at his watch when the train whistle was blowing a mile away. Then he would look at me and tell me which passenger train was coming through town.

"That'll be old 22."

I learned that the morning train going east was Number 22; the afternoon train going west was Number 21. All train whistles, freight or passenger, sounded the same to me. But if the train was going west, the whistle would get louder until I couldn't hear it anymore; and sometime I could faintly see the smoke from the engine rising above the trees far to the south of our place.

On my way home that night, it was good to think of other things, things that weren't frightening. I could remember my first train ride to Old Fort on Number 22, when I was four years old. By the time I came along, horse and wagon was being used mostly for farm work. The only respectable way to get somewhere too far to walk was by automobile. Other than that, the only nearly respectable way to get anywhere of some distance was by train. Oh, you'd have to sit in a segregated *Colored* railway car all right, but you'd be in the company of sociable Black people. At the bus station, regardless of how long we'd been there waiting in that narrow petitioned off hallway that served as a waiting room for *Colored* passengers, we'd still have to stand back until the last White passenger had boarded and taken whichever seat he wanted, often leaving empty seats that we couldn't use up near the front. Then we'd crowd into the seats that were left, but always at the back of the bus and always behind the White passengers. For Black people, the only thing equal about train or bus travel was the fare. Regardless of the differences in conditions, the fares were the same for all passengers, Black or White. *Maybe that's what they meant by "separate but equal."*

Within a few minutes I'd be at my back door. But I remember nothing that happened after I crossed the stone bridge that night. I don't even remember entering my house. I do remember how good I felt when I got to the bridge. From the minute I found myself alone on the road alone that night, I hadn't shed a tear, hadn't cried out for help, and not once had my foot stumbled along the way. I knew Papa would be glad to hear how I had the courage to come on home alone, and Mama would be proud that I could find my way through the dark. Even if she did take most of the credit for some special common sense, I'd inherited from her and give the rest of the praise to her Cherokee ancestors, I was glad I had made it.

But I can't help thinking now, 'It would have been so easy to have spent that night with Granny, or Miss Callie, or Aunt Bell.' I was just too proud to knock on anybody's door.

And I can't help wondering: 'Was Wallace really poking along behind me somewhere? Was he waiting for me to rush in the house, scared to death, complaining to papa about how he had run off and left me and how I had to find my way through pitch blackness by myself? Was he planning to eavesdrop on my tattling and then rush through the door behind me to make me look like a blubbering idiot? 'Maybe. But if we hadn't come home on time, Papa would have come looking for us with his heavy cane, his pistol, and a flashlight. But he had to go to work the next day. How many times had I watched him hoist that heavy blue metal toolbox onto his right shoulder, knowing he would have to walk a mile or two to get to his job? He was always building something for somebody in town or way to the south of town at the Richardson's or the Spate's; and he needed his rest. I didn't want him out blundering around half the night looking for *me*.

Besides, Wallace and I had to go to school the next day; and poor as we were, we never went to class without our book satchels. We didn't expect our teachers to dole out pencils and paper to us, and the other students didn't either.

Besides, what if some kind neighbor or a relative *had* taken me in for the night? How on earth would Papa ever have known where to find me? Nobody in our community had a telephone.

Aunt Bell's house was the last place where I could have stayed on the way home from church. Aunt Bell would have known to leave her front porch light burning to signal to Papa where I was. But in 1939, that thought never crossed my mind.

CHAPTER 10: MOUNTAIN GRUDGES & FANDANGLED FAMILY FEUDING

I can't tell you when it all started, but I can tell you it was way before I was born in 1931. The feuders are not even two different families, but members of Papa's maternal and paternal relatives, all mixed up by blood and marriage. Some of them moved up North, but the ones that stayed in the Swannanoa Valley kept the hostilities going until they died off. Let me tell you this: If you ever need somebody who knows how to hold on to a grudge, call on a mountaineer; If you want somebody who knows how far to carry a grievance, call on that mountaineer's cousin.

Papa always said, "Let not the sun go down on your wrath." [See Eph. 4:26, KJV].

You wouldn't find him in church on Sunday morning, but Papa could quote the Bible as well as or better than most of the regular church goers. Being able to quote the Bible is one thing; having the determination to live up to its mandates is a horse of a different color. Generally speaking, our mountain people, loving, kind-hearted and God-fearing as they were by nature, being so fiercely aware of principles that must not be breached, could also hold on to a grudge and not release it on this side of the grave. And they had no qualms about proving that it had not been released (by the one blessed with more time to forgive) by refusing to go to the funeral of that dear soul who got the call to leave his business unfinished and be off to eternity.

Furthermore, if an old timer was offended by the pastor for a misdeed he had committed, or was accused of some misdeed he hadn't committed, he might write the church off, too, and go there no more until the church bell called the people together to bid him farewell. The people were sure to answer, being eager to hear how the poor preacher would manage *with a straight face* to speak a good word for someone who had not set his foot inside the church door in so many decades, or they might look forward to being amused by the eulogizer "preaching the man into heaven" to appease the grieving family.

Now, appealing to the villagers waiting to go to that funeral, the church bell would faithfully toll, and the people would carefully count the number of times the bell rang to announce the years that dear soul had been given to set his house in order.

That mournful accounting, if it couldn't be disputed, would stop the guessing about the age of the deceased. On the other hand, if people doubted the count as tolled out, they would raise the question of whether the bell got it right and why not, if it hadn't; as it as an awful thing for an untruth to be knelled out from the belfry of the church, of all places. Nevertheless, at the appointed time, the people would rally together as if that departed soul had remained as faithful as any other church goer; for in the community, his standing had not changed anyway, as *blood was thicker than water*, they said. For in our old neighborhood blood kinship was pretty thick; and more often than not, loyalty to kinship outranked concepts of right and wrong.

Even the most bedraggled neighbor, unless he had recently done something deserving of a special reprimand, was to be greeted with genuine kindness. Though his choice of lifestyle could be thoroughly frowned upon, he would hear in passing another neighbor the warmest "How you, son?" or a "How you, ...?" followed by his neighborhood nickname if he had one. He most likely had one, as all of us did. And that question anticipated little or no response but sent the passerby on his way with a bit of cheer, the greeter—most likely a woman, would surely wag her head in pity for a life being wasted.

Among the remarkable ways of these wonderful people was their ability to be just as tolerant as intolerant, and just as forgiving as unforgiving, depending on which way the wind was blowing. And for that very reason, a reprimand by a pastor who was native to the mountains could wield a harder blow than if it had come from a newcomer, a newcomer being anyone who had not been born there, and newcomer he might remain, so long as the old timers ruled the roost in our community.

Yet, unforgiveness had no pets. From my mother's side of the family, I heard of a daughter who had refused to go to her own mother's funeral because of a festering hostility about something the mother, who had been ailing ever since she delivered her twelfth child just four months before she passed away, had done or failed to do. The ailing mother should not have been expected to prevent the illness of one of the youngest of those twelve children, eight of whom had already survived infancy.

Seeing as how the woman had managed to raise nearly three fourths of those children, you would have to say she had done a pretty good job of mothering. Still the oldest daughter blamed her for that illness and wouldn't set foot in the church on the day of the funeral.

From my father's side, the story spread from county to county and from town to town about a compassionate old midwife and herb doctor who, for some reason, refused to visit the deathbed of her estranged second husband. What we did hear was that he was a Cherokee who was known to shy away from hard labor. Now his unwillingness to provide for his own bread and board would have been reason enough for my paternal grandmother to decide he wasn't worth the salt she'd have to put in his bread, or that he wasn't worth kicking out of the road—whichever idea came first to mind.

The old man, it was rumored through Buncombe, Rutherford and Polk counties, to the town of Black Mountain and back to Rutherfordton, was known for certain peculiar personal traits: first, he would not work for a White man, which meant, basically, he had invented an excuse for not having a job at all; and second, he would not eat a chicken that had black feathers. Yet, in spite

148

of this apparent aversion to anything that might appear black in color, Uncle Andy Hayden, and most likely his parents before him, had abandoned his Cherokee land to live within a Black and Cherokee community; and he had managed to marry more than one woman possessing considerable Native American ancestry, my paternal grandmother being the third of his African American-Cherokee wives.

In that way, living among and intermarrying with African slaves and free Black and other Cherokee residents, a number of Cherokees, including my maternal great grandmother, Sarah Payne (Uncle Andy's first mother-in-law), managed to escape being driven out of Western North Carolina during that infamous march known as *The Trail of Tears*.

In this part of the state, populated by three tribalistic groups African Americans, Native Americans and Scotch-Irish Americans, feuds and grudges prevailed, even between cousins and in-laws. I have chosen one that is close to me and too colorful to be kept in the family closet.

The Makings of Two African American Clans

Over the years, from childhood, I was sure to get bits and pieces, sometimes the middle, at other times the beginning, and more often the tail end of an event that had happened way back who knows when. Then it was up to me, using common sense which I, like everybody else, was believed to have been born with, to fit the pieces together into some reasonable order or to fill in the missing parts from what else I had heard, had seen, or might live to see. Having come on the scene in the early 1930s, I stood where I could look backwards and forwards, between the former slave's life and his challenges of freedom and those of his children; so I was in rare position to collect a fair share of common sense about those times; for in those times, it had not occurred to anyone that common sense might be something other than a natural gift with which each of us was endowed along with the first breath of life.

I cannot remember how young I was when I learned that the Burnettes to whom I was related through African blood had come from one plantation, and the Stepps to whom I was related by Scotch-Irish blood had come from another — that my African paternal great grandparents Squire Alexander Burnette and his wife Rosanna Burnette had been freed in 1865 (*at the Surrender*) and that altogether they had six children: Phoebe, Squire, Mattie, Hardy, Samuel and George, the only one who had not been born into slavery.

Studying two pieces of information, I surmised that the oldest of those children, Phoebe, probably was not Rosanna's child. First, Aunt Phoebe and Grandpa Squire were born in the same year; and second, as the informant for Aunt Phoebe's death certificate, my father had sid he didn't know Phoebe's mother's maiden name although he well knew that his paternal grandmother's name was Rosanna Burnette. He often laughed about how stout Grandma Rosanna was, too stout, he said, to walk forward through a doorway, a feature that forced her to turn sideways in order to pass from one room to another. And nine years earlier he had told the death records clerk that the maiden name of his uncle Hardy's mother was Rosanna Alexander. Could it be that Aunt Phoebe and her younger siblings did not have the same mother? I had never once heard Aunt Phoebe referred to as a half-sister to anyone.

Great Grandpa Squire, who held onto the surname "lexander" even after he landed on the North Fork plantation where slaves took the last name "Burnette," was considerably older than Great Grandma Rosanna, so I'm guessing that his former wife, or whoever Phoebe's mother was, had died, if she had not been sold, and that Great Grandpa Squire Alexander had taken Phoebe and raised her-- however much child raising a slave has the time to do, right along with his and Rosanna's children. Though I didn't arrive on the scene in time to meet any one of those children, including my grandfather Squire Jones Burnette who was killed in a coal mining accident more than seventeen years before I was born, (or his older sister Phoebe who departed this life the year before I was born), I felt that I did know five of them—Phoebe, Squire, Hardy, Mattie and Samuel. I had to pass by four of my grandfather's siblings' property on my way to and from school every day: and three of the old homes were still standing and being used, two being occupied by members of original Burnette families—Uncle Hardy's and Aunt Mattie's daughters. I felt that I knew my Uncle Sam because Papa frequently talked about how he had learned carpentry and furniture making from him; and I knew Grandpa Squire because Papa and Mama talked about him all the time.

My mother adored Grandpa Squire and spoke often of his refined manners, his neat style of dressing, and his penchant for looking after neighbors who might otherwise have "gone hungry." And one of the reasons for my familiarity with Grandpa's four land-holding brothers and sisters was surely related to their having bought sizable lots along or near Cragmont Road, the main thoroughfare through the Black community. From the stories passed down to me, I would guess that each great aunt or great uncle was able to borrow a little money to buy one or two acres of land and lumber to build a little house along that main mail route.

I heard that after Aunt Phoebe was freed from slavery, she eventually got a maid's job in town that paid ten dollars a month, and with that income she was able to borrow two month's wages and buy two acres on which she built a two story house. Aunt Phoebe worked with at least one other maid who had never seen an electric light before she landed her job. Surely all the maids knew that candlelight and lamp light could be extinguished by puffing out the flame. So when that maid was reminded to "cut the light off" before leaving the room she had cleaned, she took the business end of her broom and was giving that ceiling light a good fanning when somebody came along who knew how to pull the chain attached to the light fixture.

Former slaves understood the importance of owning land. They had no choice, for rental property was a rarity at that time and for decades to come. The old Burnette sisters had bought land fronting the main road and lying between what is now Brooks Road on the east and the old Faust candy store on the west. Uncle Hardy' barren land lay at the top of the hill above Aunt Mattie's property, and Uncle Sam's place lay along a little stream just across the road from the east end of the Old Thomas Chapel Cemetery. Long before I was born, Papa had either bought or been given the deed to Aunt Phoebe's house and land, had sold it to a tobacco farmer from Tennessee and bought more land farther back towards the foothills of Mount Allen. Aunt Mattie's house, one of the two rental homes in our Black neighborhood, was occupied at times by Mattie's daughter, Irene. Uncle Hardy had built his three-room cottage with its two attic bedrooms high on the hill above the main road, and his daughter Isabella occupied that house until she died. Only Uncle Sam's house was no longer standing. His land, a strip of flat green meadow running along the bottom of that steep hill to the east of Clear View Grammar School, had been willed or deeded to the Baptist Church before I was born. But for me, it was still 'Uncle Sam's place.

Phoebe, Hardy, Mattie and Samuel stayed in Black Mountain as long as they lived. Squire and George could be forgiven for not staying. They took the train to West Virginia to earn their living as coal miners and neither lived to finish his work and come back alive. In December of 1914, Grandpa Squire claimed his lot in the old cemetery and his grave is marked by steel head and foot-stones, made in Papa's blacksmith shop where the headstone was ornamented by the three-ring emblem of the Odd Fellows.Unfortunately, George had no child to claim and bring his body home.

Phoebe married but had no children; Samuel was a devout Baptist: he was not married and, therefore, had no children. Hardy was married and had one child, Isabella, who ruled that hilltop after Uncle Hardy passed away in 1921. Mattie married a member of one of the branches of that enormous Stepp clan, and she and her husband had three children, Elijah, Irene, and another daughter named Ruth. Neither Elijah nor Ruth lived long enough for me to meet them. Tragedy was no stranger to the old Burnette family and George was murdered by one of those typically strong African American women of that era. She had either overpowered him had surprised him with the knife she used to end his life. Papa once described the scene for me, and I got the impression that the woman had killed my great uncle in a fit of jealous rage.

Grandpa Squire married a Stepp, Mary Elizabeth Louisa, the second daughter of Hannah Stepp, the old plantation midwife. He and Grandma Mary Elizabeth had three children to survive infancy, Garland Alfred Andrew, my father; Margaret, who was named for her aunt Margaret Stepp Littlefield Hemphill, detested the nickname Maggie, and little Ada ,who died at the age of eight, whose keepsake dishes always sat on a shelf with Aunt Phoebe's ancient cake plate in our dining room.

All generations of the Burnettes related to me or all whose names were handed down to me as relatives had descended from one father, Squire Alexander Burnette, and supposedly from one known mother, Rosanna Burnette, her "maiden name" and her married name being the same. In 1930, the clerk who had written "Black" for Aunt Phoebe's race and "1849" as Aunt Phoebe's year of birth apparently overlooked that significant connection to slavery and asked Papa for her maiden name; and he, being caught off guard, answered, "I don't know." It was common knowledge that slaves took the surname of the slave master; therefore, no such thing as a "maiden name" existed for a slave woman. Yet, officials who had been so careful to keep things pertaining to race separate had hopelessly muddled the matter of creating death certificates for former slaves.

The absence of a method of tracing last names for slave men and women is tragic. I will always wonder how many times my great grandparents had been sold before they came from Fairfax, Virginia around the end of the 18th century with their final owners, the Burnettes, to be freed near Black Mountain in 1865. Was Alexander a former plantation name? Was my grandfather's middle name, Jones, also a former plantation surname? I was sure of one thing, Burnette was to be spelled with an /e/ on the end, for Mama said that's how Grandpa Burnette had spelled it.

On the Stepp plantation, I heard, there had been nine slave women, only one of whom was allowed to have an African American husband. With so many different mothers and all but one of those mothers, bondswomen, bearing many half-Black/ half-White children because of their subjection to the moods and whims of the slave master and his sons, Grandma Mary Elizabeth, who didn't bother to give me the name of any such child's father except her own, could rightfully claim some degree of paternal kinship with the offspring of seven of those mothers, her own mother being an eighth part of that group. Although the task of determining kinships among members of that clan through their fathers' side has often left us in confusion, I believe that each set of those children knew exactly who his or her own mother was. Certainly, Grandma Mary Elizabeth did: her mother was Hannah Stepp. And some of those children would have known their fathers, too, just as Grandma Mary Elizabeth did...

Slave schedules created for tax records are available, but they list bondsmen, bondswomen and their children somewhat as they did the farm animals, by skin color, age and sex. All had names; even farm animals had names, but names were not included on the slave schedules I had studied. Yet, those records can be helpful when we know who we are looking for Grandma Mary Elizabeth, the last person who would have known the names of all nine of those women and how their Stepp offspring were related to one another passed away in 1956. I didn't have the curiosity to find out their names before she died, and now it is too late to raise the question. Suffice it to say that given the identification of her own father, whose name she personally gave to me, Grandma Mary Elizabeth Stepp Burnette and one Mr. Lank would have had the same grandfather, making them first cousins or a fraction of that relationship. I never heard anybody use the term "half-first cousin."

CHAPTER 11: COUSIN ISABELLA AND MR. LANK

Ages ago something had happened between Mr. Lank and our Cousin Isabella, Papa's first cousin, not a great distance in kinship, but more distant in personal relations (and this I could say of both). What it was, was never explained to me but what may have had a causal relationship was something that would not need to be explained, as it could not be hidden. A child had been born. And the child grew to be a woman who had a child of her own and possibly her child produced grandchildren, though I have not yet chanced to meet any one of that younger generation.

As with any society, I suppose, which has a narrow worldview because it is strapped by poverty, oppression and a hard and humdrum life, people need a distraction. Somewhat like the Puritans who entertained themselves by creating witches and adulteresses, and occasionally finding one to be punished, our people seemed to be preoccupied with the identity of a newborn child's father, whether the mother was single or married. If they found what they considered to be a mismatch, no punishment would be meted out except for the idle gossip that entertained its makers. And the popularity of that subject would linger for many extending into decades.

Naturally, if a child was born to an unmarried woman, an event not to be winked at in those times, people would seek for a father suspect if none made himself known voluntarily. If, in the rarest of cases imaginable, a child was born to a widow, they would seek a father suspect provided that the woman's husband had been dead too long to have sired that child. If a child was born to a married woman, they would—as in any case--seek for familiar physical features or color matches to admire and finding none that could satisfy their ability to determine positive resemblances, they would revert to seeking for a father suspect to condemn or a racial type that could have produced a child with a particular complexion or texture of hair. And common practice was to suspect trouble in the woodpile; for among unschooled country people of those days, the knowledge of how genes were passed on from parent to child was a mystery of the far distant future.

In spite of their broad experience with planting, with seeds and seedlings, of seeing seeds of hybrid red flowers reproduce pink and white flowers, and seeds of white flowers reproduce pink or red flowers, none of that knowledge counted when it came to a child whose skin color or hair texture was strikingly different from that of the legal parent or biological parents. When that

happened, they believed, somebody was surely guilty of producing a woodscolt. I don't mean to imply that our people had no morals and had to be watched so keenly. Not so. Morality is what the people took interest in, having so little of anything else to occupy their minds except for their work which they could do with both hands tied behind their backs—so to speak, and blindfolded to boot; for they were remarkably well vested in manual skills, a fact that had ensured their survival under severely harsh conditions so common to their times, common to their station in life and, consequently, to their race which made conditions inevitably tougher.

"Aunt Bell"

Cousin Isabella Burnette White

I do not know what caused the initial conflict between Cousin Isabella and Mr. Lank. What I'm guessing is that a heated discussion had arisen in the church regarding morality. Cousin Isabella, being a strict disciplinarian, probably was not pleased with her brother-in-law's response to questioning and invited him outside where she could settle the dispute physically. Whenever gossip questioned the morality of a church member, that member would be called in for a hearing. If the evidence was strong enough to prove guilt, that member could be "churched", or ex-communicated. So, the church service was the place where the trouble between my cousins hit the fan—cousins to me but not to each other. Actually, neither of them was ever called "cousin." Cousin Isabella was called "Aunt Bell" because she didn't like the sound of "Cousin Bell," and we called her what she wanted to be called because we knew better than to call her anything else; and my mother bolstered that arrangement by calling her "Aunt Bell" in our presence. Mr. Lank was "Mr. Lank," because every grown person, relative or not, had to be addressed with a title. Of course, we children knew that a title with a first name was the acceptable way to use the name of an older person, especially a relative. Title and last name meant the person was not kin. The point is, the two of them, those uncousined cousins, had gotten into a noisy row way back when.

Mama said that if Mr. Lank had not had the good sense to decline Cousin Isabella's invitation to "Just step outside, Sir," their dispute may have advanced to the next level with Mr. Lank in tow. For it was said that Cousin Isabella was much of a woman who would not hesitate *to grab a man in the collar.*

Besides being physically strong enough to protect herself, Cousin Isabella may also have felt no need to kowtow to any man because she always lived under her own roof.

Being the only child of both parents, Uncle Hardy Burnette and his wife, Aunt Harriet, she had inherited their house and land and no man, not even her own husband--if she'd had one, could lay claim to her property. Well, she had had one, a husband, a Black man whose surname was White, a name she held onto for the rest of her life. But I never knew what became of him, whether he had died, or Cousin Isabella had run him off. Either is possible, but given that, I never knew Aunt Bell to visit Mr. White's grave, that women often outlive their husbands and that Cousin Isabella ruled her roof with an iron hand and took no guff from any man. I may never know the truth, so I'm guessing that Cousin Isabella said to the man one day, "Get out and don't let that doorknob hit you in the back."

Cousin Isabella's mother, Aunt Harriet, already had a precious little girl named Hester when she married Uncle Hardy, and Hester had grown up and married Mr. Lank. As the tiny feet of saintly little Hester never dared to venture near a questionable line between right and wrong, the Burnettes took her and Cousin Isabella's side of the issue. After all, Cousin Isabella was Papa's first cousin on the African side, and Mr. Lank was Papa's second cousin on the Scotch-Irish side. That twist of kinship placed Papa squarely in the middle, between his father's side and his mother's side, and left him leaning heavily towards his father's side. This leaning may have been a cultural carryover from West African culture. Even if it wasn't, Papa and his sister Margaret had been reared by their paternal grandparents and shared a close relationship with the aunt and older uncle who had no children, Phoebe and Samuel. The two who had helped them to get on in the world more than their own father could because he was away in the coal mines. Aunt Phoebe and Uncle Sam were always there, and Uncle Sam was highly skilled in iron and woodwork, skills he passed on to my father.

Of course, the Burnettes who were blood relatives of the Stepps acknowledged that Scotch-Irish kinship—it couldn't't be denied, but that kinship was born of an inherent weakness, that was, the lack of a strong father presence, or a father who could be expected to assume responsibility for their existence outside the master and slave relationship. Although I would not expect that a slave mother and a slave master father could a close-knit family make, given the peculiarities of the slave culture, exceptions may have occurred.

To my knowledge, neither my grand parents who were born into slavery, nor those born free had any Birth certificates. Grandma Mary Elizabeth and Grandpa Squire marked their years of birth by their ages at the date of the Emancipation Proclamation (1863, Grandma) and the date of the "Surrender," (1865, Grandpa), the year both were actually set free.

My free born maternal grandpa, Grandpa Payne, had a greater opportunity for literacy and knew his exact month and day of birth in 1838. My parents, born in the late nineteenth century, knew their dates of birth but had no certificates to prove it. But by 1850, census takers were recording the ages of free Black men, women, and children, those who were present in the home when the census clerk arrived; and by 1880 or earlier, even non-literate African American parents were recording the births of their children and other family members in the family Bible. For many decades, old Bible records and Grandma Mary Elizabeth, a midwife, were verifying dates of birth for employment or for military service and were doing that as late as the beginning of World War II.

Because slave masters could freely chose mistresses from amongst the slave women, many children were born of these unions. Although these children were sired by the slave masters, they did not enjoy the slave master's status. The slave master's Black child was still a member of the slave class and lived with his mother. While he may never be sent into the fields, he does assume daily duties as a slave. This child does not relate to the slave master as a father, even though he has that understanding. This was true of Black children born of White fathers on the Stepp Plantation, and it was true of my maternal grandmother, Mary Elizabeth Stepp.

Growing up, I often heard Grandma Mary Elizabeth Stepp Burnette Hayden speak of a sister Margaret, who died before I was born. But until I began studying census records and was recently shown a page from an old family Bible belonging to cousin Nora, one of my father's cousins, I thought Granny was speaking of another of the Stepp slave children, many of whom addressed one another as brother and sister and did so knowing that they had neither the same father nor mother. Why? I don't know. In spite of my observation of sibling estrangement, it's only fair to say that Margaret's children were close to their mother's sister Mary and the sisters' children were close to each other. In fact, my father and Ben Littlefield were more like brothers than first cousins.

I have no idea when any of my fore-parents were captured and enslaved, nor have I any proof of where they lived before being dragged to this country in chains, but the region was most likely West Africa; and I have heard that West African languages have no word for "cousin." Nevertheless, that practice of the Stepp slave children of calling one another sister and brother, has kept succeeding generations in confusion to this day.

But Margaret was my grandmother's sister and so was Easter, for they had the same mother, Hannah Stepp. Grandma Elizabeth told me so, but I have no idea of what ever happened to Grandma's younger sister, Easter. On the other hand, the older Burnettes who were blessed with both parents of the same race were inseparable. They had had the good fortune to emerge from a slave plantation as a family of seven, and four of those slave-born siblings settled close together and remained close for the rest of their lives. I know that, by itself, the dispute between Cousin Isabella Burnette and her half sister's husband, Mr. Lank, never rose to anything above an exchange of words immediately, but the gorge between his relationship with Cousin Isabella and with Papa ran deep, if not noticeably wide.

Mind you, the wedge that held the chasm in place could give and make room for exceptions, even adding the senseless murder of Cousin Isabella's only child, eighteen-year-old Robert, who was not related by blood to the Stepps as Papa was and as I was. With that event the crevice deepened. Still there were exceptions.

Although it was one of Mr. Lank's first cousins who pulled the trigger of the murder weapon, that didn't stop Papa from trying to befriend the shooter's brother late one summer night.

Mountaineers, being used to thick darkness after sundown, accustomed to seeing just an occasional flicker of foxfire (phosphorus) among the treetops in the forest, blessed with lighted roads only when the moon shone brightly in its cycle, and having learned to see on moonless nights with the help of other senses and organs, their minds, their hands, their feet, their ears and sense of smell, could easily find their way at night through pitch blackness; and a stalwart mountain man could follow a footpath across a whole mountain at night even without a pine torch.

Yet, it was said, the time would come when a man, however robust, having been a heavy drinker in his youth would, if he lived, become too old to handle his liquor. That man, Cousin Log, was known for his love of the bottle. Although he was not in the habit of visiting them on better days, he had to know that he had two cousins who lived somewhere in our neck of the woods. That night he had had too much to drink and even in the light of a full moon had lost his way home.

His home was a good distance away to the west of wherever he had been drinking that night, being nowhere near that part of the hills we lived in, and still far enough away to allow him to sober up by the time he could reach his own door. The main road he was taking, old Cragmont, wound this way and that, but led towards the west most of the time until it seemed to take a sharp turn north near the entrance to the Black neighborhood, as if veering away from Cragmont Road. Instead of following that paved road around the curve until it headed west again, Cousin Log lumbered on straight ahead and entered a dirt road that turned sharply right to begin its ascent to Mt. Allen. That road led due north past the old Gragg and Hooper homes, two of the homes owned by Black families living farthest east on our side of town.

But he hadn't continued north towards his Stepp cousin Mr. Lank's house. And Mr. Lank, who was not known to touch the bottle except for a hot toddy, may well have turned him away. Never mind that. It must have occurred to Cousin Log that to get home before daybreak he needed to quit the north-bound road and go west. Well out of hollering distance from Mr. Lank's house, Cousin Log bore to his left and fell onto the wagon road branching off to the west between the small bungalow belonging to the pastor of Mills Chapel and his family and the large two-story family home of the White minister and history teacher at the high school up town, a way that would lead in time back to the main road he had blundered away from, but not until that blunder had cost him an extra hour of walking time at his gait and with little distance gained for his trouble.

Still, that old mountain dew had left him in control of enough of his senses to keep him headed west most of the time. At the top of the next hill where the woods stopped, the wagon road right-angled and headed north, too, continuing up a steep slope past the Daugherty, Carson and Whiteside homes to the crest of the mountain where it stopped short near the edge of dense woods. But at the foot of that slope where another wagon road spilled off to the left, the same road Mr. Lank used for taking his cows to pasture, Cousin Log bore left again. And when that road split a few yards ahead, he took the low road that led straight to the door of another kinsman, the wrong one, however. He was conscious enough of where he was to stop under the shadow of a black cherry tree and call out to Papa by name to ask if he could spend the rest of the night there, calling out to avoid coming to the door and knocking, and taking the risk of being turned away at the door—an awful insult to bear from a relative. And Papa, unable to see the face hidden in the shadows, had called back to his cousin by name. Despite their being on oppos-ite sides of the feud, Papa was willing for Cousin Log to sleep in his favorite chair, a big, handmade, pale blue recliner on the front porch. I heard Papa call back, "No, Log, but you can sleep in that big armchair out there on the porch 'til daylight."

No drunken man, kin or not, was going to enter Papa's house in the dead of the night, or even in daytime for that matter. It was a summer night.

That's not to say Papa was above taking a few snorts of corn whiskey in his own home, but not with another man and in the presence of his wife and children. So off they would have to go to be in seclusion behind the barn, or at the blacksmith shop, where they could feel free to talk however men talk among themselves and to swear, as they surely would, without offense to anyone within earshot.

But there would be no drinking at the blacksmith shop that night. There never had been with Cousin Log. And duly offended at not being welcomed into the house, Cousin Log who hadn't heard "armchair" stumbled on, mumbling that he wasn't gonna sleep in nobody's d...n barn.

At the edge of the onion patch behind the blacksmith shop, he had to turn left again; and to cross our land, and the Brooks land and get to another rutted wagon road that led back to Cragmont, he had to stay in a narrow footpath angling due south along the ledge of another hill. I knew the path like the palm of my hand and didn't need the high bank on the right, or the saplings growing along the left, to keep me in the path. How Cousin Log kept to it without a blunder that would have brought him tumbling down to the meadow at the bottom of the hill, or into the stream that ran beside the meadow, is more than I can say—except to remind you he was mountain born and bred.

Early mountain people were poor, but too proud to beg. Lacking the means to take care of many of their needs, to care for the sick long term, or, often, to prepare their dead for burial and get them in the ground, they practiced looking after one another: they looked after each other's children without pay; they relied on one another to share what they could afford without being asked; whatever was not being used could be loaned to a neighbor—a piece of furniture, a farm tool, a farm animal. They exchanged vegetables from the field or cooked foods from the kitchen as freely as other kind deeds, and survival in the mountains relied on these rules of human kindness which most of the people followed most of the time. That's how they had lived long before

165

the feud between the two sides of my fathers' family began, long before dear Robert was born, and that's how they continued to live after he was killed.

For that reason, I believe, not even the brutal murder of her unarmed and unsuspecting son, hindered Cousin Isabella from opening her door to another of Papa's Stepp cousins, a young woman who had decided to leave home after her mother passed away. She had told Cousin Isabella she needed another place to live. She most likely missed her own mother and desired to be under the watchful eye of an older woman. She could not have made a better choice: Cousin Isabella was well known as a disciplinarian. However, that choice ruffled the feathers of some of the girl's close relatives, particularly her father's whose nest she had deserted.

Although the feud had started many years before that, Robert's murderer was closely related to Mr. Lank, and might have been agitated by the church trial. What I believe had calmed it was the disappearance of the man who killed poor little Robert. I cannot say "killed in cold blood" because cold blood does not run through the veins of a true feuder. Fortunately, the man had high-tailed it out of town before his gun cooled, had gone four hundred miles away, and never returned.

As late as the early 1930s, a murder suspect didn't need to go far to discourage the Law from making a labored search to bring him to justice. I happen to know that Robert's murderer was not the first suspect to avoid being brought to trial for murder by merely leaving town. Another one, they said, one unrelated to the Burnettes or Stepps, went only thirty miles away to escape being caught for killing two men.

No one had ever seen or heard of *that* small ruddy-skinned, naturally straight-and-raven-haired Black man before he came striding up to his cousin's house one day. It must have been a well-kept family secret that the woman whose home he fled to was his first cousin on the Freeman side. That cousin's husband, my father, unwilling to see another Black man go to the gas chamber or electric chair for trying to defend himself—just about the only known cause for a Black man to risk his life by attacking a White man—or even for being accused of it, had given refuge to the run-away. Now I guess that either the man was no longer considered a suspect or some White man of considerable influence had put in a good word for him; for it was not long before his younger brother, unrelated by blood or marriage to that maternal cousin—my mother or her husband, appeared out of nowhere some days afterwards to tell the suspect it was safe to come back home.

Of course, the husband who took that refugee into his home paid a dear price for his kindness. That younger brother took a shine to his oldest daughter, my sister; they eventually eloped and endured until death did them part after nearly forty years a loathsome marriage which the father was forced to tolerate until his death because his daughter would not permanently leave her husband, believing as she claimed, that marriages were made in heaven and the vows not to be taken lightly.

But in this case, my Stepp cousin's decision to go up North and never come back stopped the physical skirmishes of the feud. With the killer being out of reach and residing within a jurisdiction that probably took murder more seriously than the one he had fled; and with no citizen having the means to hunt him down, then the onerous duty to avenge Robert's death was lifted to wait for the great hammer of justice to fall naturally; for the apple not plucked from the tree would surely fall when the time was fully ripe.

I bring out these unpleasant details for one purpose only—to depict the strange inner workings of a feud among Black people of the mountains. For it was different in every respect from that historical White American feud waged for nearly one hundred years, give or take a few, between the Hatfields and the McCoys of West Virginia and Kentucky. To preserve our own long earned peace, I have withheld names well known to me to prevent any finger from pointing at the dead. May they rest in whatever peace they have earned beyond the grave and without interference from the living, for the living also have their own deeds to account for in the hereafter if they don't get it done beforehand.

Not from anything I had heard about the feud and the circumstances surrounding Cousin Robert's death did I dare imagine much like those earlier feuders some of my own relatives were, until I began to ponder my cousin's death with the probable causes of it and to realize that the death of even one cousin, particularly a male, was a great loss for the tiny Burnette clan. They had produced only sixteen members by the third generation, many of them had already died of natural causes, and only one male of the third generation had lived to reach adulthood. Unlike those famous feuders to the north, our feud did not stretch across state lines and none of it was ever recorded in a court of law or published in a library. All members of both sides of our feud belonged to the same community, most were members of the same neighborhood, and all were either members of or connected to the same two churches that faced each other from opposite sides of the same road, with the doors of both being open to members of either congregation. Consequently, our feud with one exception was relatively mild, self - contained, of relatively short duration around fifty years; and, being right in the midst of it, I was fond of members of both sides.

Cousin Isabella, one of the feuding parties, the oldest living Burnette, daughter of Grandpa Squire Burnette's oldest brother, was a bright thread of kinship running through the fabric of my life. Whether I liked it or not, she was a sturdy fixture in my existence, and I adored Mr. Lank, the other feuding party, a more distant relative, and his wife Hester, an unwilling benefactor of the feud, who was not related to me at all so far as I can tell.

So, whatever may have caused that quarrel at church back then was of no consequence to me. I was accepted by both sides, Burnettes and Stepps, as if nothing had ever happened and both sides were acceptable to me, being ignorant as I was of what had happened and caring even less than the little I knew about it—except for my feeling of sadness over the mystery of Robert's untimely death.

And much of that mystery has always centered around questions unasked and unanswered. *When had my Cousin Isabella become so strict, so determined to make young children behave like little cherubs? Had it happened before or after she lost her only child to a gambler's reckless gun? How could a woman who was able to control her cousin's children by merely lifting an eyebrow, my Aunt Bell, who dared me to squirm on a hard church bench after two or three hours, how could she allow her eighteen-year-old son to go alone to a gambling den on Saturday night? Did she know where he was going? Did she have any idea who would be there? Had Robert lied to his mother before leaving home that evening? How did she find out he had been murdered and how long had he been dead when the shocking news reached her? Nobody had voiced these questions, but they hung in the air.*

And what had prompted the older gambler, armed with a pistol, to take the life of a slightly built, helpless teenager except for that child's being on the wrong side of the feud, away from his own neighborhood, away from the protection of his mother's people? Now Robert, come to think of it, had no doubt been kept in as much ignorance of the feud as I had, but his ignorance of it cost him his life. On the other hand, I, sandwiched between the feuders by blood, was allowed to observe and sort it all out.

What I had heard and all I had heard about the murder scene was the murderer's facing little Robert and asking, "N------r, don't you believe I'll shoot you?"

To which poor Robert most likely answered "No."

Who would have believed it? Consider a time when any wound can be mortal, a time before telephones are in use in rural Black neighborhoods, when health insurance is unheard of, when no ambulance will be called to take a dying Black man to a hospital sixteen miles away to beg for his admission, when the result of a shooting at close range is to watch the victim bleed to death. Then, think of the murderer running away, leaving his victim with frightened onlookers watching the wounded young man bleed and struggle with death without a relative close by to pray for mercy or to comfort him. None of this was ever voiced to me, but who could help thinking about it?

Now the old Burnette men were very black and small of stature but possessed with unusual strength and physical endurance. Papa used to laugh about balancing Grandpa Squire on the palm of one hand and sometimes did until his father, growing tired of his son's fond jesting and display of power, demanded "Put me down, sir!"

And the women were strong, too, judging by the tale of Great Grandma Rosanna and her sister adding to their stock of winter meat after Great Grandpa Squire passed away. Some misfortunate black bear attracted by the smell of fresh meat came down out of the mountains to rob their log cabin of the hog they had just butchered. When that bear stuck its paw through the crack between the logs, one sister grabbed the animal's foreleg, put both feet up against that wall and reared back in readiness for the ther paw. The bear didn't disappoint her. Then, the other woman, trusting her sister's sturdy grip, picked up the ax, stepped outside and went to work on that bear. Pretty soon, Papa said, those sisters were skinning and cleaning that animal, too, so they could hang its carcarcus up beside the hog.

Robert had inherited the Burnette body structure and the black skin, but probably not the physical stamina. And I can't help wondering whether the sight of Robert's black skin had whetted the appetite of the murderer's vindictiveness.

It was well known that something of a color caste existed widely between Black people of light skin colors and those of dark skin colors. Though it could not have happened in our neighborhood, we had heard about the brown bag parties being held elsewhere: of a host tacking a brown bag beside the entrance to a social gathering and admitting only those whose faces were as light as or lighter than the color of that bag. Ours was a close-knit neighborhood and the people were of many colors. It would never have occurred to any one of the old people to risk offending a friend, neighbor or relative with such a silly scheme. Skin color consciousness existed among us, but not to the extent of consciously excluding another Black person from a neighbor's house because his complexion was darker than the ombre of a common lunch bag.

Now I myself wouldn't have passed the brown bag test on a warm summer day after my skin was tanned by playing in our unlit meadows and fields. And to my surprise, I completely failed church angel test one summer afternoon. Being naïve I hadn't noticed that color consciousness, like everything else, had found its way into our church where it was practiced by one of the blackest members, black in skin color only. One of Papa's first cousins on his mother's side, a kinder person could not be found, but she had us waiting like outsiders in the churchyard. My classmate Edith Daugherty and I were sure to be called as promised to take our places in practice for a church pageant. To our surprise, we weren't called in at all. Instead, we experienced the exclusion of a twisted all-White-heaven mentality. The wait-outside strategy must have been designed to shield us from the shock of watching those angels being chosen from among girls with lighter skin colors and selected by a cousin whose skin was much darker than my own. My cousin simply rejected us, and she did it without so much as making an excuse to either of us, Edith or me. More embarrassed than hurt, I felt bad for Edith. It was Papa's cousin, a grown woman with a high church position who had misbehaved.

By the age of ten or eleven I was so well exposed to that kind of mentality that I soon forgot the disappointment of not being in the pageant and never bothered to mention it to my own mother. It wasn't worth mentioning— something so trite as telling Mama I'd just found out that water was wet. And I was too young to even onsider the mystery of someone with rather black skin being firmly convinced she was going to heaven while holding onto the belief that all angels if not physically White must have light colored skin. I just left it alone. At that age, getting chosen as a temporary angel draped in a white bed sheet to stand speechless beside the pulpit was not a pressing priority of mine anyway.

Being shunted out of a pious angel pageant was a mere slap in the face to a friend and to me, born in the middle of the feud. On the other hand, Robert, because of no known offense, had lost his life. Robert was a Burnette, born on the opposite side of the feud; he was outside our neighborhood, on the wrong side of town, with the wrong people. His skin was much blacker than that of his murderer and he had no relative there to protect him.

Whatever had first caused the rift had driven a wedge between the old Burnettes and certain members of two branches of the Stepps, and now that wedge would hold fast as long as those members lived.

And it didn't end with Robert's death. In childhood I would catch just the end of a dispute between Mr. Lank and Papa regarding a field of wheat Papa believed was being damaged by our neighbor's chickens. Mr. Lank, taking the neighbor's side, voiced a different opinion, "Nonsense," he said, and added that chickens could not harm the wheat. Then came an exchange of words with the threat, "Why, I'll break thee old fool head with a stick," words that sent the wheat-field owning cousin into his house for a pistol. My brother Garland chuckled as he mocked Mr. Lank's "Why, I'll break thee old fool head with a stick."

Our Mr. Lank had such a comical way of speaking. But I don't think Mr. Lank was holding his ground when that cousin returned with a pistol to the scene of the squabble. Yet, nothing more came of it; and that fall, when the neighborhood wheat threshing took place on Mr. Lank's property, our wheat, mowed and sheathed, went there as if nothing had ever happened. My youngest brother and I went along, too, to play freely around the threshing machine on dear old Mr. Lank's land.

Under normal circumstances, mountaineers as I knew them could harbor a grudge forever without ever allowing their animosity to interfere with the usual flow of life and certainly with the opponent's livelihood. For while personal spats prevailed and memory of Robert's murder was never erased by time, no entire family was consumed by the animosity related to it. On the contrary, some of the best of relationships, friendships and marriages did thrive within small groups closely related to others who had been holding a grudge for decades.

CHAPTER 12: WAR TOO, BRINGS
A JOYFUL MOMENT

Mr. Lank, like my father, first generation born out of slavery, had bought land, and he always kept several head' of cattle, too. On any morning of my summer vacations, I could wake up to the clanking sounds of hollow bells in motion. They would announce the arrival of Mr. Lank, a marvelously typical old mountain man, leading his cows by the only route available from his barn to that steep grassy hillside beyond the woods to the northwest of us. He would be dressed in clean but faded blue coveralls and a checkered cotton shirt that had seen brighter days. Pushed slightly back on his head, a mousey brown worn leather hat partly shaded a round face burned to a rich chestnut by long hours in southern suns of many summers gone by.

He was a pleasantly plump man with the bulge of his belly taking up the slack in front of his loose-fitting overalls, starting with a long curve that began just below his shirt collar. As the morning sun rose behind him and its rays filtered through the trees at his back, the brim of the hat lifted one way and flopped the other, dipping forward over a large round right eye, while the other side rolled upward to let a ray of sunlight play on the end of his pudgy red nose and bounce onto his bushy reddish-brown mustache below. The mustache bulged like a muddy cascade beneath his nose and flowed over his upper lip from side to side. The whole picture of him, focused in front of tall London Poplars as he stood on the wagon road, all of that, created for my childish mind the perfect portrait of a gigantic but gentle leprechaun.

My fairytale view of that very real man was reinforced by the mystery of his mother's having gone off to California in a covered wagon with a White family when he was a child, with my question of whether that wagon ever reached California and whether that White family with their Black servant, a former slave and mother whose own children, two little boys, were left behind, was ever heard of again (for letter writing was not common among people who could neither read nor write.) And overhearing that Mr. Lank, who at some stage of his young life had reclaimed the last name of his mother's clan, the name handed down by the slave master, the surname of the grandmother who had reared him and his brother, nine years younger, who also used the clan surname, made me wish that Mr. Lank, truest spirit of the mountains I knew, had not abandoned his father's harmonious surname, one so befitting Mr. Lank's character, McConaughey.

Mr. Lank and his bovine charges wouldn't pass the time of day with my siblings and me, but if my mother, who had had nothing to do with the feuders' quarrel at church or its causes, now if she was home, then he would stop the patient cows, ease the length of their steel chains to let them graze along the road, and he and my mother, a neutral party married to a vocal partner of the feud, would call back and forth from her back porch, her backyard flower garden, or clothes line, to the old wagon route to pasture.

In that road, Mr. Lank walked on property considered to be public; he was older than my father and possessed the right to do as he pleased. It didn't matter who started the conversation between my mother and him, whichever of the two saw the other one first, I suppose. My mother was surely privileged to greet him first as he was passing by her home, and anybody who passed a   neighbor's house or watched a neighbor pass by his own property and failed to speak would be deemed a sure candidate for Goldsboro, the eastern town offering asylum for mentally ill Black people; for even the insane were segregated by race.

But Mr. Lank also was privileged to speak first. He had been born not far from the soil he stood on; he was old enough to be my mother's father; and, my mother, was not from our part of the mountains at all. Although Mr. Lank would not set a foot inside his cousin's house, nor would my father set a foot inside his, the old man was not going to miss a chance to hold a conversation with my mother.

"Mornin,' Miss Hattie. Reckon we're gonna git some ra-i-in?"

"Ye-s, Mr. Lank. It shore looks like it, don't it?"

And he, referring to something of which he swore—"Faith and by-gods," he had recently heard on the radio [his *by-gods* pronounced as *be-gods*], would take their conversation to a deeper level, "Why, *the* god, A-bove, Miss Hattie, what do thee reckon's a-gonna happen ne-e-ext?"

[The first part of that statement—*The God A-bove* with its high-pitched nasal intonation meant *Times is bad enough for us now*. And the rest meant *What will we do if conditions get worse?*]

And shaking her head at the thought of anything worse, or maybe just to dramatize her empathy for his concern, the answer would come, "Oh, Mr. Lank, only God in heavens knows."

At another time, one of them could begin with, "Pretty day, ain't it?" and the other might return with, "Be good to git some rain, though, wouldn't it?" And from there, either of them might delve into what had been planted and which crops needed the rain most, with my mother properly limiting herself to her vegetable garden plantings, the woman's domain.

No matter how often I heard it, I marveled at Mr. Lank's use of the Biblical "thee." Habitually, the peculiar enunciations of his speech would be inter-rupted now and then by a generous spurt of dark reddish-brown tobacco juice, almost the same color as his lush growth of mustache. On the wagon road, too, he could spit as much as he liked.

These were the days before telephones came to the homes of Black people on our side of the mountain, the days when some Black people didn't even own a good radio. Grown people talked to one another and we children lis-tened and learned what life was like for them and what it would surely be like for us if we didn't do well in school. Even the cows benefitted from this benign conversation as it allowed their grazing to begin early; and the occasion for an unexpected moment of socializing with a neighbor obviously delighted my mother and Mr. Lank as well. What's more, it gave them a brief relief from the day's drudgery.

The scene I cherish took place about three years into World War II and Mr. Lank proudly dominated that one. Every man, Black or White, married or single, who was healthy enough and not too old was being drafted. Mr. Lank's brother had three girls and eight boys, and six of those sons went to serve their country. My three oldest brothers had answered the call, and my adventure-some youngest brother was trying to go. But at 16, he was too young, although he was two years older than my father had been when he tried to enlist for the Spanish American War. Now, Mr. Lank's son, Oss, his rather shy youngest child, the one who sometimes accompanied his father to the pasture, who stood silently close to the older man on the wagon road, and whose fair skin flushed a bright red when a neighbor spoke to him, was eligible for the draft and had reported for duty. Naturally, the old man was fearful of the war. All of us were yet patriotism knew no color lines. Mr. Lank was making his con-tribution of one son to the greatest war since 1865, and he was eager to boast about it.

October came. Along the ridge of the western hill, the late afternoon sun lingered behind a row of tall trees and forced its brightest rays past their leafy limbs just changing from dark greens to crimsons, deep golds and yellows. Where the tree trunks and branches managed to block the sunbeams, soft shadows emerged and crept across the valley below. Still Mr. Lank had time enough to lead his cows' home from pasture, get them milked and foddered and have his own evening meal before the air raid siren in town sounded well after sundown, signaling "Lights out!" It was a practiced black out that sent us into the usual pitch blackness we had become accustomed to, living outside the "city limits." Still, we'd wait for the all-clear signal to rise over the woods to the east.

At this time of year, a setting sun could sink rapidly behind the hills, but Mr. Lank would risk just a few extra minutes on the wagon road that evening. So excited he could hardly contain

himself, he dug his heels into the road above his cousin's blacksmith shop, reared back, and bumping the brim of the old hat upward to reveal his furrowed brow, he staged his lines. Born in 1868, he was an old mountain sage, unschooled, but he had mastered the art of telling a story, the telling being more important than the story, which the listener understood as well as the teller.

Now Mr. Lank's wife, Miss Hester was a true homebody and never came along with her husband on these trips to and from pasture. Had she been there, my storytelling would truly be complicated for she and my mother were longtime friends and both of them welcomed any chance to talk to each other.

Our old people always addressed close friends and relatives by title and a given name or nickname, particularly in the presence or in earshot of children, and the children followed that practice for the rest of their lives.

When Mr. Lank saw Mama and me, the cowbells clanked to a halt and he began: "Well, Miss Hattie, what do thee reckon?"

[Meaning, Guess what?]

Then, clutching the cow chains with his right hand and flipping the other hand backwards to rest on his left hip, he waited for his next cue.

It was wartime. News could be bad. Night after night, Mama took her seat near the radio, listened to Walter Cronkite report the war news and prayed. Her lips barely moving, she announced her grief with chin on chest, right hand cradling her forehead, left hand limp, resting in her lap, a symbol of helplessness. My two oldest brothers had "shipped out" to God knows where overseas; and except for the New York or San Francisco postmarks on their envelopes, we had no idea of where they were or which battles, they might be closest to. Both wrote home as often as conditions allowed, I guess. My second brother, as faithful to his country as he had been in helping Papa with the farm work long before the war, wasn't going to violate an army regulation; but my defiant oldest brother, determined to let Mama know where he was, would faithfully send us letters marred by the censor's bold black marks blotting out many of his sentences, which served to escalate our anxieties about his situation and to raise unanswered questions: Where on earth was he, and what was it that he was not allowed to tell us?

As mama sat praying, Papa walked restlessly back and forth across the living room, wanting-- I sensed, to let his fiddle bespeak his uneasiness; but respecting my mother's sorrowful countenance and not wanting to invoke her criticism for playing a few joyful tunes to lift our spirits at a troublesome time like this, he would keep that feisty fiddle quiet until Mama ended her solemn prayer sessions, took her sadness and went off to bed.

At the back porch that afternoon, in response to Mr. Lank, Mama stood up, cradling a lap full of string beans, she could march down the steps towards the wagon road. Mr. Lank's "What do thee reckon," had promised a serious story and Mama's acknowledgement came fast.

"Why, what happened, Mr. Lank?"

That was just what he needed. "Why, the other night, me and the Hess hadn't been long gone to bed when we heard footsteps on the porch. Hess nudged me and said 'Lank, that's Oss.' I said, 'Noooo!'"

He quickly gestured the "No." Then his head jerked to the right again as a spout of tobacco juice formed a glowing rustic arc against the fading sunlight. No doubt he spat to buy time for his tale. But he had held onto his Noooo long enough for his excitement to register deep within my mother's ear. Not only was the resonance of his No close to an apology, it was an humble admission to my mother that he should have known better and was relenting for doubting a mother's recognition of her own child's footsteps, a gift my mother also was blessed with. (My smart aleck third brother would sometimes remove his shoes and tiptoe to the front door to deceive her, but she quickly caught on to him.) Now, as for Mr. Lank, bantering, too, was practiced between members of the older generation and from them down towards the younger generation; yet my mother would surely have chided the old man for blundering into her bailiwick with his domineering male nonsense, doubting a mother's perception and daring to admit it. But Mama was caught up in the wonder of his voice and waited.

Mr. Lank continued. "Hess says to me, she says, 'Yes, 'tis." Good! Mama must have thought. Miss Hester had corrected him. What mother in her right mind would waste time trying to explain how she knew her own child's footsteps as soon as they landed on her own front porch, after bedtime and in wartime, too?

He continued, becoming more excited, "Well, be-gods, Miss Hattie, by that time, the scutter [a term of endearment, also indicating the quickness of the footsteps] was at the door!"

He needn't have said more. My mother's mind could quickly supply the sound of those footsteps coming across the front porch in the night and match them with her own voice calling out the name of the child to whom those footsteps belonged, and she could add the memory of leaping out of bed and rushing to the front door, then the huggings and the tear filled eyes examining the feet, the hands, the face, to see if war had left its marks, and she could envision father and son following her to the kitchen for the needed snack for a hungry child who could not find a restaurant that would serve a Black man, not even one wearing a United States Army uniform—not even if one had been open at that hour.

The old man stared at my mother with wise and discerning eyes, bLanking suspiciously as if he had watched from the wagon road and had seen her praying after dinner in the evenings and understood her longing to hear that her children were alive and well. He couldn't have watched. He was never on the road that late and our window shades would have been drawn against any

180

passerby; but he did know that her spirit had instantly joined his wife and him in the ecstasy of that moment of their army son's first visit home.

"You musta been awfully glad to see your boy, Mr. Lank." Appeased by my mother's answer, he stood there staring, nodding, saying no more. His telling had "hit home," as the old mountain people would say. My mother knew the joy of a son's coming home in wartime. My mother understood Mr. Lank's humble need to boast, and he knew it. Cowbells clanked. He rushed on towards home and the hollow tones disappeared behind the woods.

The beauty of that rich encounter should have caused a mature soul to shed tears. The depth of it was too much for a teenager to grasp. Unable to appreciate the marvel of words unspoken between two old people of the mountains, I viewed that moment as an instance of sheer comedy and conveyed it to Howard, my schoolmate, as soon as I saw him. He doubled over cackling, and for some time afterwards, as we stepped off the school bus in the afternoons, he would look at me, mimic Mr. Lank, waving one hand and shaking his head as if in disbelief. He believed, for he knew of Mr. Lank, but Howard's family lived on the far west side of the hill, so he rarely, if ever, saw the man.

Just as much as they loved music, mountaineers loved language and could revel over the simplest sample of rare speech, particularly one coming from a colorful character. Mr. Lank was a rare unpolished gem, and I never saw anybody do more with a good laugh than Howard could.

CHAPTER 13: THE DARK SIDE OF THE MOUNTAIN

For my mother, another side of those well-scripted conversations with Mr. Lank, a more subtle side prevailed; but being mountain born and raised herself, my mother knew it and played out her role, yet not without deep resentment; for it was a sorely humiliating position to be placed in through marriage.

"Don't matter how long you stay here," she complained to me one day while making her bed, "you'll never be one of them." And I understood that her "you" meant she, not me, for I was three times one of them—once by birth in that area and twice by kith and kinship to fifteen of the oldest twenty-four African American families to settle in the North Fork-Black Mountain region after the Civil War. A mountain product myself, I also understood that my maternal relatives in Mama's village held the same kind of prejudices, for I had seen a somewhat different side of that game played out in Shiloh, the little village near Biltmore.

I was not an object of the game, of course. On my mother's side I was blood kin over there, too; but I did witness it in a conversation between Uncle Will Payne and one of his helpers in the blacksmith shop behind my uncle's house one day. The younger man was refusing to accept money for his work, saying in the only way he knew to show his great respect for my uncle,

"Uncle Will, you ain't gonna give me no money"; and playfully, "Why, I'll bust you in the head."

What surprised me was the man's addressing my mother's brother as "Uncle Will," and when the conversation ended and the man had gone on his way, I asked 'How is that man related to us, Uncle Will? Straightaway, my uncle replied with unmistakable scorn for the thought of it, "That old n----r is no kin to us."

But the Burnettes and Stepps were not the only feuding families related to me by blood. Recent census record studies uncovered a rift between two branches of Payne's that lasted way over a hundred years.

It must've started when Sarah Payne II's husband abandoned her and moved in with one of her cousins. That's when that cousin's mother went to live with Sarah Payne II Hayden. And Sarah II's descendants must have stopped claiming kinship with the descendants of her cousin. Then this denial of kinship was kept up down to my children's generation because nobody I knew could trace the other Payne's back to any one of Sarah Payne I's seven children.

Well, Sarah Payne I was in hiding herself, so she kept pretty quiet about who her Cherokee related kinsfolk were, especially her siblings. We never heard of any one of her kinfolks until Grandpa George Payne gave his deposition in 1908, 120 years ago. That's when he alluded to an unnamed Cherokee great grandfather, a named grandfather (Sarah I's father), and just mentioned his own mother, but his historic and unnecessary secrecy earned him a denial of the compensation he sought. nearly 20 years after his mother (Sarah Payne I) had passed on and he couldn't get any better information.

But now that the old mystery of who was or wasn't kin to those other Payne's "over there" has unraveled, we have only one person to blame. But I'm not blaming that poor old soul, the old geezer that ran away from my great Aunt Sarah Payne Hayden (Grandpa GW Payne's only sister) and later went traipsing off across country though five states with another woman (wasn't it Aunt Sukey?) and named their five daughters after the states they passed through, going who knows where only to come right back to where they started from. I did hear about that and heard the names of those five girls, Arkansas (pronounced ArKANzus), Kansas, Louisiana, Missouri, and Texas. (Mama could count them off in the order of birth.)

The problem was, Sarah Payne I was not the only child her dad Joshua Payne had, and nobody bothered to tell us that Great Grandma Sarah One had a sister and that sister had children, too. No, we were misled into believing Sarah Payne I's children were the only ancestors any Payne kinship could ever come from.

I'm just glad it's over and I can now claim the kin I didn't know I was kin to for about 89 years.

On another visit to Shiloh, observing my mother's sister Sarah's attitude towards certain younger women in that neighborhood who also connected themselves with the old Payne family, I realized the blacksmith shop helper had not merely addressed the older man as "Uncle" to show respect for his age, but more so because he, along with others of that neighborhood, derived some personal dignity from identifying himself with a family that had been born free in a time when most other Black men and women and their children were enslaved.

The seven branches of the free-born Paynes were the six sons and a daughter of Sarah Payne, the Cherokee wife of the slave trustee, Londen Mills, and their offspring; and anyone who could trace his own beginnings back to a blood relationship with one of those seven was kin to all, down to the umpteenth generation. For Payne cousins were not to be counted by number of descents —third or thirteenth was all the same. Even the three school children of my generation, James, Nathaniel, and I, who could trace our genealogy back to the exact branch of that old Payne tree would occasionally flaunt that knowledge among ourselves at recess time at Clear View Grammar School. They had descended from Sarah II, their great, great, great grandmother. Sarah Payne Hayden was the only sister of my maternal grandfather, George Washington Richard Henry Lee Payne and his five brothers.

After a time, the Burnettes were so few in number that genealogical tracings were not necessary. In Black Mountain, the child descending from the Burnettes was surrounded by the mother's or father's kin. That kin presented themselves by land, in life, and in gravesites within the old cemetery purchased in 1897, by former slaves who started the Stepp and Burnette clans and by other Black settlers of that area. In blood and culture, the Burnettes were generally more African than the Stepps; and all of those surroundings made up my immediate family. The rest was a nurturing neighborhood wherein older siblings, other relatives and certain neighbors could scold and punish, while others could only scold, give advice and report to my parents if I rejected their advice—which never happened. When an older person spoke, we children listened and obeyed.

Now none of my mother's resentment for being the low man on the totem pole on our side of the mountain was ever directed towards Mr. Lank. He hadn't created the laws of mountain culture and was as much a victim of it as she was. Furthermore, Mr. Lank was older and deserved her respect. And he respected her as well, but she was an outsider who was to receive his gestures of acceptance in an arena where both she and he knew she would never be the same as kith and kin. It was a kindly condescending custom that worked best on the unsuspecting resident of even forty years who, after so many decades, could not envision such apparently primitive people having acquired such delicate social manners. I would not label that practice as a farce, for they were absolutely sincere in what they did.

CHAPTER 14: UNCLE HARDY'S STEPDAUGHTER: MISS HESTER

Miss Hester, too, enjoyed company, as did most of the old mountain people I knew. She was a sprightly woman, head and shoulders pushed slightly forward by an adorable hump just below the base of her neck, causing her thin protruding shoulder blades to make angular ridges against the back of her neatly patched cotton dress, pale and worn by years of being boiled in an iron pot, rubbed with a chunk of homemade lye soap and scrubbed and scrubbed on the washboard. The hump at her back coming from age or hard work or both seemed unrelated to bone troubles I might associate with a limp or a walking cane. Unimaginable! Oh no! Miss Hester was both spry and nimble as a wood nymph, and to my mind, she was the perfect companion for Mr. Lank.

In spite of her age, Miss Hester still had a full head of silvery white hair, the whiteness contrasting remarkably with her smooth as leather sunbaked skin. The length of her hair was braided and bundled at the back of her neck, the front of it softly framed her angelic face, while the bulk of it clung to each side of her head in well - defined waves, while the waves themselves sent off fine unwieldy sprays of wispy silk to create a soft halo over the top of her desaserving head.

The dear little woman had a small face on which she wore an aging pair of spectacles above a finely chiseled nose and well above deep furrows of wrinkles pursing her mouth into a tight little coil that could instantly relax into the sweetest smile. She rejoiced at the sight of one of her neighbors coming to her house and would receive him, her, or it as if it was the highest honor imaginable for a neighbor of any age to set foot inside her door. And it was not uncommon for children, unaccompanied by a parent or any other adult, to visit older members of the neighborhood wherein everyone knew everybody and to which everybody belonged. Back then, nobody was homeless, and nobody felt the need to lock his door, even when away from home.

I liked Miss Hester's and Mr. Lank's rambling one story bungalow, the most unusual house in our whole neighborhood, I thought. The well sat in an open, unshaded spot not far from the kitchen end of the house, and both well and house wore the same once-painted-green, with the soft green of the house and the white around the windows slowly fading and melding into the rich green of the lawn spreading around it in all directions.

The homey, sweet smell of fresh buttermilk drifted through the house whose rooms had been added at different stages of the family's growth, from a son, a daughter, to another son and then to the two girls of the daughter who had passed away. And similar to a family of different ages and heights, the floors of the rooms were not all at the same level. Actually, from the living room, I might have to step down into the dining room and step up into the kitchen, descending or ascending one or more steps thoughtfully built here and there to accommodate the differences in elevation.

I was a child still in elementary school, so Miss Hester was not obliged to sit and entertain me. Being a child I had the freedom to follow her about the house as she did her chores and to listen to her talk like an excited young girl whose long lost playmate had just stopped by, that playmate sometimes talking too much once she got started.

But it was her house, I was her guest and she would begin: "Well, honey, I reckon ye school's out now for su-um-mer-m?"

It was customary for us mountaineers to wring out three or more syllables from any one or two-syllable word, and particularly in polite conversation when the word landed at the end of a question and the voice should not be raised. Only a rude or angry person or one not familiar with our manner of speech would commit the offense of raising the voice at the end of a question. But Miss Hester's syllable stretching took the cake, as the people would say; for she did it with a peculiarly fine nasal twang produced by closing her mouth before the question ended and blowing the rest of it out through the nostrils.

"Yes, Ma'm.' Miss Hester had made a statement. It was late May, and school was out. Miss Hester would know that.

"Miss Hester, we had another play this year.' Miss Hester hadn't been to church to see our play last year, nor the year before that. The church was a good three-quarters of a mile from my house and Miss Hester and Mr. Lank lived nearly another quarter of a mile farther away, a long walk for a couple born between 1869 and 1870. Besides, they no longer went out after dark anyway. And to my knowledge, they didn't come to church even on Sundays, at least not after the feud started. Fact is, after the squabble at church with Cousin Isabella, I never heard anything more of Mr. Lank's darkening the church door and I'm certain that I never saw him there. At least, that's what I thought.

Miss Hester, "A pla-ay? My goodness! What in the world was that all *abou-ut*?"

"About a prince that was looking for a princess in a flower garden.'"
"Well, Lord, who ever heard of such a thing as *tha-uh-at*?

"Well, all of us girls in the play was dressed like different flowers'

"Now how on earth did they manage to do *tha-uh-at*?"'"My sister Rena, she likes to sew, and she made me a costume: a cap that set right flat on top of my head with long, white petals and a yellow circle sewed in the middle; and she found some chinz about the same shade of green as a real daisy leaf and cut me out a dress and then she made green covers for my black patent leather dress shoes and sewed big green bows near the toes, to match ma dress.'

"Now that must have been awf'ly per-dy."

"I was Meadow Daisy. Miss Ollie's girl, Edith, was Tiger Lily; and she thought the prince was gonna marry her, but he chose me instead.'

"Well, you'uns is both mighty per-dy girls. I don't see how he coulda picked one of ye over the other."

"Cause, the prince said Tiger Lily was too haughty, but Meadow Daisy was humble.'

[Chuckling] Oh, merciful heavens! A prince looking for a humble wife in a flower bed. Lord, lord! We never got to do nothin' like that when I was in school."

"You didn't?'

"Lord, no! Way back yonda when your papa and me was young 'uns? Why, we just had three months of schoolin' a year. An' then we just got a little of the three R's, --readin, ritin' n 'rithmetic."

I knew Papa couldn't do long-division, but he had a way of dividing and sub-dividing until he got an exact measurement, and he could build a chimney, a wall or set in a window as straight as anything you ever saw. And with all his tools of black smithing, wrought iron work, brick masonry, rock facing and carpentry, he knew how to use a square, a spirit level and *a plumb bob* (plumb line) so his corners—squared or mitered, would always be perfect angles and his lines always straight. And I didn't understand how he could do all that a bit more than he understood how I had learned to do long division.

At Clear View, school closing activities, singing, reciting speeches and act-ing, were commonplace. We looked forward to it and our parents and other relatives looked forward to coming out to watch us perform, to see which child got the biggest part in a play or which one was the most promising speaker. Papa had already told me about his three-month school years of the 1880s. Still it was hard to imagine being sent home for a whole summer with-out some kind of fanfare.

"Why was *that* Miss Hester?'

"Why, honey, crops had to be planted in the spring, fields worked in summer, 'n everything gathered and stored for winter in fall, and then the butcherin' to be done soon's winter set in. An' nen they was quilting and feather–bed and straw-tick making. By then it was Christmas time, so we never got back to school 'til the next year."

"Ooooh.' I was no stranger to any of that, not even to an occasional mattress made of straw, and certainly not to quilt making and ticking with the testy lumps of feathers that gathered in clusters in the comforters and could never be coaxed to separate when the bed was made; neither was I stranger to planting and gathering crops, nor the butchering of hogs, calves or goats.

Hog-killing time generally took place in late November if the weather was cold enough but certainly by late December and preferably before Christmas to jolt the excitement of that joyous but poverty-stricken season. The weather had to be cold enough to chill the meat until it was cured, for no such thing as a refrigerator belonged to us; and ice boxes, if we'd had any, were not made to hold great slabs of fresh meat that had to be cured in the smokehouse.

But I had never thought of school as something to do only when the farm work was slack. School was my life and I couldn't imagine life without it. We had to be in school for eight months of the year and nobody made us stay home to help with the work. We did help in the afternoons and on weekends, carrying kindling and dead branches from the woods to keep the fires going under the big black three-legged wrought iron pot where animal fat was rendered into lard, or to keep a supply of cut white potatoes handy to toss a handful now and then into the bubbling fat to keep its clear yellow color from getting cloudy and to rid it of much of its natural stench, particularly that portion of it that had been stripped from the animal's intestines. As a reward for our labor, we could glean the crispy fried potatoes from the pot and eat them; for at no other time of the year was oil to be used to deep fry "Irish potatoes," one of our most plentiful and cherished crops. Potatoes could be boiled, stewed with other vegetables, especially green beans, added to soups, creamed, mashed, baked, scalloped, pan fried with onions and even with other vegetables such as okra and tomatoes, or roasted in the hot coals of the fireplace for an evening snack, but never deep fried. Deep frying potatoes was a way of cleaning grease, not a way of cooking them for a meal.

On another day we would have to carry more wood to put under the iron pot brewing part of the animal fat mixed with Red Devil Lye for home-made laundry soap that even the neighbors envied. And some of them were sure to come with a dime to buy a chunk of it from time to time.

The difference between Miss Hester's land-owning generation and mine was that her peers and she had not only helped with the work, they had also learned how to get that work done in their own households and under almost the same conditions known to the older generation. My generation had limited our involvement to mere participation under the illusion that education promised us a far better life, and so, we would never need to learn how to survive by our wits and with whatever nature and the land combined with common sense and physical strength provided; and true to form, we would become homeowners but landless, as compared to our parents who knew how to eke out a living from the land, to make it supplement their meager earnings, and to provide food that could be stored for those times when no money was in hand to buy any. Yet we spurned that lifestyle in spite of knowing that without the land, we could not survive. The older generations loved their land, were proud of their land; my generation possessed neither value nor simply took for granted far smaller plots of land as sufficient.

In all fairness to my generation, I should explain the amount of work that made it possible to have a pitcher of molasses on the kitchen table for breakfast. First the field had to be plowed, then harrowed so that the sorghum cane seeds could be sown on smooth ground. When the plants had grown and were ripe with cane juice, they had to be cut and taken to the grinding mill that Papa himself had built at an area reserved for that important fall harvest. [I knew of no one else, far or near, who owned a sugar cane mill.] Attached to pulleys connected to the mill, the horse or mule circled around the mill, that motion caused the two heavy iron grinding wheels to turn and crush the stalks of cane being fed into them. The juice from the stalks flowed down a spout attached to the mill and filled a waiting vessel. As one vessel filled to the brim, another replaced it.

Meanwhile, close to the mill, a fire was built in a six-foot long fireplace that had its own smokestack. The sweet, watery juice from the receiving vessels had to be cooked until the water evaporated. In its pure state, it was poured into a metal tray about six inches deep and almost 6 feet long - the length of the fireplace, and the tray was placed directly over the fire. When the liquid began to boil, it had to be stirred by yard-long ladles that allowed the stirrers to stand well away from the heat of the fire. The tray had two wooden handles at each end so that it could be safely removed from the fire. When the pale, thin juice had thickened and turned a reddish brown, it was poured from the tray into barrels and stored to fill numerous quart jars of that iron-rich element of our diet. From the jar, the molasses pitcher was filled and brought to the table where that delicacy was mixed with homemade butter and sopped up with Mama's hot biscuits. And everything used in that entire process—except for the cane seeds, the horse and plow, the glass jars, the barrels, and the metal molasses pitcher, was also assembled and made on the farm. If only we had realized how blessed we were to have such skillful parents, and how well off we were to own land! But we were not unlike those stalks of cane being crushed to undergo a drastic but inevitable social and economic change.

But I wanted to hear Miss Hester talk some more.

"Miss Hester, Mama told me something funny about Papa's school days.'

[Cautiously] "What was that honey?"

"Well, Aunt Phoebe told Mama that Papa used to skip school sometimes. People would see him out playing in the woods on school days, and they would say, [mimicking] 'Well now, I reckon he thinks he knows more than the teacher does.' [Giggles.]

[Chuckling] "Lord, that Miss Hattie, I declare!"

Then catching herself, rubbing the back of her right hand across her mouth, bLanking her eyes thoughtfully, not willing to poke fun at a grown man in the presence of a child, especially not his own child. Indeed, she must ever be mindful not to stir up the embers between her husband and his cousin who had stood up for her long before that child was born.

"Well, I kin tell you one thing: that Mr. Garland's a mighty smart man. Do might'- nigh anything he sets his mind to. Allus could. Now you come on out here in the kitchen wi 'me an 'git you a big red apple. Right over there in that basket, honey. Just help   yourself to as many as you want."

'Thank ye, Miss Hester.'

This was the better part of it. I wasn't expected to talk anymore. I could sit and watch as Miss Hester maneuvered from the kitchen to the porch the heavy wooden churn with its other wooden parts, the churn lid with the hole in the center, the thick dasher with the long handle, and the contents of the churn giving off a familiar chug of thick curds of sour "sweet" milk and whey sloshing around inside as the churn rolled forward on its round metal-rimmed bottom edge.

I dearly loved that porch that ran from the south side of the house, passed by the kitchen door, wrapped around the east side and didn't end until it was well beyond the front door. It stopped at the northeast corner of the house, for no doorways had been built on the north side of the house. Near the kitchen door, I could sit and watch as Miss Hester turned that household delicacy, clabber, into milk that could be offered to others outside the family. (Clabber itself was for the family only.) Occasionally she lifted the lid to peek at the size of the globs of golden yellow fat collecting on the thick cross-shaped dasher attached to the handle protruding through the center of the lid.

When the bulk of the butter had gathered into a mass on top of the milk, she would scoop it out of the churn, place it on a dish, rinse the milk out of it, chill it with cold well water and then pat that delicious mass into a wooden mold about the size of a woman's bath powder box. The time of year and what the cows had been eating made the difference between a deep gold or a   pale-yellow butter. The firm molded butter would bear the imprint of a golden sheathe of ripened wheat, suggesting plenty. Without salt, the butter was sweet; but Miss Hester would blend in a pinch of salt before molding it.

From the churn, the milk, holding on to little specks of butter, would be poured into scoured and scalded gallon jars, and sold or given to neighbors whose cows were "dry," that is, waiting to deliver a calf.

At times, I could expect Miss. Hester, looking up from her churn, to acknowledge my presence with a smile, a twinkle in her narrow gray eyes. After all, the company of a child was better than no company at all. And the child's company could be exchanged for something only an old woman or old man could share, something the child would never learn about in school, or a broader version of something she had heard about at home.

CHAPTER 15: CURTAINS: THE FINAL SCENE

Like a great play that had spanned decades, it all ended at last, the feud, that is, for this lifetime at least. But the drama itself didn't have a proper ending. The characters just died off, one by one, as they were called to go. And the strangest part of it was that the one character who never consciously played a part in that drama was the only one who was actually murdered. Many years had passed before a cousin on the Stepp side told me that the cousin who shot Cousin Isabella Burnette's Robert had been crushed to death in a trucking accident. An accident! The apple had not been plucked from the tree. When the time was ripe, something had shaken the tree and the apple had fallen, to be crushed beneath the tree.

I was away at school when Cousin Isabella died peacefully at her home in the fall of 1947. Not to say that they didn't, but I had never known her and her half- sister Miss Hester to visit each other; and whether that distance in their relationship was created by Miss Hester's loyalty to Mr. Lank, I will never know. I would like to imagine that Mr. Lank, at least, had stood at Cousin Isa-bella's deathbed, and that they had grasped each other's hand in a final peace making, but I had no proof of that, either. But neither of them had killed anybody and Cousin Isabella had kept up her church membership until she was no longer able to manage the steep hill from her house down to the main road and couldn't climb that other hill from the east end of the cemetery up to the Baptist church door. She was the only contender in that feud who had remained faithful to the church and had kept it up for most of her sixty-nine years of church membership. Nobody at Mills Chapel knew the old common meter hymns better than Cousin Isabella. I could always hear her strong voice rising above the others when she was there. The voice would be silent now.

The feud had passed over us like a storm with its one strike of lightning, but most like a moody cloud, scattering raindrops in some places, allowing the sun to shine in others. Still, a dark and foreboding side of the moon was rising over our mountains. Four years after Cousin Isabella passed, Papa came down with a terminal illness. In October of 1952, he and Mama sold the home place and moved to California. The past with its hateful moments of violence along with its amiable encounters, its customary kindnesses and cherished friendships were vanishing scene by scene, stage by stage. After Papa died, Mama came back to visit, and she and I drove over to see Mr. Lank and Miss Hester who were then in their 80s, feeble, and ailing. When it was time to go, the old couple followed us to the edge of their sprawling well-cropped lawn.

Close friends, friends heartily welcomed, could not be given their farewells at the door. In better days, days when the most despicable thing imaginable was an insincere gesture, days before we could actually see the old ways dying out, before we owned telephones, refrigerators, and automobiles, they may have walked even farther, a piece way, with us; but now age and illness excused any perceived abruptness or breach of hospitality. Walking with visiting neighbors or relatives beyond the front or back door, that way of prolonging the farewell was proof of a visit sincerely welcomed, a genuine sign of friendship with no other gestures expected. For children, that practice merely extended the time of parting after evening playtime, for sleepovers were not part of our social life.

The old mountaineers were emotionally strong people who mourned or grieved deeply. As we finally turned to go, Mr. Lank looked at my mother and wept like a helpless child about to be taken away from the rustic life he had known and loved. And if he hadn't loved it, it was all he had ever known. Gone were the bright mornings sending sunshine filtering through the treetops at his back on the wagon road when he was younger and strong enough to lead two or three cows to pasture; gone were the gentle cows with bells tinkling, gone were the cLanking sounds of steel chains falling to the ground to allow the cows to nibble at the tall grasses growing beside the road; gone were the pleasant conversations held between the wagon road and our backyard by two mountaineers so different, one a rustic old Baptist farmer, the other a Methodist minister's daughter reared under gentler circumstances, who despite their differences in age and upbringing, held deep respect for each other. Evening, with its shadows, had come. Mr. Lank in that moment of recollection may have wished he could recall pleasantries of younger years between his cousin and himself. And I would like to think that letters asking forgiveness had passed between Papa and him. To my knowledge, there had been none, and Papa was gone, buried three thousand miles away. It was too late. Mr. Lank wept as if he had suddenly realized he and my mother would never see each other again on his soil or hers, or wept for something I'm sure neither he nor the other characters had ever been conscious of—the tragedy of a life lived in feuding.

More than once I had seen elderly Black men, more men than women, in fact, shed tears in public, particularly in church where crying could be construed as an expression of religious emotion.; and I thought it must have been more acceptable for a man to weep openly, perhaps because the woman was expected to endure pain in stone silence.

At least, I knew that was how my mother believed. Not even half Cherokee, she wholly embraced the concept of pain and suffering being endured in silence. To behave otherwise was to openly reveal some weakness of character; and that, according to my other, was as shameful as receiving poor grades in school, or as disgraceful as being punished by the teacher for misbehaving.

Neither Miss Hester nor my mother tried to console Mr. Lank. The four of us just stood there absorbing the finality of that scene, soaking up its sorrow, its gloom, though not yet realizing the meaning of it all. I cannot recall Miss Hester's last words to my mother. She must have fled back into the house in sorrow. The heavy curtain was closing. I would visit Miss Hester again, but never more would the three of them--Miss Hester, my mother and Mr. Lank, meet together on this earth; nor, for that matter, would any of the other characters meet again. Just as I, alone, had lingered safely in the shadows and observed the stage, I, alone, survived the drama.

**

CHAPTER 16: THE TEACHER THAT MADE A DIFFERENCE

Mr. "James" Charles Carleton Ulysses James

My last Clear View teacher, Mr. Charles Carlton Ulysses James, taught the fifth, sixth, and seventh grades — all in the same room and at the same time. Given the tenor of the times, the support of the parents, and his own genius for classroom control, Mr. James juggled his three grades through periods of recitation, last minute preparation for recitation, and quiet time. So I was blessed for three years to sit in the same room and receive all subjects of three grades from the same teacher, listen to reviews of the previous grade's lessons, and preview the lessons of the next grade. Roll call must have been the easiest duty ever for Mr. James, who was the finest schoolteacher I have ever known. Here was a man, a young man who when unable to carpool, came to school on time after a sixteen-mile bus ride from Asheville, walked the nearly quarter of a mile from Old U.S. 70 at Blue Ridge Road to the school on Fortune Street, took roll, gave assignments to keep us occupied, built a fire in the stove to keep us warm while he scouted around the community looking for truants of any grade level, taught at grade level, and taught well beyond grade level in a manner that we could grasp.

He seemed to enjoy telling me that I was his *first* student. He had explained to us that he was right out of pre-med school. He had become a teacher because he did not have the means to continue his studies. Back then a college student might not know much about writing essays, but no matter how he spoke it, he knew the King's English backwards and forwards, regardless of which subject he majored in. Mr. James was a perfectionist in every subject, it seemed; and he taught us students like he thought he might be the last teacher we would ever have. And he wasn't all wrong about that either, though many of us students would go on to college. Mr. James knew that hardly any of our parents had enough education to help us with our schoolwork, so he made certain that I understood my assignments well before I left the classroom each day.

His misfortune at having to stop his own education surely became our blessing. However, years later when I reminded him how he had prepared me for higher education, he admitted a flaw not unlike that of *Dr. Faustus* who admitted to the people as they turned out to praise him that *he had killed as many of them as he had cured.*

In other words, Mr. James's demands for excellence in the academic setting had driven some students from the classroom forever. He admitted that he had been compelled to lower his standards. What a dilemma: *Maintain your high standards of achievement and lose many of your students or lower your standards to the disadvantage of high achievers but keep mediocre students in school longer.* That's enough to drive a conscientious teacher to drink.

On sunny mornings of a bright mountain spring day, the tall windows obediently sent broad beams of light from the west, skimming across the long blackboard embedded in the wall at the front of the room and casting a glare on the other long one at the east wall. At the end of the school day, those very same beams of light betrayed wide columns of dust rising from unpainted floors where their boards, aged and shrunken, pulled away from each other, making cracks that filled with dirt, straits of dirt that always managed to elude the daily sweepings by two or more of us students. Sometimes we could go to the utility room for water to dampen the bristles of the broom. The dampened bristles would prevent the dirt that fell captive to our sweeping from sending its dust into our nostrils, or not so much of it. We students not only swept but also washed the black boards and took the old erasers outside to beat the day's chalk from their worn sides. Blam! blam! blam! and the grainy chalk came out in sheets, coating the face of a dark gray river rock jutting out from the side of the building.

Once we had beaten the erasers soundly, we would return them to the chalk trays, sticking out like pouting lips at the bottom of the blackboards. The chalk trays, too, waited to be wiped clean for the next school day. Except for the blackboards with long manila manuscript charts of the upper and lowercase ABCs tacked above their maple crowns, and the one large framed picture of George Washington, the pale, scarred plasterboard walls of our classrooms were bare.

Other than the coal burning stoves in each room, our desks, the teacher's desk, and the lone school piano used for morning devotions, for school play rehearsals, and for one teacher's whimsical winter marches, a room might also boast of one bookshelf, sparsely supplied with a few scraggly donations, mostly outcasts from the big brick schools uptown.

From the ceiling, three rather dim electric lights, operated from a switch somewhere, descended upon us at the ends of long black cords. On cloudy days the lights came on, or on an occasional evening when the school raised a few dollars by showing an ABC movie, an appropriate Old Western, Cowboy vs. Indian film with the script running along the lower edge of the screen. Our teachers were not insensitive to who we were, but for these films, it didn't seem to matter that some of us could trace one or more ancestors back to a Native American clan of Black Hawk or Cherokee. These moving pictures were entertaining, they brought in a few dollars for the school; and except for them, some of us would never see a movie of any kind. The closest movie theaters Black people could go to were sixteen miles away where they would be ushered to segregated seats in the balcony.

***

Mr. James was a brilliant and dedicated teacher. With my own students, I tried to emulate him, knowing I would never surpass his achievements in the classroom.

Over the years, after I began teaching English, we corresponded, and from Washington, DC or San Francisco, or wherever I was, I would call his home in Asheville to let him know what academic pursuit I was engaged in. By letter or telephone, Mr. James always responded with words of praise and encouragement.

I can't forget that day in 1964: I was parked across the street from 115 Fortune Street, just above the entrance to Carver Elementary, our last segregated school. I had no idea Mr. James was inside, clearing his office for the school's closure due to integration. He saw me and brought my 1944 final exam history paper out to the car: Twenty hand-written pages, with all questions answered in complete sentences and the entire exam written in strict number-letter outline order.

He designed his exams so that we could not possibly earn credit by guessing. He did not accept Yes or No written nswers, nor did he give multiple choice tests. And he had taught us Standard English grammar along with the correct syntactical structure of every English sentence, according to purpose and form.

Looking over that paper he had kept for 20 years, I recalled the day he said to us students, "And when I receive a letter from my own brother and see grammatical errors, I mark them in red ink and send the letter back to him." Remembering those words, I felt sure Mr. James had read my paper although he not made one red mark on any page.

It was that day, standing there with him in front of his last segregated school, I had the opportunity to tell him, face to face, what a wonderful teacher he was.

Actually, It was his thorough teaching methods that made higher education easy for me. So easy, in fact, that I was able to complete my undergraduate college work in only three years, and finish master's degree courses in the fourth year.

For he had seen our pitiful plight as children still mired in the poverty of the Great Depression and submerged in Jim Crow's pandemic oppression. He had been to our homes and he knew we had come to him from parents who had left elementary school to help support themselves. As young as he was and with no prior teaching experience, he knew what he had to do, and he faced that gigantic challenge fearlessly.

Mr. James had come from Delaware, he told us; but all of us spoke a dialect of English hardly understood in an outside world that didn't know we existed. Some of us wanted to rise higher; some of us just wanted to earn a living. But I never heard of any one of his students going to prison.

At Clear View, Monday mornings began with school-wide devotions, whatever religion we claimed to be, all praying together and singing the same songs harmoniously. And for my seven years at Clear View, those devotional activities continued with full community approval and parental support. In Mr. James' classroom, each remaining day of the week began with a reading from the Holy Bible. After the reader had finished, returned the Bible to Mr. James and had sat down, the teacher would remain standing and looking on us he would quote, "For there is no speech nor language where their voice is not heard." [Psalm 19:3 KJV]

He must have come to our little African American elementary school in

Southern Appalachia determined to make a difference in our lives. For those of us who longed for change, Mr. James made a difference. Some of us went on to college, graduated and earned advanced degrees.

Mr. James was surely proud of his student who also rose from low beginnings yet made outstanding academic strides and became a Professor of Biology, William Douglass Moorehead.

A brilliant light can illuminate the darkness, or--for those who lack vision-- it can appear to make the darkness more alluring. The reaction is not the teachers to control.

A few male students, unwilling to meet Mr. James' demands for excellence, left school and found work in a local factory. As the drop-out trend continued, Mr. James was compelled to change his manner of delivering instruction.

Nevertheless, he remained the best academic teacher I have ever known.

When I called his house from Los Angeles in 1986, his wife said he was gone. The realm of teachers had lost a bright jewel.

CHAPTER 17: A LIFE CHANGING TRAIN RIDE

"Aunt Sarah"

Sarah Frances Payne III (1883 - 1969)

Aunt Sarah, nine years older than my mother, had stayed in Ohio ever since she had gone there as a teenager to live with her oldest brother, George, Jr. She recalled that it was around 1897 when things began to change in her life. Around the time that Uncle Billy escaped from that trouble in Shiloh, Aunt Sarah had been planning to go away to school. In those days, a young woman could finish normal school, take a teacher's training course, and become a primary school teacher. But Grandpa remarried five years after Grandma Frances died; and the stepmother, Victoria Caldwell Payne, saw no need to spend money to send Sarah Frances away to school.

Although Grandpa had bought new clothes for Sarah Frances and her trunk was all packed, he listened to his new wife. Aunt Sarah was so disappointed that she just left home, went off to live with Uncle George up in Cleveland. In Ohio, everybody who was old enough to earn a few dollars had to work. So Aunt Sarah didn't get the chance to go back to school, but learned to cook and to do laundry. A few years later, she met and married Laurence Bratton and they built a home out in Painesville, Ohio. That was before I was born, but as far back as I can remember, Aunt Sarah came to see us every other summer.

Although she had lost her chance to be a teacher, Aunt Sarah never stopped acting, speaking and dressing like one. I loved to see her come walking up in the front yard, looking as if she had taken plenty of time to dress and had good clothes to dress in, too. I would look her over from head to toe. And because I loved and longed for pretty shoes particularly, I wanted to see what kind of shoes she was wearing. Whenever she traveled, stylish as she was, she was also sensible and always wore sturdy, low-heel navy or black oxfords that showed off clean, unwrinkled shoelaces. But her ankles would be swollen from sitting on the train for so long, she said.

Yet, she always showed up with a smile on her face, and she always brought gifts for my brothers, and for me, pretty dainty things such as I had never seen before, like a beautiful box of dusting powder and one time a set of bronzed metal double bracelets etched in floral patterns and held together by a little golden chain. What's more, as long as Aunt Sarah was there, my two brothers and I would have hot lunches every day while Mama was at work. Mama would always fix dinner when she got home.

Whenever she came to North Carolina, Aunt Sarah would visit Uncle Will Payne in Shiloh, sixteen miles away, and she'd take me with her. On summer evenings after dinner, I could sit quietly on the front porch at 965 West Chapel Road and listen to Aunt Eldora, Uncle Will's wife, Aunt Sarah, and sometimes Cousin Agnes talk about the family. They talked about who moved where, how long ago, and how many children they had, including all seven of Uncle Billy's. Aunt Sarah, born in 1883, was especially good at this kind of story telling; and through her I learned many things about the Paynes which my mother didn't know or couldn't remember, as she was younger than Aunt Sarah. At home, most of the stories about family would be about the Burnettes. My paternal grandmother told stories, too, but more about the frighting experiences she had faced as a young woman growing up in the wilds of our mountains. And since I was the only one of my siblings who heard many of these stories, I thought it must have been meant for me to try to remember all I heard, in case one day somebody might ask me what I knew about the family on the Paynes or the Burnettes, my parents 'paternal sides of the family. Their maternal sides were the Freemans and the Stepps.

When Aunt Sarah came to visit, she always spent most of her time at our house in Black Mountain, cooking, cleaning, and helping Mama all she could while she was there. Being from another mountain settlement, living way up North and not well known by our neighbors, Aunt Sarah didn't visit the families who lived near us, and she rarely went to church with us either. In our settlement, people were always kind and polite to strangers, but even as young children we knew who was either born there into one of the old settler families, or who was an outsider, just married to a member of one of those families.

I can't speak for my six brothers and sisters, but for me, Aunt Sarah was the queen of the whole family on both sides. Whenever she came home, when she first got to our house, I would run to hug her, take her coat and the big black leather handbag with the round double straps [handles]. I liked to smell everything. [Before the war, leather handbags and shoes were made of real leather that smelled like leather.] Then off in a room by myself, I would cuddle her coat (always a summer soft black or navy blue serge woolen) up to my face and inhale that mysterious fragrance of the train, an oily odor of coal smoke and the faint smell of cigar smoke mingling with a delicate perfume.

The heavy odor of the coal smoke told me she had just got off the train, the faint odor of the cigar smoke meant she had been sitting in a coach where some man had been smoking a cigar, but not recently. I knew Aunt Sarah didn't even smoke cigarettes. To mountain people, only certain kinds of Black women smoked or, worse, drank alcohol in public, particularly in the presence of men who were not members of their own family. With my eyes closed and face buried in that coat bundled up in my arms, I would take a deep breath and wonder what it would be like to leave the mountains, get on a train and go all the way out of the South. Every other year I could have my private daydream with my head nestling in Aunt Sarah's coat, but I never even guessed that my time to leave would come so soon.

Now the summer of 1944, was not Aunt Sarah's year to visit. Besides, she had recently married and moved from Cleveland to Middletown in Southern Ohio. But Mama, who had seen only two of her seven children get anything close to a normal high school education, was hoping that her youngest child would go farther. Mama was thinking of my future, my education, my health, when she allowed that no daughter of hers was going to walk nearly a mile to the main highway, stand in the cold to wait for a raggedy school bus with a burned out engine, weak brakes and no heater, sit shivering for 16 miles to the county seat, and catch tuberculosis and die as her teenage sisters Florence and Laura and nephew Emanuel had done. Between the ages of 17 and 19, they had all died of galloping consumption: Galloping it was called because by the time the doctor discovered it was tuberculosis, they had just six weeks to live.

So when I finished the seventh grade that spring, Mama wrote to Aunt Sarah and in late summer, Aunt Sarah came right down on the train to get me so I would be registered in time to start school in Middletown in the fall. Aunt Sarah's visits had always spelled happy times for me. But this one was absolutely the best. It wasn't her arriving, but her leaving that I longed for: This time I would be going back home with her.

I was excited about taking a long ride on the train, nearly four hundred miles from Asheville to Cincinnati, with another 30-mile ride north to

Middletown. By train, I had been no farther than the next town to the east, Old Fort. That was only four miles away. Between Black Mountain and Old Fort, I could see one thing other than a tunnel and mountains: The Old Fort geyser that sent a solid spout of water up into the air. Making a figure that looked to me like a giant question mark, the waterspout rose high into the air and curled back towards the earth before breaking into a spray that created a rainbow against the sunlight. Somehow, as I recalled my first train ride at the age of four, the image of that old geyser brought to mind a disturbing rumor about schools up North.

My excitement about going to live up North was slightly dampened by my misgivings. As my mother would have put it: my anxiety had "dampened my tail feathers." I knew that I could keep up if I was given half a chance. But we had been led to believe that northern schools were so perfect and demanding. What's more, two of my school mates had already moved away to New Jersey to live with their mother, and I had heard that southern Black children who entered schools in the North would surely be demoted. I had worked hard in the seventh grade. In fact, for the last three years of elementary school, I had been writing 20-page mid-term and final exam papers all from knowledge of the subject, and in a strict number-letter outline form.'Could anything be harder than that?' I wondered.

At Clear View we had been tested on what we should know and had learned, not on how well we could guess. Nothing in my elementary school training had included an objective test or much time for classroom discussions. But the time came to leave, and I was not backing away from this opportunity to get a better education.

One late summer afternoon, at the station on Sutton Avenue in Black Mountain, Aunt Sarah and I waited to board westbound Number 21. Black Mountain was a small town, but not a flag stop where the ticket master had to put out a sign for the train to stop. As the train ground to a stop, its metal wheels screeched against steel rails, a little bell made a nervous-sounding

ding-ding, ding-ding, and the engine hissed and puffed as if to say "Hurry up: I've got other places to go tonight. Hurry!"

I do remember staring at the side of that train, the olive green panel on the side of the train behind those dusty big black letters that spelled S- O-U-T-H-E-R-N, and the opening doors to the coaches. A Black railway porter came through a door, swinging to the ground as if it was some kind of game and set a metal step below the door. The Black porters would stand at the doors of the front coaches, and the White conductor stood near the rear coaches, dividing the passengers by race. The coaches reserved for Colored people were always next to the engine. Train engines then were powered by steam, generated by coal fire. That thick black coal smoke from the engine boiled up out of the smokestack rising out of the engine in front of the train. As the train chugged away towards Biltmore, the first stop, it gathered speed and that smoke puffed out in great clouds and the wind pushed it backwards over the passenger cars. Cars closest to the engine caught the heaviest fumes from the smoke, and those cars were always the dirtiest, had the grimiest windows and, I guess, were the ones most in danger if the train wrecked. I couldn't tell which was heavier, the smell of the coal smoke or the stale odor of cigar smoke, though no one was smoking in our coach on that trip. Now my clothes would smell like Aunt Sarah's. The dirt and the grime of the coach didn't matter so much.

CHAPTER 18: THAT HOUSE ON MAIN STREET

O I looked over Jordan

and what did I see
comin' for to carry me home
A band of Angels comin' after me
Comin' for to carry me home.
Chorus
Swing Low, Sweet Chariot,
....
Negro Spiritual

I came to meet the ghost on South Main Street in Middletown in a roundabout way. The truth is, I wouldn't' even be writing about a scary time in Ohio if it had not been for conditions in Black Mountain that affected my education, a good twenty years before school integration began in the South. No middle school in my hometown was going to allow me or any other Black student to enroll under any circumstances, and they certainly were not going to let me sit next to a White student in a classroom, no matter what my grades and test scores looked like—not in 1944.

It wasn't the hardship of transportation my mother objected to, it was the danger of exposure to cold weather that her sisters and she were so familiar with. Although tuberculosis was all around us, brought to the mountains by new residents who could afford to come to this climate for treatment, young people were no longer dying of galloping consumption. Whatever the physical hardship for me, I was expected to go to school—if there was any way to go. Older members of the family had given up on education after the seventh grade because they had no way to get to the school sixteen miles away. But by

1935, when the county provided a school bus for Black students, older boys and girls had gone on to high school and several went on to finish college.

For me, stopping was not an option. I was determined to go on to school, my family expected me to go and so did the whole community. The strange part of it is that our families had no money for higher education and even high school was a financial burden.

But I, the great granddaughter and granddaughter of slaves, had a better educational opportunity than those who had come before me and was expected to make every possible effort to grasp the few advantages of my time. Back in 1889, with no prospect of going beyond the third grade, Papa had quit school. But he said if each generation would go as far as they could, their children would go farther, and that's how the race would move forward out of slavery. That burden, that obligation to the African American race was not one that every student felt. I suppose I did because I never thought of education as a means of making money, only as a way to a better life. From elementary school, my schoolmates and I were taught to serve the community.

So, in the summer of 1944, Mama wrote that letter to her sister in Ohio, and Aunt Sarah came right down on the train to get me, so I would be registered in time to start school the next fall. At the train station on Sutton Avenue in Black Mountain, Aunt Sarah and I waited to board a segregated coach on the westbound Southern No. 21. I'm sure Papa was there, maybe Mama and Papa both were there. I don't remember. My old Clear View classmate William Moorehead was there. I was too excited to say a decent good-bye to anyone. I was, I suppose, much like one who feels he is leaving this earth behind and is going straight to heaven. But, you know, they say "Be careful of what you wish for."

I loved listening to the clickety-clack of train wheels. Other than that, the train ride was long and there wasn't much to see. The Southern Railway going west went right through the thickest part of the mountains of Western North Carolina, Eastern Tennessee, and on north through Kentucky. That evening, at dusk, a Black family left our coach. When I looked out the window on the exit side, my eyes bumped right up against a mountain so high I couldn't't see the top. Through the windows next to my seat, I could see only a thick row of bushes growing beside the tracks.

Aunt Sarah had been making this part of her trip from Cleveland to visit us every other year for as long as I could remember, so I asked, 'Aunt Sarah, where are those people going?'

She said in a matter of fact way "Either up that mountain or into the river."

Well, that's how it looked to me, but I didn't want to believe it. I had always lived in the mountains, but I had never seen such a rugged looking place. We lived in the Swannanoa Valley, still the foothills of the Appalachians, but at least some places were level, not just gorges between mountains or between the mountain and a river.

Aunt Sarah said we would cross the Ohio River at Lexington, Kentucky the next morning. Now that I had to see. That was the enchanted river, the River Jordan that we had sung about in the spirituals at church: the river that slaves had risked their lives to cross to get into a free state. And the band of angels coming to get them, I understood, were the abolitionists who hid them from slave catchers when the Black Codes made it necessary for runaway slaves to keep on going until they reached Canada. That's where that old Black Moses promised them, *If they would just keep on going, and not stop,… they could ride the iron horse to shake the lion's paw* [cross the bridge decorated with busts of lions at the other end], as Harriet Tubman described it.

In a way I was escaping, too. I would not miss my first sight of that great symbol of freedom, the place of crossing over from bondage, as the spiritual said "Wanna cross over into campground." But when we reached the river, our train also had to ride an iron horse that had so many railings I could hardly see the river below. That was disappointing.

In Cincinnati we had a lay-over, so I had time to rush outside to get a glimpse of my first big city. The city was hilly and that didn't impress me, but I had never seen such a fine, large building with different colored stones decorating the tall domed front of the terminal. Here was surely a new world. No wonder Black folks came back home boasting about living up North in Indiana, Illinois, Michigan, Ohio, New Jersey and New York, places they had fled to in large numbers to find work. Every one of those states had claimed members of my hometown, and some I had never seen again. As sparsely populated as our mountain area was, I had known entire families to vanish, their houses left to be claimed by the elements, their property sold for taxes. For me it was different. My family wasn't moving North. I alone was coming North for education, and I wasn't coming here to stay.

On the Baltimore and Ohio train to Middletown, we could sit wherever we wished. That was new. On trains coming from the South or returning there, Black people sat in segregated coaches; and on buses going from one town to another (my hometown had no city buses), we had to sit in the rear seats, even if seats near the front were empty. If White people had taken all the seats, we would have to stand up.

Aunt Sarah's husband and his pastor met us at the train station. As we drove across town, I was startled by the *lay of the land,* as Papa would have called it. I didn't say anything as I stared out the window from the back seat of the car. *Who would believe this?* I had grown up surrounded by trees and hills. In the distance, blue mountain ranges, undisturbed and beautiful, rose and peaked high above our valley that nestled at 3,000 feet in the foothills. This valley, the Miami, was flat as a pancake.

I thought about a tale told many years before to my oldest sister Juanita by her future brother-in-law. Her husband-to-be wanted to make a good impression, so he told her his father owned 100 acres of land, and she realized that was more than twelve times what her father owned. Well that turned out to be true. But then the man's brother chimed in with "Yes, and it's all level, just as fur as you can see." Now that was really stretching the blanket.

The father-in-law's land was level, the space where the house sat. And that was as far as you could see any level ground. We heard that the young woman had to walk two miles over a sparsely used wagon road through the woods just to get to their mailbox on the main highway. But here, it really was level, just as far as you could see.

The car pulled up to the curb and stopped, and Aunt Sarah turned to me and said "Well, here we are at last."

At last? It had been a long trip, but I wasn't tired. I stared at this house so close to the sidewalk. In Black Mountain, only White people who could hire maids, cooks, housekeepers and laundresses lived on streets and in houses like this, had sidewalks in front of their houses, and their help didn't come in through the front door, either. At home, not even the main roads through the Black   neighborhoods were paved.

A smaller house, a bungalow, stood a few yards to the right, and I could see a boy tall enough to be in high school watching us from behind his front screen door; but he didn't come out to greet us. If I had a neighbor living that close back home, he would have come out and said "Hey" to us. And he would have known our names, even mine, because somebody would have told him about me; and they might have already invited him to come over to see whether he could help me with my school work, as I was only in the eighth grade. That boy just stood there looking like he didn't know what to do.

Aunt Sarah's husband saw him and bragged, "That's one of the three Black families that live on this street. But *this* is the only steam heated house in this town that's owned by a Black man."

I didn't ask, 'Don't you know the family's name? 'I knew all of my neighbors' names, and even some of the people living as much as six miles away because they came to our church. And among the old families, I knew the children, the parents 'and grandparents 'names and many of their other relatives, living and dead. Not only that, I knew what they had died of, whether an accident or of some disease, and knew who else in the family was still living with

215

the same disease. Every family had a history and people in our neighborhood knew most of it. It was hard to keep anything hid in my hometown and nobody tried very hard. Secrets got out, but we children knew what to talk about and when to keep our mouths shut.

I didn't know what *steam-heated* meant. Where I came from, Black people had fireplaces and coal and wood stoves. I could tell that this uncle-in-law wasn't used to talking to young people. He wasn't bothering to explain anything.

We were walking towards a well-built two-story home. Yet, on the outside it wore a dreary face and stood uncomfortably close to the sidewalk with hardly any sign of life about it. Why, back home our apple and cherry orchard separated our front yard from the nearest public road. And when the two great black cherry trees next to our house were in bloom, little more than our roof could be seen from the road.

The narrow lot surrounding this house had no trees, and the few scraggly shrubs growing around the front appeared to be dying. Two small squares of barren soil flanked the walkway to the front steps and served as a front yard, not a lawn, for grass no longer grew there. The outside walls of the house were covered with some kind of heavy dark grey stucco to which the white rimmed windows watching over the porch from the second level tried to add a bit of cheer. The front steps were of sturdy cement and so was the front porch. Its solid walls were high enough that no woman or girl would have to sit with ankles crossed all the time, but low enough to allow a clear view of the sidewalk, the houses on either side and the attractive homes with well–kept lawns and neatly groomed shrubbery on the other side of the street. I wondered why a house in such a pretty area had to look so gloomy. Not even the drab grey stucco and the neglected grounds seemed to be the answer.

Aunt Sarah's husband set our suitcases down at the foot of the stairs and Aunt Sarah said, "Our bedrooms are right up these stairs."

I was already halfway through a room that looked like a funeral parlor, furnished with cushioned chairs, glossy tables and fancy lamps with flowered glass shades, but not one settee or davenport to suggest that anybody would ever sit in that room. In the dining room, a China cabinet was full of pretty dishes.

'They must be for company,' I thought.

I noticed the sideboard that matched the oblong table and the china cabinet. We had a sideboard at home. It didn't match our big round table or the chairs. But it had a secret drawer, deep enough to hold a crock of Mama's homemade wild grape wine. Something above the sideboard caught my eye.

A large globe-shaped mirror held between the claws of a great bronze eagle hung there. I had never seen such a mirror before and thought it must be just for decoration because when I looked into it, a strange-looking face looked back at me—mine. In the kitchen, a white enamel gas stove stood on four tall legs in one corner. Its oven was on one side of the burners. At the other wall a big sink had a faucet over it, like the one at Clear View, and metal cabinets below it. Wow! Mama cooked on a wood stove and we carried our cooking and drinking water from the spring.

Next to the wall nearest the dining room were two wooden pieces of furniture that somebody, a good carpenter like Papa, had made. They didn't look homemade, but I could tell that they were. The table was made of heavy timber and the cabinet was built from floor to ceiling. Solid oak! The top part of it had glass doors and I could see the thick white dishes stacked inside.

"Now, that's more like it. Don't have to worry about dropping one of 'em. Probably wouldn't't break any way"

Aunt Sarah's husband had already gone to his radio beside the dining room windows, where he sat puffing away on a black pipe with a curved stem. The odor of the smoke was strange, sweet and pleasant. Aunt Sarah was calling me. I ran down the hall from the kitchen to the stairway where she was waiting. 'What's that odor, Aunt Sarah, 'I wanted to know. Papa had smoked a pipe, too, when I was a little girl, but his tobacco didn't smell like that.

Aunt Sarah's eyes twinkled as she smiled and said, "Let me show you where Chester gets his pipe tobacco."

She ushered me back down the hall and out the kitchen door. We stepped out onto a porch that was almost as long as the width of the house. "See that bush growing at the end of the porch? That's a fig bush. He picks the leaves, dries them and then crushes them for his pipe."

I recognized the leaves of the fig bush and was surprised to see one growing here, so far North. Figs didn't grow in our part of the mountains, but I had seen a bush like that at Uncle Jim's place in Nebo, thirty miles away to the southeast. He was my grandmother's youngest brother and tears came to his eyes when he looked at my mother and said, "My baby sister's baby." It took me a while to figure that out when I learned he was younger than Grandma Frances. Actually, he was the youngest boy and Grandma was the youngest girl, so they were baby sister and baby brother. Anyway, he was born in 1850; it was 1944 when we were in Nebo last, and I never saw him again. I didn't tell Aunt Sarah about that visit because she was already walking back towards the stairs. "Let's get our luggage upstairs and I'll show you to your room."

"OK."I grabbed the bigger bag and left the smaller one for her.

At the top of the stairs, she said, "Just set that one over here, pointing to the door to my right. "Your room is over there, and that door straight ahead leads to the bathroom."

It was a pleasant room with double windows facing west over the front porch. Full length lace curtains hung dutifully over the closed windows and in front of dark green window shades, a pleasant backdrop for my study table and lamp. A large dresser waited near my bed. The walls of the room were covered with wallpaper, seamlessly hung and delicately printed with tiny deep pink rosebuds scattered aimlessly over an eggshell background.

At the north side of the room, Aunt Sarah opened the door to another room big enough to walk around in and said "Now, this is your closet. Just set your suitcase down for now." At the opposite side of the room, the closet had been left unfinished, and a heavy dark green curtain covered the doorway to that deep empty space that I would not dare to enter. That doorway was right beside the head of my bed. In spite of the room's inviting appearance, I felt that something was not right. A deathly stillness hung over the house.

From my bedroom windows, I could see over the rooftops across the street and beyond that to where a high ridge rose above the houses. 'What's that ridge way over there, Aunt Sarah?'

"Oh, that's the levee. The Great Miami River runs right through this valley and in spring when the snows melt, the river rises out of its bed. The levee keeps it from flooding the city."

I remembered one summer when I was much younger. It rained day and night. Papa called it "Dog Days," and said it would rain 40 days and 40 nights. I wasn't allowed to go out of our house, but Papa said the branch had risen, the water had backed up into the fields below the house and the water was muddy. He and my brothers wore boots when they went outside. But our house was built high above the stream, and Papa said the water would never reach the house. Nobody even took me to see the little branch flowing over our summer playgrounds in the meadows, and I hoped I wouldn't't see a river flooding the street where I was living now.

I couldn't't actually see the Miami from the house on Main Street, but I couldn't't wait to go there. Aunt Sarah said we could go the next day because school had not started yet. And go we did. The levee was a little more than two blocks away.

Aunt Sarah and I crossed a narrow-deserted street running along below the levee. Then we climbed the steep hill to the top of it. The levee had been built high above the river, leaving the river far below in a deep valley of its own. It was kind of like standing at the top of the hill at the north end of our farm and looking down into the big meadow. At that point I wouldn't't have been able to see our little branch hiding deep within its banks. But this was a real river that could be dangerous.

"Well, there it is, "Aunt Sarah sighed; "And let's pray it stays down there."

But it was only September and the snows hadn't even started yet. Standing on the levee, I could see far down below and I couldn't't imagine seeing enough water to fill up that deep wide valley. Enough to rise up to the top of this hill and spill over the street below? Where could so much water come from, I wondered, as I stared at the sluggish, wide, slow moving ribbon of black water snaking its way towards the Ohio River thirty miles to the south? The Great Miami crawled, sooty and heavy. Never before had I seen a black river. The mountain streams I had seen were crystal clear, splashing over the rocks and gurgling like an innocent and happy child.

Another sign that something in this valley is not right, I thought.

When I first went to Ohio, I didn't believe in mysterious signs and ghosts, though I had heard a lot about them. The old people said the locusts would come every seven years, and when we saw them, we should look at their wings. If we saw a "P" on the wing, it meant peace would come; but if we saw "W," it was a sign of war for seven years.

Well, some years earlier, the locusts *had* come, though we never saw a live one. They would slip out of their skins and leave their old skeletons clinging to the trunks of the trees and we could tell how the live ones would look, like grasshoppers that had just crawled out of their outside skins, with eyes, wings, feet and everything all in one piece. I remember one morning my brother Wat found one of their paper-thin hides with tiny feet dug into the trunk of a big black cherry tree in our front yard. I knew that thing hadn't been there the day before. Wat plucked it off and showed me the wings, made of something like the skin that covered the sweet little yellow ground cherries that sprang up in the fields. Within the wings, we could make out tiny white veins shaping the form of a letter. I can't remember which letter we had seen but war had surely come in 1941. We had many other signs of bad luck and plenty of superstitions, like breaking a mirror that meant seven years of bad luck. But I had no proof of it as I had with the sign on the locust's wings.

As for ghosts, we had heard a lot of stories. From the days when Papa used to play for the country dances way back in the mountains, he recalled stories and told us jokes about coming home in the wee hours of the morning with his fiddle, guitar, his mandolin or banjo, and his gun. Sometimes his walks were blessed with moonlight. Sometimes he walked in pitch blackness. Once he had a pine torch to light his way. When Papa first heard the *Cuh-zip, cuh-zip* from the resin [we said *rawzum*] dripping from the torch, he thought it was a haunt and started to run. And the faster he ran, the faster the torch burned and the more the resin *cuh-zipped*. Finally, he realized he was running from the sound of his burning pine torch. We all laughed. How could anybody be afraid of a sound?

Another time, coming home late at night, Papa decided to rest in an old church 'til daybreak. When he yanked on the handle, the sagging door scraped noisily over the threshold and the rusty hinges squealed a loud and long— sque-e-a-k, and something, some things rushed out grunting and puffing, almost knocking him down, he said. But it was just a bunch of pigs that had the same idea Papa had until they were frightened by the squeaking door. *Really? How had the pigs gone into the church through a door that was so hard to open?*

Papa didn't care. He just wanted to make us laugh. One time he told us about stopping at an old abandoned log cabin on his way home. He thought it would be a good place to rest until daybreak. So he built a fire in the fireplace and was about to light it and lie down beside the hearth, when he heard a husky voice say, "Well, young man, it looks like there's nobody here but you and me tonight."

Papa said he looked around but didn't see anybody, so he reached for his hat and said to the voice "Yes, sir, and if you'll just wait 'til I get my hat, there won't be nobody here but you." Ghost stories were funny.

Then, one night a distant cousin passing by the woods near our house yelled for Papa to come quick and bring his gun. The poor man was so frightened, we could hear his voice all over the house: "Mr. Gar-land!" Mountain people had a way of casting their voices so they could be heard from one hill to the other. [My youngest brother and I used to go up on the hill and practice calling, and sometimes we could hear our voices echoing back to us.]

Papa grabbed a pistol from his trunk, rushed out of the house and on past the orchard to the Sand Road. He said Cousin Findley was just standing there, waiting for him to come and rescue him from the ghost he believed was in the woods.

"Well, what is it, Finley?" Papa wanted to know.

The man said that a strange light was jumping from one tree to another. Why, Papa explained to him, it was nothing but some chemical in the trees that seemed to leap from one limb to another and it took on the appearance of a soft glow at night. The old mountain people called it "foxfire" for phosphorus.

As much as Papa liked to practice shooting at night, he certainly wasn't going to waste a bullet shooting at foxfire. The man went on home, feeling a bit foolish, I guess. We children had played in those same woods for years, from morning 'till dusk and never had reason to fear anything.

One-time Mama had to leave suddenly to visit Aunt Sarah in Ohio. She had recently married and had taken ill all of a sudden. My brothers were in military service, my sisters had married and moved away, and Papa and I were at home alone. Sitting in our living room one night, I heard the house creak. I looked at Papa and he calmly said to me: "Now, that's just the sound of the house settling. I built this house, and nobody's ever died here. So, there's nothing to be afraid of here."

At home, the house-settling creaks were irregular, coming now and then or not at all. Nothing to be afraid of.

But Papa had said "Here." Here. *Did that mean other kinds of creaking sounds happened when somebody had died in a house?*

CHAPTER 19: STRANGE FOOTSTEPS
ON THE STAIRS

I would hear them … always around the same time every night. The footsteps were sure to come after dinner and shortly after we had gone to bed, although at different times that mysterious presence in the house on South Main Street would make itself known in other parts of the home, too—even in the daytime.

One time it happened in the kitchen. A disturbing clatter of rattling, crashing sounds was loud enough to make anyone think that every dish in the kitchen cupboard had fallen to the floor and splintered. But it was a sound, only a sound. Nothing—not one platter, bowl, plate, cup or saucer in that cupboard had been moved.

One time it happened in the dining room as we sat at the table, startled by the movement of a heavy mirror that hung above the sideboard or *buffet* as Aunt Sarah called it. That mirror, shaped like a gigantic globe grasped between the claws of a mighty bronze eagle, moved gently like a pendulum from side to side, and then came to rest in its normal position on the wall.

Other movements came without sound. It appeared once when one of the two Black teachers in Middletown came to visit Aunt Sarah. As the older teacher sat in the big armchair near the north wall of the parlor, a piece of plaster broke loose from the flawless ceiling and fell to the floor, barely missing the teacher's head. And it happened just as suddenly as the mirror had moved before our eyes or the dishes in the kitchen had seemed to shatter against the floor. Aunt Sarah told me the teacher never returned. She passed away unexpectedly.

But I was there for the nightly visitations: The strange creaking sounds on the stairs leading from the foyer on the main floor to the hallway above. They didn't pause at the first landing but came to rest in the hallway on the second floor. That was a nightly occurrence, only at night, and at bedtime.

Creak! creak! creak! Whatever it was, was slowly making its way up the stairs. Was it the sound of an old woman's or an old man's weighty footsteps, tired and weary, laboring to get up to the second floor? But for what? Then in the hallway outside my bedroom door, the creaking sounds would stop for the rest of the night. Lying in my bed, nearly frozen with fear I would find the courage to pull the covers over my head, and wait, hardly breathing, my heart racing, wild thoughts spinning through my head.

Was this something or somebody standing outside, trying to decide which door to enter? If it chose my door, would I hear the click of the doorknob and then the creaking footsteps again, this time coming towards my bed? Could it pass through the bedroom door just as it had apparently passed through the front, back or basement door downstairs? If so, could it be in my room right now? What did it want? Maybe it lived in this house as Aunt Sarah, her husband and I did, watching and waiting to torment us at bedtime. If it was in my room, how long would it be before I felt its presence beside my bed, felt a feathery touch on my shoulder, or worse, felt the covers being yanked from about my head, as another relative had felt in a house built over an old burying ground back home?

Nothing in my shallow encounters with ghosts had prepared me for these moments. As a child in the mountains, I had played games with other children along the Sand Road, next to Byrd's woods where foxfire was known to drift through the treetops at night. Sometimes on a summer day, for reasons that concerned none of us children, a soft warm whirlwind would whisk up a dusting of white sand and swirl it around for a few seconds like a toy tornado. In response, John, the oldest child, would remind his sister Helen and me, "Now we have to say these words..."; and we would whisper to the wind certain words, a eligious rebuke I've long since forgotten, something it was customary to memorize and repeat to the little dust devil; then we'd return to our games of hide and seek, or *Ain't no bears out tonight*, or we'd simply look for bright green oak balls hanging from the trees along the road. They were good to eat.

Coming home alone at dusk, fearing nothing, I often pretended to be running from a ghost; but I was on my own land, and because I loved to run and knew every step of the way, I would race over the path along the foot of the hill until I crossed over the stone bridge above the little branch that rippled across the farm. Then I would walk the rest of the way to the house because no haunt would ever cross over a stream. We children knew that.

Some nights we gathered around the fireplace with Papa where he would play the fiddle or guitar for us or tell us ghost stories, but they were always funny and never believable. Mama's strict religious upbringing didn't allow her to tolerate these gleeful sessions. She believed ghost stories were nonsense and said that believing in ghosts was nothing but old *fogyism*—one of her favorite words.

Nothing about the sound of footsteps in the house on the Main Street was playful, nothing was funny, nothing was unbelievable, nothing was nonsense —except for the absence of any sense of why it was happening. But the torture of my anxiety, my anticipations, of my imagination was painful. One thing was certain, the presence didn't annoy Aunt Sarah's new husband, that BlueBeard of a man who cackled with laughter when he described his own encounters with that mysterious resident,visitor, whatever it was. When the mirror moved on the wall, he had kept perfectly silent and made no effort to explain it away or to console Aunt Sarah or me.

It was as if he was saying, "These things happen in this house. Get used to it. Accept it. I do." He was so much like the spider, I thought, able to skitter about his lovely web without ever once getting entangled in it as creepy things do in real life. Nothing seemed to bother him.

One day, as the three of us sat in the dining room, the husband rose from his chair, went to the buffet, opened the lower right hand door and took out a photo of one of his former wives, the second one, to show us.

How weird! Is this his way of explaining the movement of the mirror on the wall? What is the connection?

No one had mentioned his previous wives, or the strange movement of the mirror several nights earlier. The woman in the photo was dressed in the stylish manner of the past century or early 1900s. She wore a silken, pleated, fitted bodice firmly buttoned at the neck. Its long sleeves puckered and puffed upwards at the shoulders. Her elegant wide brimmed hat was adorned with tall plumes of ostrich feathers. She was a stout woman, buxom, and *good looking*, as the folk back home would have said. Her broad, dark brown face wore a determined look. The eyes stared straight ahead. It was a handsome face, but not delicate and pretty like Aunt Sarah's. And the woman in the photo, like the one before her, had died childless.

Had her spirit moved the mirror on the wall because she was jealous of Aunt Sarah's beauty?

I was sure of one thing. Like a giant housefly, she had died in the web. *But, died of what? Two dead wives, no heirs, and all of this unexplained commotion in the house that Aunt Sarah kept as tidy and immaculate as a museum! Did he know that his second wife was the presence that frequented the house, or whose spirit still lurked there?*

Her name, he said, was Anna Lee. *What was going through his mind?* I looked at the picture of his Anna Lee, at him, and thought of Poe's *'Annabelle Lee'*:

To shut her up in a sepulcher

227

In this kingdom by the sea.

. . . .

. . . .

. . . .

And neither the angels in heaven above

Nor the demons down under the sea,
Can ever dissever my soul from the soul
Of the beautiful Annabel Lee.

Edgar Allan Poe 1809 – 1849 [from the third
and fifth stanzas of Annabel Lee]

Was my Aunt's husband in some way responsible for the haunting? There was no way he could have created those frightening movements and sounds that came unexpectedly and stopped only to return, we never knew when or where—except on the stairs. And at night? No, he was in his bed in the room across the hall.

Yet his behavior, his lack of surprise, his inattention to whatever occurred, given what was occurring in that house, was a puzzling combination to consider. Now the man was not clever, and of that I was certain. Although he had lived in Ohio for many years, his English was still poor. He read nothing other than the newspaper and spoke of nothing of any substance. But his actions were suspicious. And just as suspicious was the fact that the footsteps were always coming *up* the stairs and never going *down* to wherever that ghost stayed at other times. Always coming *up* the stairs and stopping between our two-bedroom doors, and then… dead silence on the stairs until the next night.

Aunt Sarah was afraid of this invisible creature, just as I was. I could tell. When the mirror moved on the wall, I looked across the table at her. She stretched her eyes and the pupils grew wide with fear. But for my sake, she didn't scream and she wouldn't talk about it while I lived in that house.

But she didn't deny it—neither her fear nor that disturbing presence in the house. And sometimes at night when I could no longer bear the suspense of that ghostly silence outside my door—if it was still outside my door, I would call out to her. She must have been lying awake, too, because I would soon hear her door close softly and she would enter my room with a smile on her face. Her expression spoke words of comfort and apology to me.

I'm here. And I'm so sorry this is happening. So sorry, but I'm right here.

Without saying a word, she would slip into my bed, and I would sleep peacefully until morning. Then off to school I'd go, as usual, and not once would I think of the previous night's horror, though I knew it would return.

***

The next spring President Franklin Delano Roosevelt died suddenly. It was a sad time. The radio reported that he had done so many good things for the country, although it seemed to me that he hadn't cared much about Black people in general. Men in the armed forces, like my four brothers, had to serve in segregated companies. I didn't need to get that from the radio or the newspapers. Not long after being inducted into the Army or Navy--only my youngest brother volunteered, every one of my brothers would send home a large company photograph. I would eagerly scan the picture, row by row, searching for my brother's face. And every face would be Black, not all black in color, but Black by race.

I thought the President showed less concern when a ship filled with frightened Jewish people fleeing from Hitler sat docked at a New York Harbor. I couldn't't understand how a President could have so much honor but ignore important problems like legalized racism and its ways of puncturing the hopes of Black Americans. I couldn't't understand how a man in the position of President could hard-heartedly turn his back on another group of people trying to escape from a tyrant in Europe.

Among the usual senseless lynching's, the newspapers also reported lynching's of Black soldiers who returned home after fighting for their country. To see a picture of a young man who had been tortured and left hanging from the limb of a tree just because a group of White people somewhere resented seeing a Black soldier dressed in a United States military uniform was horrible. And the news of those Jewish people who came to this country on that ship, begging for the President's help and protection, was horrible. The newspapers said it was Eleanor Roosevelt who helped the people on that ship, not the President.

My mother spoke well of President Roosevelt and said, "He has beautiful delivery." It sounded to me like Mama was repeating something she had heard up town. Although I understood little of what the President talked about, I thought he did make beautiful sounding speeches and in a voice that was hardly like any other I had ever heard except for Winston Churchill. And he did start the Works Progress Administration [WPA] that gave Papa a job, but only after someone up town reprimanded the White supervisor of the project for refusing to hire a Black man who owned a few acres of land.

Papa helped to create that beautiful lake, Lake Tomahawk, at the recreation center in Black Mountain. But his children could not swim in the water. I faced that bitter fact one Sunday afternoon when Papa took us to the lake for family photographs. In one of the pictures, I am crying because I cannot even dip my hands into the lake.

Racism always had a way of placing things right before our eyes and then holding them just beyond our reach, as it happened in the stories of mythology that I loved to read. And I thought the Greek character most typical of the Colored man's plight was that man who kept on pushing that big heavy stone to the top of the mountain, only to have it slip out of his hands and roll back to the bottom of the hill. And with racism, too, the punishment of the pushing and the slipping was meant to go on forever.

As I write these lines, I understand for the first time why Papa snapped the shutter on that camera while I was still crying. It would be a reminder. What must have hurt Papa more deeply than not being able to lead me over to the lake and letting me just dip one hand into the cold mountain water, was seeing that I could not understand something he would have to explain to me a few years later. And about three years later, he did explain in these words: "What this country stands for [its greatness] is more important than what this country allows today." And later he explained "So you just go as far as you can, and your children will go farther." I took that lesson to heart and loved Papa's America. I understood his words to mean that it was not the United

States of America that imposed racism on us, but the will of mean human beings who, to put it in Papa's words, 'temporarily had the upper hand,' like the local White supervisor of the WPA. But in time, a time that education would help us to prepare for, the great spirit of America would rise up and break the grip of that hand from our necks. Papa's words helped me to shake off the intended humiliation of racism, and I have never shed another tear over the effects of this great cloud of affliction.

For very much like the ghost of South Main Street, the ghost of racism suddenly moved things like the heavy mirror on the wall, back and forth, where we should have found stability. You could go to school, but you couldn't' get the same job that was open to a White person with the same or less education. Like the piece of plaster that fell from the ceiling, racism held its unjust laws over us and threatened us with restrictions and punishment. *Like the creepy footsteps on the stairs, racism always made its presence known. And even in its silence, awareness of its awful presence tormented us. It seemed to me that racism had three faces: a kind face—like the woman on the WPA board of directors up town, a blind face—like the President, and a cruel face—like the lynchers. And from where I sat, racism often wore the masks of all its faces at the same time.*

But at 14, my main interest was school. I really didn't know much about anything else. In 1945, I did know that most people back home would think I should have stayed in Ohio. They believed anybody who got the chance to get a better education should be willing to go through hell for it. Well, I had been through hell living in a haunted house for two semesters. That summer when school was out, I went back home.

My little attic room was just as I had left it the summer before. It was on the right side of the stairs, and the double windows still overlooked the meadow where I had played just a few years earlier. The head of my old white iron single bed still faced the East.

Papa said all beds should face East, just as every grave in the cemetery of the former slaves and their offspring at Thomas Chapel Church all faced East.

That little bed never looked nor felt so good when bedtime came. There was nothing to fear in the house that Papa built.

The most valuable part of my northern schooling was the advice I received from the kind counselor at McKinley Junior High school. That blessing came from a woman who had taken the time to look at my grade reports, had dismissed the racial label "Negro," and sent for me to come to her office. And that happened at a time when "Negro" labeled boys and girls in many other parts of the country, I heard, were being directed into woodwork and radio repair shop or into home economics and secretarial programs.

As I sat listening to the counselor, I didn't take a single note but committed to memory every bit of advice she gave me, and I faithfully followed it in spite of being at a different school every year. For my four years of high school, I went to four different schools in three different cities, and in three different states—North Carolina, Ohio, and California.

I'm not complaining. Going to school was a privilege. Students of my age had been conditioned to take hardship in stride. I will never forget that sunny morning in January of 1944. Our raggedy school bus broke down about six miles east of Beau catcher Tunnel. The bus driver had no telephone. I knew I would be dreadfully late for classes whether I stayed on the bus or walked the rest of the way to school. I was sure to be embarrassed.

My city-born ninth grade classmates would probably think it was funny and snicker at seeing a bunch of country kids arriving so late. I didn't know whether our bus would be repaired by the time school was out. I had the ten cents for lunch—if we got to school in time for lunch. [In Asheville a school lunch cost seven cents less than in Middletown.] I don't remember whether I had Trailways 'bus fare back to Black mountain.

For whatever reason, my buddy Shannon, born with a more beautiful voice than her mother who had sung the spirituals to us in kindergarten, and I decided to walk the ten miles back home. We weren't tired when we reached my house, so we went outside, took off our shoes and socks and played in the

233

stream running along the western meadow. Where the trees hung over the banks, the snow could hide from the sun and form little hills along the edges of the stream. Mama needn't have feared my dying of galloping consumption because of riding to school on an unheated school bus. Neither of us had a cold afterward, and Shannon still had another two miles to go before she would sit before a warm fire at her own house.

After the ninth grade, I had changed schools not just to avoid riding a dilapidated school bus for sixteen miles one way to the nearest school for Black students but more importantly to attend a school that offered the courses I had been advised to take. Never again during those four years would a high school counselor offer to explain to me which courses to take for admission to college, nor would any one need to.

One dedicated Black grade schoolteacher back home had prepared me to succeed in college; one wise and impartial White counselor at the middle school in Ohio had told me how to get there. Perhaps I had paid an unnecessary price for that gift from the counselor, anguished by the nightly visitations of a mysterious ghost whom I had mistaken for a presence of evil, and for a whole school year. But the gift was priceless.

Aunt Sarah had made a great sacrifice, too, suffering mental torment along with the physical hardship of remaining with and supporting a man who had deliberately deceived and exploited her for his personal benefit. I know that part of her conscious sacrifice was for me. The unconscious part, I suspect, was due to a characteristic weakness, that is, blind loyalty, being loyal to a fault, as when a virtue is captured as a device to be used for the vices of one less virtuous.

However, unlike the tormented spirit that trekked up those stairs night after night, driven by a force the living cannot know, Aunt Sarah's merger with the strange Mr. Lowe who kept Miss Anna Lee's picture in a sideboard and paid no attention to the nightly visits of that unsettled spirit, it was a matter of choice: For him, a good choice for an ill-motivated purpose; for my dear Aunt Sarah, a bad choice with honorable intentions proven by her loyalty to the oath, *for better or for worse.*

But when I think about that poor man, My Aunt Sarah's husband, Chester, about his strange ways, his two wives who had passed on, leaving no children, about that big empty space at the end of the room I slept in, and how that mysterious creaking appeared on the stars every night, I wonder if he planned to work my Aunt Sarah to death to collect the little insurance she had. Maybe that poor old woman's spirit was trying to warn Aunt Sarah to get out of that house before she worked herself to death, too.

Well, if Chester had been planning on collecting insurance from Aunt Sarah's death, he lost out again on that gamble. A few years later, Aunt Sarah buried Chester in North Carolina, in the cemetery of the same church Grandpa Payne had once pastored. For several years after that, she visited relatives from North Carolina to Michigan. Finally, she went on to Fresno to spend the rest of her days with an older sister, Aunt Latha. And Aunt Sarah outlived Chester by more than twenty years.

If that house in Middletown is still standing, I wonder whether anyone hears noises in the corner of the dining room where Chester sat smoking his pipe and listening to the races in the daytime, and whether that poor woman's spirit is still coming home and struggling up those stairs at night. That happened more than sixty-three years ago. And nobody today can convince me there's no such thing as a haunted house or a ghost. I lived with one in that house on South Main Street.

CHAPTER 20: LIFE IN A LONELY VALLEY

Though I knew little about money, I could tell that whoever had built the house on South Main Street had spent plenty on it. When Uncle Will heard that his sister Sarah had run into an old childhood acquaintance and was considering marrying again, he took the train from Biltmore Station four hundred miles away to meet the uncle to be in Middletown. Uncle to-be told my Uncle Will about all the money he earned as a paper hanger—and he did: in 1943, $25 a day was much more than Papa earned in a whole month. And when it came to smarts and skills, that uncle-to-be couldn't't hold a candle to Papa. But when Uncle Will heard about the money and saw that nice home, more modern than his own home in Shiloh, he was impressed and agreed that Aunt Sarah should marry the man. Aunt Sarah was a pretty woman but — with the exception of her stable breadwinning first husband—she had developed at a knack for attracting gamblers.

Shortly after marrying the paperhanger, she had a nervous breakdown and the paperhanger hired a registered nurse to take care of her. Yet she sent for Mama. Now my mother would sleep well anywhere. Once she went to bed, nothing was going to wake her up before time for her to get up. Mama had grown up on farms in Hendersonville and Edneyville, and after she married Papa, they had lived in rough coal mining towns in West Virginia and she had to learn how to shoot a rifle. Mama said she had to learn to use both ends of that gun.

One time some tough older mountain woman making passes at Papa was foolish enough to make a threatening gesture towards Mama and did it while Mama was standing there with the rifle in her hand. But the butt of that rifle stopped that woman cold in her tracks. Mama said the woman took her to court. Oddly enough, all the evidence went along, too. Papa was allowed to sit right in the courtroom with the rifle across his knees and the old plaintiff came in with the side of her face bruised and the skin still peeling away. The Judge saw that Mama was a decent young woman; the older woman had a bad reputation, and that was that.

Mama would so to speak, "take a bull by the horns," but not Aunt Sarah. She wasn't really a coward, just timid and afraid of snakes. But she wasn't sickly. I wondered what had caused Aunt Sarah to get sick.

When school started, the giggly talkative seventh grade boy living in the big red frame house down the alley behind our weed-bearing garden walked me to McKinley Junior High. The school wasn't far from the house on Main Street. I felt happy walking through paved streets to school. That couldn't happen back home: only White kids lived close enough to walk to middle and senior high school, and Black kids couldn't't go there at all. Besides that, I had walked much farther when I was just four years old, and for seven years I had walked what must have been many times that distance going to and from elementary school over narrow grassy paths and dirt roads.

McKinley was a beautiful three-story red brick building sprawling over a broad green lawn. The students were Black and White. The principal and all the teachers, even the people who worked in the cafeteria, were White. I didn't have trouble keeping up with my schoolwork, but I was confused by the bell schedule. At Clear View Grammar, I had stayed in one room all day and received all my subjects from the same teacher. When the bell rang, that is, when some student ran around the school ringing the bell, it was time for recess, for lunch, or time to go home.

At McKinley, hearing the bell ringing inside the building, I would go to the large glass double door entrance to the front hallway and look out. Not a single soul would be on the grounds. One minute the halls were bustling with students; the next minute they were empty. Frustrated and fearful of being late for class, I would show my class schedule to a teacher in the hall, and any one of them would always walk me to my classroom. Eventually I got the hang of it, and I continued to get good marks all through the eighth grade.

But not everything at McKinley was hunky dory. I was used to seeing Black students respect and obey our teachers. All of us looked up to our Black teachers, -- except for one or two students who acted like they were a little touched in the head. Most of my Black school mates and I would have obeyed a teacher of any race or color, anywhere.

In Ohio, day after day, I saw students talk back to teachers and act up in class in a way that was shocking to me. Much of the time they acted as if no teacher was in the room, and when the teacher reprimanded them, they talked back. I saw no meanness on the teachers' part, but somehow, I knew that a wide gap separated the Black students from their White teachers. I just couldn't explain it. These kind teachers never gave me a note to take home asking to come over for dinner like the teachers back home, and they didn't show up at my church like my last Black teacher did.

In spite of the gentleness of the White teachers in Ohio, something was missing. Something I had been accustomed to, perhaps had taken for granted. What was it other than race that separated us? It was 1944. I knew of no African American who held a high position in our nation's government, no state governors, no mayors that I knew of. All positions of power were held by White people, and my White teachers could identify with those people in power. I couldn't' I couldn't't really identify with anybody at this integrated school as I had in our segregated school back home. There I had known that I belonged in our two-hundred-year-old-neighborhood and in our school. I didn't have that feeling of belonging to anything in Ohio except for my Aunt Sarah. So, wasn't it power that went along with race? A power that could make sure a Black person didn't belong to anything?

Could it be that the other Black students felt that emptiness, felt they didn't really belong in a White world during the day, when they had to return to a Black world in the afternoon? Is that why they acted out in class, disrespected the teachers and seemed not to care about learning anything? But, for me, learning was more important than anything else.

Though most of these poor Black students dressed better than I, and had more money to spend for lunch, they didn't have what I had been used to. I had gone to shabby schools where only Black teachers taught more than they found in books. Even being forbidden to teach us about the history of slavery, they taught us who we were and what was expected of us .... These Middletown students had probably attended fine schools all their lives. But what had it done for them? I was a country bumpkin in their environment, but I knew how to make the good parts work for me. They didn't. I had learned to put one foot in my Black world and one in a White world and not stumble. I had learned that from my parents and my Black teachers. These students hadn't learned it from anybody, and they acted as if they didn't know that Black people everywhere faced a lot of challenges.

I knew that we were not the only people in the world who had been slaves, and who were still being persecuted. I had heard a little about that madman in Germany who was persecuting and murdering a group of people whom the old Black people at my church in Black Mountain had admired and looked up to. God had led them out of slavery, and we prayed and sang about how God would deliver us. A cloud and a flame had led the Hebrew children out of Egypt. My people were coming out of slavery, but a cloud of bondage still hung over our heads. In the Deep South, Black men were still being lynched, not in great numbers but it seemed that nobody was doing anything about it. The old Moses women of the past century, Harriet Tubman and Sojourner Truth, had died; and our race had no leader. Papa had always said the Black man would rise. But when would that time come?

My White teachers could often be even outwardly kinder than our Black teachers, but a bridge stood between us. And between them and the other Black students in my homeroom and other classes, the bridge seemed awfully wide. I saw that these teachers tolerated more nonsense than Black teachers.

That's the word, tolerated. They would punish the students physically, but not in a way as to make them change their behavior.

One time on our way home from elementary school back home, my brother Wat got into an argument with a group of sassy older girls. I swore at one of them, knowing she wouldn't't dare to strike me and face my sister Rena. But the next day she told the principal I had cussed her. He called me into the cloakroom and gave me a good lecture about a Sunday school girl cursing. I was embarrassed. Another time, at a general school assembly, he called the names of a group of students whom he had seen dipping into the school's lunch supplies of apples and raisins. He did that before the whole school, and you could see the students 'teachers looking around at them in disbelief. That was real punishment. Black teachers knew how to make us want to change. They made us feel they loved us and cared about what happened to us even away from school.

I had a good relationship with my White teachers because I didn't give them any trouble. They taught, I learned, and that was good enough for me. They didn't need to love me, just teach me and be fair. That's all I asked.

One afternoon at McKinley, several students were acting out in class. The teacher said the whole class would remain after school. So, I did. I sat there for a while, growing angrier by the minute. Then I stood up and quietly walked out of the room. I thought about it all the way home. I had done nothing to be punished for.Furthermore, I didn't even know those students who caused the trouble. It was like being lumped with a bunch of criminals without a trial, without even trying to find out who I was and that was not fair.

I thought about the day Johnny Stepp pinned the donkey tail on my seventh-grade teacher's coattail. Mr. James punished the whole class. But I had giggled, and I was not innocent. Besides, Johnny had stolen part of our lesson time, and I had encouraged him by giggling. I deserved the lick I got across my back that day.

And that Bible teacher who used to come to our seventh-grade class, calling us Nigras? We couldn't't stand her. BUT..., we kept quiet until she left. Our teacher told us he wasn't in position to correct her. We understood that. If he had challenged her or if any one of us had been rude to her, she would have reported that uppity young Nigra teacher who couldn't't control his class. Before the White Board members, it would have been the word of a White Bible teacher, a woman, against that of a young Black male teacher, and we would have lost the best teacher I had ever had. Even as seventh graders, we could understand that our feelings of being insulted weren't a drop in the bucket when compared to the importance of a Black teacher's job. A pitiful few Black man were being hired to teach anyway. So, when little Miss What's-Her-Name asked us to stand up and recite the names of the 66 books of the King James Version of the Bible in chronological order, we politely obeyed. But not for her —for our teacher.

Growing up in a segregated southern town, I had experienced injustice only because I was Black. But I had good reason to conform. Black people were lumped together and held together by chains of racism, inequalities, and discrimination. Rebellion by any one of us would make things worse for everyone else, especially my parents. They were poor and didn't have money to pay a lawyer who probably wouldn't't win the case anyway. Black children learned early to accept injustice to protect their community, their family, their parents. If one Black person misbehaved, it was believed to be typical of all Black people. Good behavior, they believed, was the exception. So, we heard left and right, "She's Colored, but she's intelligent," or "He's Black, but...," followed by some complimentary remark about a characteristic not associated with a person of African descent. We children understood that each one of us represented all other Black people and that we should, as my seventh-grade teacher put it, "become a committee of one and a representative of many."

In Ohio, I had walked out of the classroom that day because I couldn't't take the injustice and didn't believe I had to. Sitting in a room full of strange students on punishment when I had earned none just didn't make any sense to me. A little Black country girl from the Deep South, I had no relationship with those city-bred students, Black or White, and the teacher had broken her connection with me by punishing me as a thing in a collection of things.

I was in tears when I reached home and told Aunt Sarah what had happened. She listened quietly and I could tell she understood how I felt. And Aunt Sarah was polite, but she didn't bite her tongue when the teacher called to say I had earned some kind of demerit for leaving the room without permission. I heard Aunt Sarah say plainly and firmly "But the child told me she had done nothing to be punished for." I'm sure Aunt Sarah helped the teacher to understand that because the penalty was dropped.

I knew about the gap between the other Black students and me: I was Southern born, country bred, and this was the first time I had ever set foot in a city school, so they looked down at me. They had been out of the South longer, had lived in the city longer, but I could see they weren't doing all that well in school and didn't seem to have any sense of direction in life like my Black schoolmates back home.

Most of us had an idea where we were going even if we didn't know how we would get there. Most of us had what Papa called "vision." We understood that school was important and behaving well in school and doing our best with the books was important, too. Truth is, most of the time, we had no books, but we paid attention to what the teacher said, copied the lessons from the blackboard with our mouths shut and didn't mumble back at the teacher.

Mr. McLaughlin, our tall, balding, Irish homeroom teacher had a paddle just like one of my Black teachers had used, but the punishment didn't seem to take on these students. Was it the war in their blood, the way they were raised? Why did they bother to come to school? What was the difference between them and me and the other Black students I was raised with?

Outside of school, I kept my distance from them. That was easy because they lived somewhere on the other side of town. Anyway, I didn't have much time for socializing. Schoolwork came first and, besides, I didn't care for them. The Black kids made fun of the way I talked. They thought my pronunciation of the word w-a-t-e-r as w-a-t-a-h was hilarious, though the way they pronounced w-a-s-h as woursh and w-a-t-e-r as wourter didn't sound much like English to me, either. Uncle-in-law's grown nephew, James, already a widower in his thirties, told me that was the way people talked down in Kentucky. But never mind, I could run rings around them in the classroom.

I went to church on Sundays. During the week, I had loads of homework that kept me busy evenings and weekends, and I didn't miss a day of school for anything.

One of the best things happened at McKinley. One morning Mr. McLaughlin leaned over my desk, gave me a note and whispered, "Go to the counselor's office."

I didn't know what school counselors did, had never seen one, and I wondered what she wanted. I certainly hadn't broken any rules, and I had no bad grades. When I entered her office, she greeted me pleasantly and offered me a seat. Then she opened a file of papers on her desk and asked, "Mary, do you want to go to college?"

'Ye-es, 'I answered softly. I had learned that northerners didn't say Yes, ma'am and No, ma'am. But it was hard for me to say just plain 'Yes' to a grown person and make it sound respectful, too.

Of course, I had no idea where any money for college would come from, but she hadn't asked me about that. She asked whether I wanted to go. I had heard that it didn't matter how smart a Black student was, White high school teachers would try to steer him or her into a physical or manual course of studies. I found out that rumor was like the one about Black students from the South being "put back" a grade or two in the North. It didn't happen to me.

The McKinley counselor explained to me that I should take a college prep course all the way through high school, and she named every subject I was to take from the ninth grade through the twelfth. I never had high school counseling before, nor after that and I never forgot what she said, either. As she suggested, in high school, I would make certain that I studied Latin for at least two years because I wanted to be a doctor. I was not to follow a program in home economics or in business, but to take the required courses in English, social studies, math and science, especially biology.

Middletown was a good place for a student to live. Aunt Sarah worked hard all week, and on Saturday mornings she went to the market. Usually I went with her, and one time we saw some of my soap carvings from the eighth-grade art class on display in a store window downtown. Aunt Sarah was pleased, and I was surprised. In Black Mountain, nothing a Black student accomplished would get shown off in town. Black students didn't even use the public   library in my hometown.

And, yes, segregation was thriving in Middletown, too. Aunt Sarah played bridge with the Black teacher and the principal of the tiny elementary school for Black children on South Main Street. They said the parents had asked for that school. But they had not invited other kinds of segregation.

It was wartime. Black men and women living in the Deep South were leaving, going to Norfolk, Virginia and even farther north to fill defense jobs and earn more money than they had ever seen before. I heard that in Norfolk, people working at the shipyards shared the same bed on different shifts, and some homeowners had tenants sleeping in their bathtubs. But it wasn't going to last forever, and people were there for the money while it lasted.

My Payne cousins in Tennessee had a Cousin Mildred on their father's side who worked in Dayton. When she came to Middletown on a visit, she took me to the movies. Mildred paid for the tickets and I saw her look at them and frown. Then she asked the girl at the ticket window to call her manager. Mildred with her big round face, hazel-gray eyes and her gentle southern voice, said to him "Sir, we didn't ask for balcony tickets."

The manager's face turned red and without saying a word to Mildred he told the employee to reissue the tickets. We were the only Black people sitting on the main floor that evening. Other Black people were at the movie, but they sat in the balcony, the section reserved for African American moviegoers in the South. Later Mildred explained to me that forced segregation was illegal in the State of Ohio.

Ohio was different. Everything was made easy. I could walk to school even when it snowed. I was not part of an excluded group of students who couldn't use the town's drinking fountains or toilets, who had to sit in the rear seats on the city buses, who couldn't do this and couldn't't do that because my skin was Colored. It was a worthwhile trip—going to Middletown, that is, so far as school was concerned. Yet, I found another reason never to forget that valley with the sluggish black river running through it and the lonely house that stood too close to the sidewalk on South Main.

CHAPTER 21: MY BROTHER CHARLES: A SCAR OF CONSCIENCE

"Chuck" Charles Andrew Burnette 1919-1990

We were eight in all, four girls - Nita, Marj, Rena and I: and four boys, Rinky, Chuck, Brud and Wat. Rinse, 21 years older than I had left home long ago because he detested his siblings, the youngest ones, at least, and spurned farm life. Charles, called Chuck by the older siblings, the second boy, was only twelve years older than I, the youngest; but he became the pillar that Papa leaned on. Marj lived in New York, but the rest of us were at home. Our family consumed the crops our farm produced, so Charles took care of the animals and tilled the soil while Papa built houses for other people. Somebody had to work to buy the seeds that Charles planted.

My earliest memory of Charles comes from that summer day when he rushed to the car to rescue me. A curious two-year-old, I had crept out of the house unseen toddled up the hill to the blacksmith shop where Papa parked the old Willis Knight. The windows had been left open to keep the sun's heat from breaking the glass. I climbed through the window and looked around. A round wheel was right in front of me. That's what they held onto and turned when the car was moving. And just behind the wheel something bright and shiny was sticking out from a wall below the big glass window in front. Whoever sat behind the wheel looked out that window the whole time the car was moving. But what was that shiny thing? I would find out. I yanked on it; it moved towards me and a growling noise came from somewhere under the car, maybe from that metal part beyond the big window. I panicked. Screamed. In no time, Charles was lifting me from the front seat. Without a word, he carried me back to the house. I was safe. Papa's children didn't get punished for trying to learn.

Two years later, Charles was the one who settled this trusting four-year old into the saddle of our blind horse, handed me the reins and said, "And when you want to come back, just say 'Go home, Dan.'"

He slapped Dan on the rump and off we went. When Dan passed our property line and headed east towards town, I uttered the magic words and that horse turned right around in the middle of the road and came right back to the spot we had started from and stopped in his tracks. I could depend on anything Charles said.

But it was a winter's evening, months later when the incident occurred. Unfortunately, I was in the house. Had it been spring or a summer's night, I might have been on the front porch or farther away beyond the orchard, at the edge of the woods, playing "No bears out tonight," with my future schoolmates, Johnny and Helen, who lived on the hill above us. But, no, winter's months bring darkness early in the mountains. I was inside.

Why didn't Charles, that good-natured, kind and playful sixteen year old, choose that time to teach me something, to tell me more about the school I would go to across the hill, to sing one of our church songs to me, or to teach me one of the school songs he knew? He did that sometimes. Instead, this evening, he darted into the bedroom, opening the door, saying "Boo!" and closing it quietly before I could touch the doorknob. Why had that silly game made me so angry?

From somewhere I found an augur bit that should have been in a toolbox, better still in the blacksmith shop. But, no, it was in my aimless hand and when the door opened again, I flung it at the open space. The door slammed shut and I heard Charles groan, "Oooh!"

Oh God, what had I done? I wasn't afraid for myself. I had hurt my brother. Before long, my father was in the room with me. The doctor followed, carrying his big black satchel. After the doctor entered the bedroom, the groaning stopped. What did the silence mean: was my brother dead? Papa looked at me. At least he looked at me. My mother wouldn't. I tried to read Papa's face: his eyes wide, his nostrils flaring, he looked straight at me and said, "Go to bed."

What was he thinking, was it anger, fear, disgust? It was his own steel bit in his daughter's careless hand that hurled it at his son. How grateful I was to be out of sight, covers over my head, ringing in the darkness, wishing I never had to come out.

In the darkness of the bed covers, I could hide for a while. If only I could be that little bug that hid in its hole beneath the grass. Next summer my youngest brother and I would go back to that special plot where the Black-eye Susan bloomed. We would kneel in the grass, find a tiny opening to a burrow, and Wat would say," That's a doodle-bug hole. If we sing to him, he'll come out." And we'd sing, "Doodle-bug, doodle-bug, house's on fire, children burning up."

The doodle –bug wouldn't't come out. He was a bug; he didn't have to come out; but I did. And how would they look at me tomorrow? And how, after many tomorrows? I had done a terrible thing.

I heard my mother say "The doctor said the point of the bit missed the center of the eye. He's gonna be all right" Thank God! My brother would not be blind in one eye.

In 1942, with perfect vision but a scar on the left eyelid, Charles went off to war. When he came home on his first furlough, I wanted to please him, to show him how proud of him I was. I couldn't read a note of music, but I could find the chords to many pieces of music that I heard. I sat at the piano, carelessly banging out the chords of *The Star-Spangled Banner*. He joked, "Better close that lid down. Anybody passing will hear that and report us for being unpatriotic."

Gratefully, I slid off the bench. In all these years he had not once mentioned his eye to me; neither had any other member of the family. We were in the same room, and the piano stood just a few inches from the door that had opened and closed, where the face had appeared in the space and the mouth had said "Boo!" Charles was teasing again. One day I would try again to please him. One day I would get it right.

Somewhere in Germany, at times he had to sleep between two olive drab wool blankets on the snow, he told us. But he was sending money home to help me through school. I spent it gingerly. Instead of a thirty-two-cent feast in the Ohio school cafeteria, I would order the lunch of boiled white potatoes, stewed dandelion greens, bread, meat and milk for only seventeen cents. In 1945, the government subsidized the school lunch program, and my spending money lasted longer.

After the war, uninjured—except for the scar on his left eyelid, Charles came home and parked his green Buick in the front yard. He had been giving me driving lessons, but I still couldn't do reverse on a stick shift. Not yet. One day he came through the front door dangling his car keys. "Here, Thel, take the car and go to the store for me."

At the age of twelve, he had already been teaching himself to drive. And Mama said when he swooped down by the house in that old Willis Knight and took the front steps with it, Papa just replaced them with heavy blue granite rock. It would take a tractor to move them. I was older, I should do better. As

I opened the door on the driver's side, Charles called out, "And if you drive towards a ditch, make sure you don't go in with both front wheels at the same time."

I had to do better. Heck, I could keep the car in the road, just couldn't back up. He had to know that. Mr. Faust's little candy store had a driveway that looped right past the store and back into the big road. No need to back up. Charles knew that, too. I brought the car back without a dent. When I handed him his keys, he gave me a look of "I knew you could."

I looked at the scar. *Oh, I wish I hadn't done that.*

After I finished school and landed a college teaching job in the nation's capital, he drove four hundred miles just to pay me a surprise visit. He was so proud of my accomplishment. He still had that scar.

It was March 7, 1990 in Los Angeles, the day after my birthday. The telephone woke me from a deep sleep. 'Hello.' I said. A voice answered with my nickname, nothing more, and then went silent.

'Hello, hello!' I lay there thinking 'That sounds like Charles.' Before I could dial his number, the phone rang again. It was my youngest brother calling from Oregon, this time in a different voice, his lines sure but vague in detail.

"Charles is dead. Yes. His landlord lives in the apartment below and she heard him fall. By the time they got to his apartment, he was gone. They think it was his heart. When will you be leaving?"

Had Charles tried to call me? Had death snatched him away from the telephone?

Our parents had died, my oldest brother Rinky had died exactly seven years after Papa passed away, and within the same hour, Brud told me.... Our oldest sister, Juanita, had died, too. Only five of us remained now, Marjorie, Rena, Garland Jr., Wallace and I. And hadn't Papa said, "When I am gone, you must look after one another?"

Marjorie couldn't make it from Tennessee; Rena was recovering from surgery in Ohio. The three of us, his two youngest brothers and his youngest sister would be at his side. We had scattered to the wind for work, but we would come together for weeping.

In Oklahoma City we planned. Charles had earned more medals of honor than any of his brothers, and he would have a military funeral. His co-worker would deliver the eulogy; his family would serve. A niece and nephew would sing. We asked Wat to read from the Bible.

He turned to me. "You ought to do it," he insisted, "you're the best educated."

'But I can't. I have to play the organ.'

As the family car pulled up to the church, I watched as soldiers removed his coffin from the hearse. *Step-step, halt; step-step, halt.* Charles would have loved the precision of that ceremony. My nephew sang in B-flat major that lonesome melody to which words appropriate for a church service had been assigned. To me it was still *O Danny Boy* with the same refrain: *"But call me back when summer's in the meadow...."*

The service was over. I lingered at the organ, not eager to look for that last time into my brother's face, but they refused to close the coffin until I came out. The others were already outside. On my way to the gravesite to receive his Flag, I didn't stay long at the casket. The lid had cast a shadow over the left side of his face. I couldn't see the scar, but I knew it was there. If only it had been summer back, then.

CHAPTER 22: AUNT MARY HAYDEN
MY GRANDMOTHER'S PROPHECY

"Granny" Mary Elizabeth Louisa Stepp Burnette
Hayden 1858 -1956

"And I was five years old when the man rode up to
our cabin and read that paper to us...."

How she loved to tell me about it, about the day she first heard that her mother, her older sister and she were free. An old Black Mountain newspaper carried the report of a Black man seen *reading* the Emancipation Proclamation in 1863. If Granny was five years old that year, then she would have been born in January of 1858. She knew her month and day of birth, I know not how. But she was right in calling the Emancipation Proclamation *that paper*. For other than to help me determine her year of birth, its reading was mere ceremony. Slaves in the North Fork-Black Mountain area weren't *freed* until the Confederate Army surrendered two years later. That's how Granny's husband, my grandfather Squire Jones Burnette, established his own age, saying to my mother, his teenage daughter-in-law, "I was sixteen years old at the Surrender."

So, my grandfather was born in 1849. My mother admired him, a man with refined manners who liked to dress well and cared about the welfare of others. She would say to me, "Why, just let him hear that a family was hungry, and he would go right and buy food for them to eat."

I knew that Granny helped sick people and I wondered ow my paternal grandparents, having been subjected to slavery from five to sixteen years, could become such marvelous human beings, though I understood that people who were ignored by the government and had no protection from the laws of the land had to survive by looking out for one another. In our settlement, we still lived by the law of exchanging and sharing nearly everything we owned with neighbors.

In her later years, my grandmother Mary Elizabeth Louisa Stepp Burnette was known for miles around as "Aunt Mary Hayden." Granny had learned to read and write after she, her sixteen-year-old sister, and her mother, had actually been set free. Granny could say her ABC's backwards faster than I could say mine forwards. And she knew many things, things about people, nature, and plants—which ones could poison you, which ones were just weeds fit for the pigs to eat, and which could heal; and she remembered many other things, too.

Granny didn't have a single book in her house and had only one picture that she kept on her dresser. It would be years before my childish mind would grow to appreciate it, to begin to understand it. Even back then I would often study that picture of a few birch trees turning bright green at the tops, their paper thin white bark peeling away from trunks marked with moldy shadows of gray, trees that stood tall and straight, clustered in a quiet corner of the woods where dry yellow grass leaned this way and that to cover the spacious ground between them. No sky was visible, but the sun was surely shining somewhere. *Was it spring or fall, or both?* Did that peaceful scene symbolize Granny's world of greening hopes in a dying past? I wish I had asked Granny for that picture, wish I had kept it; but at that time, it was meaningless to me.

She always remembered hearing the Emancipation Proclamation being read to her, her sister Margaret, and Great Grandma Hannah, the plantation midwife and herb doctor, read by a man seated on a horse. And I could sense the pride in Granny's voice when she'd tell me how her mother—Granny called her "Mammy"— "took us and left that place." That's what Granny called the plantation, *that place.* Of slavery, she recalled no tales of horror or cruelty to herself, but clearly had no sweet memories of it, either.

The day that should have brought the happiest time of her life must have left her with the deepest disappointment. Yes, she was only five years old, but I would bet that every five-year-old on that plantation understood what freedom meant to their parents and grandparents. They had just heard

the Emancipation Proclamation read openly; the height of its excitement matched only by the depth of the dispiriting events that followed. I can imagine the man on the horse with that great paper in his hand signed by President of the United States, Abraham Lincoln, galloping away in haste after stopping to read at the last cabin door. I can visualize black, brown and almost white faces of grown women and teenage girls, heads bound in bandanas, some holding infants, their long skirts sheltering small frightened children peeking out from cabin doorways. And I can imagine the hopes of the adults and teenagers shrouded in the dust of the horse's hoofs because the highest power in their world, the slave master, refused to budge from his chair that day. The same man who years earlier had defied the Union officer that held a pistol to his head and demanded to know where he had hidden his gold would again defy the highest official in the land to hold onto his legal property until the confederacy fell and its army surrendered.

The Emancipation paper had been read, but Black people still in slavery didn't have a church bell of their own to ring; and if they'd had one, they would have needed permission to go and ring it. No feasting on that day. The hand that held the keys to the larder was the hand that controlled the chains of bondage. A deathly stillness clinging about the big house could mean only one thing: a broken-hearted people would languish in solemn servitude for more than two years longer.

So, Granny didn't tell me about the mental suffering that followed the reading of the Emancipation Proclamation. Instead, she told me about the physical suffering of two other slave children, one a little Black girl whose mistress had driven a needle into her hand; the other, an older child whose mistress had cursed her and forced her to keep on working after the child had complained of being sick.

Granny had said to me only this: *The man sat on his horse in front of our cabin and read the paper to us.* Then she added, "And Mammy took us and left that place." Well, she did. But not that day. How we love to pamper our morbid memories with fairytale fallacies of dreams trampled in the dust.

Granny had told me nothing in detail of the cruelty and hardheartedness of the mistresses of those two children. Possibly the first mistress was enraged by the child's facial resemblance to her own husband. That's my guess. I know of a great grandmother on another plantation who was manumitted from slavery before 1850, because her fourth child had been sired by the slave master. Even though slave women had no choice in the matter of who would father their children, the wife of the slave master, when forced to accept the addition of her husband's Black child as an increase in the plantation's slave property, often resented the innocent child and its helpless mother. Well, that resentment earned Great grandma Sarah Freeman her walking papers. Once free, she dropped the slave master's last name, Wright, took the name Freeman and gave that name to all five of her children, Alfred, twins Polly and Nancy, Frances, and James.

And of the young slave girl who was forced to keep on working after she had complained of feeling sick, Granny said sadly, "She died." Before she drew her last breath, her mistress had called her a Black b...ch. But if Granny knew where those two slave girls suffered those acts of brutality, whether in her mother's old home state of Alabama or on the plantation where her own mother would live and work for most of her life, she never told me. I'm guessing it was not on the Stepp plantation: it was not known as a brutal place, though slavery, of itself, is brutal.

Granny Hayden had heard of other tales, too. The problem with Granny's stories was, they almost never had a happy ending. Oh, she always outsmarted some wildcat that picked up her scent and stalked her when she was coming through the woods at night. And there was the time when she went blackberry picking and was scared nearly to death by something long and black that suddenly slid across her shoulder and chest and fell down over her waist. At first, she thought she was being attacked by a big blacksnake hiding among the berry vines. But, telling the story, Granny would relax, clap her hands, shake her head in a show of victory, chuckle and say, "Well, gen[t]le-men! It was just a braid of my hair." Even in old age, her long straight hair hung below her waist.

She never told me *Uncle Remus* [Joel Chandler Harris, 1895] stories about animals that dressed in loose-fitting hand-me- downs and talked and played tricks on stronger animals, nor about little people like *Hansel and Gretel* who had to find their way out of the dark woods at night more than one time. Granny's stories were real, the people and the places were real; and with the exception of the animals she escaped from, Granny's stories had really awful endings.

Well, was it my grandmother's fault she was born and had to live her life in a neck of the Southern Appalachian wilderness that had a dark past? Our mountains were bespattered with treacherous trails of breaches in human decency lurking behind the shadows of that heavenly beautiful place. When

Granny was born, every other Black person she could have known was a slave, too. If it could get any worse, she was born at a time when the life of a Black man was nearly worthless after he left the slave auction block; and most of Granny's life would be a time when a Black man realized little or nothing would be done if he killed a member of his own race.

In the early days, our area of the Appalachians had been known as Grey Eagle, named after a Native American chieftain who was stabbed to death by White settlers. They believed they had the right to live on Indian lands; and since they could no longer make slaves of the Indian and legally claim everything he got his hands on, they must have believed the easiest way to get his land was to kill him—until they could get the government to drive him away.

All of that land in and around the Swannanoa Valley had belonged to Native Americans and some of it had belonged to my mother's Cherokee grandmother and her people. Common knowledge was that Jackson's soldiers had marched the Cherokees off their rich lands to get the gold and minerals for the taking. Before the 1830s, to escape being driven off like cattle 1,500 miles away to the Southwest and maybe die on the way, Grandpa George Payne's mother and a number of other Cherokees just walked off their tribal lands, gave up their Indian names, their culture, their language, and disappeared through marriage to Black men and women, bond and free.

In those days being married to a White person, or being half-White/half-Indian, offered the Cherokee no protection from the "Indian removal." On the other hand, Black people were under no threat of being driven out of the state. A native American passing for Black, Colored, or Negro and her children of mixed Native American and African blood generally would be safe. My mother's paternal grandmother, Great Grandma Sally Payne, must have known that when she agreed to marry slave trustee Lonnie Mills, but since she herself had never been enslaved, their seven children were born free. It was a good way to hide, and my dear old Great Grandma Sally Payne didn't leave North Carolina until 1892. That's the year she finally closed her eyes and drew her last breath in Grandpa George's house, not long after my mother was born. And I'm proud to say that she and my great grandfather, Londen or Lonnie Mills, were loyal to their marriage 'til death did them part.

Granny Hayden knew some of those Cherokees who had come to live among the Black people. She had even married one of them. That's how she came to have the last name, Hayden.

Granny Hayden was a tiny woman. She stood about four foot-eleven and had hair almost as long as she was tall. Her fiery black eyes peered out from beneath bushy black eyebrows, her nose was straight as a ruler, and she had a small mouth with lips that puckered and flattened from old age, from being pressed together in pain and sadness, or pressed together to force the snuff into place in the hollow of her lower lip. She loved to talk and would talk to anybody, Black or White, male or female, old or young. She even talked to herself when she thought nobody was listening.

Like many other southerners, particularly the older ones, Granny's favorite part of the house in summer was the front porch. I knew three ways to get to Granny's porch—from the north, coming from the big road, from the east, taking the wagon road that passed her garden and led to a path heading directly to her front steps, or from the south, a direction that led onto the porch past her kitchen door. Not only was the south entrance well out of my way, it shunted around below a vacant gray house where Granny said a man had been murdered in the kitchen. Besides, Granny would have quickly spotted me if I had chanced to come by the east or south paths. She usually sat facing southeast, from the north end of the porch, and high above the garage at that side of the house.

As a child I was given to snooping. My world was like a basket filled with balls of yarn wrapped around mysteries, and as soon as one unraveled, I faced another one. I thought maybe snooping and eavesdropping would help me unravel the knots sooner, and sometimes it did help. I learned that if I crept up to Granny's house and stopped near the garage, I could pick up a few words of her private conversations with an invisible visitor. I didn't always understand what I heard, and when I relayed some of it to my mother, she told me Granny Hayden had suffered a nervous breakdown in mid-life. I didn't know what that condition was, but breakdown told me it wasn't something to look forward to common sense told me it wasn't a piece of mountain music played on a country fiddle.

But something else I overheard Granny say one day made me feel sad, and I think I stopped listening after that. I had been standing below the porch, looking up at Granny sitting in her rocking chair with her back turned to me. As it was her habit when speaking to anybody, I knew her right hand was stretched out like she was going to shake hands with fingers and thumb held close together, pointed towards her listener, and her hand moving up and down to hold attention. That day, she spoke as if explaining to someone what had caused the great breach in her and Grandpa Squire's marriage, and she sounded angry, saying "[Yes], we fit. He hit me. I hit him back"

On one of those rare occasions when my mother was not praising Grandpa's wonderful character, his kindness and generosity, it had slipped out. Granny and Grandpa had actually fought. Physically fought at times. But according to Mama, Grandpa didn't always get the best of it. Granny, tiny little creature as she was, was not a bit frail; and she would grab Grandpa in the collar and swing onto him like a wildcat. I didn't see how Granny could get in any good licks from that angle, but it was true to her character. When she was young, Granny had outsmarted mountain lions that stalked her through the hills at night; and when it came to confronting a man, she was nobody's weeping willow.

So, Grandpa Squire was *not* a saint. Still my parents loved him, and I would have loved him more if he had lived long enough for me to be born and to get to know him.

I hid my sadness, not wanting Granny to know I'd been eavesdropping, then I walked around to the front steps and bounced up on the porch with a "Hey

Granny," like I had just got there.

Granny's conversations would stop the minute she saw me. I was named after her and my mother. Nobody in the whole neighborhood ever called me by her name, and I don't ever remember her calling me by my middle name. But as soon as she saw me, she would greet me like she was glad to see me. She was always glad to see me, and if a stranger passed by her porch while I was there, she would proudly introduce me, saying "This is my boy's baby chile," never bothering to mention my name.

Granny wasn't crazy by a long shot. Just lonely, maybe. Maybe heartbroken because Grandpa had divorced her. He married again in West Virginia. Granny did, too. But Mama said she screamed when the telegram came with news of Grandpa's accident in the coal mines. Mama said Granny had already left her second husband, Uncle Andy Hayden; and when the poor man sent word from his death bed that he wanted to see her, Granny didn't budge.

Some of my most memorable childhood moments were spent on Granny's porch, listening to her stories. Awful as some of them were, I believed them. She had no reason to lie to me. I well knew that when old people didn't want me to know about something, they just wouldn't mention it to me. No doubt as many secrets as bodies were buried in those graves surrounding the Old Thomas Chapel African Methodist Episcopal Church. The old people didn't *hide dirt*, they just kept their mouths shut when something was apt to get out way down the road and harm somebody who was still living.

And Granny knew people's lives, knew the wild oats they had sowed and their diseases, some of which she had cured. She also knew about things that had happened to people, things they didn't cause and things they could do nothing about. And Granny knew that two kinds of people couldn't be trusted with Black folks' secrets—children and White folks. Children tattled and talked too much. And secrecy from White people who could do them harm was the only weapon for African Americans living in a society that paid them no respect as a people and offered them no justice as individuals.

On the porch I would pull up my chair close to Granny's, inhaling the aroma of strong soap, herbs and snuff coming from her clothing as I listened. Granny always wore a big white homemade apron with pockets she'd cut and sewed nearly to the hem (I never saw her with a pocketbook—doubt that she owned one), and she would have worn a spanking clean apron over her old black dress when she went to church. "Too much pridy," Granny believed, was not good.

I understood. Granny in her day had been a member of the servant class. with her European features and long straight hair, she had to tone down her looks. No rouge no makeup, hair pulled back without a wave or ripple and knotted tightly at the back of her head, and no earrings. A bondswoman had no protection from the whims of the slave master; and a free Black woman with no husband, brothers or close cousins had no protection from any man, Black or White. Granny's drab appearance in her youth was meant to repel men of both races, to please pious churchgoing black women and to appease the better class of White women who needed maids, cooks, and housekeepers to take care of their children. Those women had learned caution from their mothers, their grandmothers and great grandmothers who had seen half-White children crop up all over the plantation. They couldn't stop the infidelity on their husbands' part, but they could be careful not to hire temptation.

Granny along with many of the older people in our settlement knew that four-fifths of the Black children on the plantation where Granny was born had been half-White. Siring slaves was a prosperous business. The good part of it was that I never heard of that slave master selling one of his own or one of his sons' Black children. But a different kind of story was to be told on my mother's side of the house. And Granny Hayden, Papa's mother, knew about that, too.

She didn't bother to tell me about how my great grandfather Lonnie Mills' was sold away from his family in 1844, and what happened after the Civil War. Granny Hayden was the youngest of my grandparents and outlived all the rest of them, so she knew about the ups and downs of their lives. But I guess she had enough of her own history to think about and figured she'd leave something for my mother's people to explain to me.

*Remnants of Granny Hayden's Cottage built on
the G.A. Burnette place before 1950*

Granny would talk for a while, then fall silent, looking into the distance like she was thinking about what she had told me or would tell me next.

I studied the side of her face. Did I dare disturb her thoughts? But I wanted to know about the old slave plantation legend. Granny was young when she left the plantation, but surely, she had heard about it.

'Granny, did you ever hear about how the slave master looked that Union officer right in the eye and lied to him about where he hid his gold?'

'Well, honey, who ain't heard that tale? You see, the war was going on and nobody knowed which way things would go. Plantation holders had paper money, but if the war ended with them holding the short end of the stick, why then them horse blankets wouldn't be worth a speck of cold water in a gnat's eye. So, them that could, started to hoard gold. Then if the South lost, they would have something to fall back on. ``

'Granny, did you ever see a horse blanket that was used for money back then?' How annoying my ignorance must have been!

"Lord, chile, to my knowledge, no kind of money was known to pass through a slave's hand. Now they was trustees, like your Mama's grandpa Lonnie Mills who could go off the plantation and earn a little money, but the slave master could lay claim to every penny of it if he had a mind to do it an 'was mean enough. An 'I'll tell you something else. It seems like the slave masters' sons got their finger in the government's eye, so they was laws rigged up to protect the kin of the slave master and his wife, to keep his Black children or any other slave from holding onto anything that was passed down to them by the slave master or the mistress, even in a will.

For years, my mother had worked for a lawyer, and I had heard her say that a legal heir could break a will. Somehow, I always knew when Mama was quoting the lawyer because she didn't have the book learning to know about these things otherwise. Still, that seemed wrong to me. If a person wanted somebody to have something that belonged to him and put it in writing, the court ought to uphold that person's wishes, I believed.

'That wasn't fair.'

"Hmf, slavery wasn't fair. It's the way things was. The slave master let one Colored woman live in her cabin after the Surrender and he even gave her a cow. But after he died, his sons came and took the cow away. But now let's get back to the story 'fore some of it slips my mind."

'Did anybody ever find the old slave master's gold, Granny?'

"Well, I reckin *he* did. He was the only one to come back from that burying alive. Took that poor old slave and a dog way back in the hills, made him dig a deep hole, then he throwed the gold in, shot the old man and the dog and pushed them in on top of his gold."

An old man and his dog...back in the woods. Where on earth did the old slave master get that idea? Did he know about Rip Van Winkle? Had he read that story as a boy growing up in Ireland? Did he hear about that story on the ship that brought his family and him to America, or did he hear about it after he landed here?

But because he was Black and helpless and nobody cared how he died, or if they did, they could do nothing about it, this old man, the slave, and the slave master's dog would never come home again. I would always wonder about the good side, the human side, of a person who committed crimes, of a man who could use other human beings as slaves and make them work for him without pay until they died, or kill them for his convenience.

Granny didn't flinch. My stomach turned over and tightened. 'What was that for, Granny? Couldn't he just hide his gold without killing the old man and the dog?'

"What you have to understand is ... back then a heap of people was buried in the woods, here and there. Nobody was gonna disturb a grave. All he had to do was mound up the fresh dirt like it was a little grave. Maybe a little child's grave. If anybody went poking about back in the woods looking for that gold, what would they find? Nothing but the rags and bones of that poor old man, and the dog. But the slave master already had blood on his hands. He didn't mind the extra dirt of scrounging through the dust and bones to lay hands on his sack of gold when the time was right."

I could visualize that grave in the woods. Maybe it was like the one where Granny Hayden's mother, Great Grandma Hannah Stepp, was buried in 1897, way over at the northwest end of the cemetery, more than two decades before Old Thomas Chapel was ever built.

But in the cemetery, most of the trees had been cut down. Long before that day on Granny's porch when we talked about that grave in the woods, I had gone to spend the day with her. After a snack of her wheat hoecake and homemade blackberry jam, she was ready to walk about. She took me by the hand and led me out to the big road. We turned left where the pavement stopped in front of the last house owned by a White family. That's where the main road started to wind through a long stretch of the Black community. It led us past the Black Walnut Tree, past the little candy store, and on up the hill past the old Methodist chapel. That's where we left the big road, turned into the cemetery and didn't stop 'til we came to a grassy spot below a thick row of green hedge bushes. Granny stopped and I looked down at her feet. She was standing close to a small natural rock marking the head of a grave facing east. Looking at the few graying headstones standing in that burying ground, I could see that all the graves faced the East, to face the rising sun as the old spiritual said. Standing there in silence, her head slightly bowed, Granny pointed at the ground and said to me "Here's where my mama is buried."

I was about five years old, but I knew we had not always had a cemetery of our own. After slavery, when they stopped burying the slaves somewhere near the White church cemetery, our old people got buried wherever their families could find a free plot of ground. It seemed reasonable to me that Black people didn't just stop dying between 1865 and 1892, to wait for two former slaves, Granny's relatives, to save enough money to buy a plot of land and donate it to the community for a burying ground. Grandma Hannah Stepp was buried there in 1897, the same year the people got enough money together to pay for that land and get a deed to it.

But those that died before 1892, who knows where they are buried? Well, Granny did, and she knew whose houses had been built over a few of those nameless and unmarked graves after the free plots of ground had been bought and resold as lots, but that was another secret to be kept.

Granny was silent again. I still wanted to hear more about the hidden gold. 'Granny, since the slave master was the only one to come back from that grave alive, how did the tale get out?'

"Well, honey, they's some secrets you never want nobody else to know about and then they's others you need to share in case something happens to you. Now, just think. What if the slave master had died before the war

266

ended and the confederacy fell? Whether he lived or died, that family was gonna need that gold to live on. He must have told one of his sons, whichever one could be trusted the most."

Granny was silent again. I waited. Then she started. "Now they's something I wanna tell you and I want you keep your mouth shut 'til the right time comes.

"The Bible says *Keeping mercy for thousands, forgiving iniquity and transgression and sin, and that will by no means clear the guilty; visiting the iniquity of the fathers upon the children, and upon the children's children, unto the third and to the fourth generation. (Exodus 34: 7 AV)."*

I had never seen a Bible in Granny's house, but she could read. Even Black people who couldn't read could remember what they had heard and what others read to them. The Bible was the only book that could be found in many homes; and whether the people could read or not, they prided themselves in quoting the Scriptures to prove a point—not just unquestionable and easy to remember commandments like *Thou shalt not kill (Deut. 5:17 AV),* but verses a person had to chew on, really think about.

'What does that mean, Granny?'

"The Bible says *[V]isiting the iniquity of the fathers upon the children, and upon the children's children, unto the third and to the fourth generation. (Exodus 34: 7 AV).*

"Never mind how that tale got out. That slave master's scandalous deed set off a rumor that's been told over and over and miss-told in different ways to this day, ever since I was a child. Regardless of how or how often it's told, it just goes to prove the Bible prophecy. It was cold-blooded murder of a slave who might have thought he was helping his master hide his gold as, unbeknownst to him, he was digging his own grave. And that one foul deed set off a whole chain of murders among the slave master's Colored offspring that's been going on for a long time."

"Was somebody else killed, Granny? Somebody we know?'

It didn't matter what I thought or how little I understood, the story had to go on. "The Bible says, ... *visiting the iniquity of the fathers upon the children, and upon the children's children, unto the third and to the fourth generation. (Exodus 34: 7 AV).*

"Now you keep this under your hat. That slave master, the one that set off the iniquity, he was the father of it. The rest of the murders, barring any element of mystery, are just as bad.

"This comes from right close to the horse's mouth, from one of the old master's right close kin. Now one of the slave master's Colored sons, a chile little older than me and born into slavery just like I was, growed up and married a Black woman. He come home one day and saw she had a new dress hanging up on the wall. When she couldn't explain to his satisfaction how she'd come by that dress, he politely beat the life out of her. After beating her senseless, he draped her limp body over his horse and took her back to her family—to bury. The slave master's own son, that was the first generation."

I was beginning to take hold of this old bear by its tail. On both sides of Papa's family, it was well known that, in cold blood, a gambling grandson of the slave master's favorite Colored slave woman had shot and killed Cousin Isabella's son, Robert, a young man only 18 years old. To escape revenge from Robert's next of kin, the murderer fled the state and never returned.

'Granny, whatever happened to that man that shot Aunt Bell's son in cold blood?'

"The Bible says, ... *Vengeance is mine, I will repay, saith the Lord. (Rom. 12:19, KJV).* Years later, that man was crushed to death in a trucking accident. Don't matter whether a body gets caught and jailed or not, nobody gets away with foul deeds. They's a higher order to be reckoned with. Now mind you, chile, a grandson of the woman that bore most of the slave master's Black childern, the one that shot poor little Robert, that was the second generation."

The ball of yarn was unraveling. Even I knew some of that man's, the murderer's, brothers. But the Bible had said, "...unto the third generation...."

Had the curse skipped over that generation? Wouldn't Granny know about it if there had been another murder in her time? How long would these murders go on? I came to understand the kind of questions Granny didn't like, so I didn't ask.

She had a strange way of ending her storytelling suddenly sometimes, and I would ask 'Is that all?'

I mean, you don't just kill somebody and that's it. I wanted to know but wouldn't ask, 'How could there be no punishment, nothing, for killing another human being?' One time after Granny ended a story about another woman who was murdered by her husband, I did. I asked, 'Then what did she do, Granny?'

Granny stared at me as if I'd accidentally left something behind that cold March night when her skillful hands guided me into the world. She just looked at me in pity and asked "What could she do? She was dead."

At other times, Granny would fall silent in her rocking chair. The chair would stop. Then she would fold her upper body over her lap, look down at the floor, forearms resting on her thighs, hands folded loosely between her knees and pat her size four foot up and down in no particular rhythm, just as she might do while waiting for a pot of water to boil (Granny said bile) for a cup of catnip or ground ivy tea at bedtime.

Was she reading my thoughts, waiting for my next question?

I would keep quiet, watching her. Then she would raise her head high enough to look off into the distance, the right foot still ....

"Well, chile, I was born with one eye wide open. I've lived in these mountains a long, long time, and they's not much to happen around here that don't find its way to one ear or the other.

Sometime at night you can see foxfire (phosphorus) in these woods and at times it 'pears to be leaping right over the tree next to it. But foxfire'll stay in the woods. You watch. It may not happen in my time, but you may see it light on another tree in your lifetime. You just watch. See where it lights."

Unto the third generation..., the Bible had said. Had it happened secretively and never been found out? And to the fourth generation, the Bible said. That would be in my own time.

Well, maybe that was yet to come, so Granny might never mention it, might not even live to see it. The old slave master who murdered that elderly slave in cold blood to save his gold was Granny's own grandfather and his son was her father.

Everybody around knew the slave master's name, and Granny told me her father's name, too, but I was never to mention it in public. Whatever the reason, a promise is a promise. But one thing was certain, the Bible was surely being fulfilled and more was to come. Mark Granny's words, "You watch."

FINAL LETTER TO COUSIN ELIJAH

Dear Cousin Elijah,

    I still haven't found out why you left us so young, but I know you were important. Whenever Papa would say "Me and Lige," his face would light up. Because I didn't get a chance to meet you, I wanted to make certain that your name was not forgotten.

    What I do know is that the house and the land on which the old Black Walnut Tree stood would have been inherited by your sister, Irene and you. I heard she married a man whose last name was Underwood. They had no children and eventually separated. I knew Rena, knew her well. I called her 'Cousin Rena.' She and Uncle Hardy's daughter Isabel used to meet at the candy store after church on Sundays.

    Now, Cousin Isabella never gave me one red cent that I can remember; but Cousin Rena used to give me a nickel every Sunday; and then she would sit and watch to see how I spent it. Her wages were pitifully small, and she worked hard for every penny. She liked to see plenty of plain foods on the table—stews, potatoes, green beans, and other vegetables. She didn't value fancy foods or clothing. Once a person had his own house and land, his money was not to be wasted, but to pay taxes and to keep that property in the family.

    Cousin Isabella lived in Uncle Hardy's home until she died in 1947. Cousin Rena kept the family home and land almost as long as she lived. Sometime after she died in 1945, the old Black Walnut tree died, too. Another one sprouted up near where the old one stood, and it's tall and strong. I know that when Cousin Rena was old, she deeded the house and land to a cousin on your father's side, Cousin Lester's daughter, Arcie. That cousin sold it to another cousin on the Stepp side, Cousin Arthur. Now he's gone, too; all of his children are gone. Today, Cousin Irene's house is gone, and the land belongs to strangers.

The old tree that I played under dropped her fruit onto the yard she shaded; the daughter tree lets much of her fruit fall on the public road below. I still visit the Black Walnut Tree when I come home, and my nephew tells me the squirrels carry the walnut seeds all about town, and young trees are popping up all over. I guess that's a sign of the times. Thank you, Cousin Lige, for the old walnut tree and the house with its long, dark bedroom next to the stairs where I spent many a night huddled under the covers, edges of the blankets wrapped about my nose, as I listened for those strange noises coming from the attic. Many times, in my childhood, I sat at the table next to the window in the kitchen, looking at that grassy plot around the well, and waiting for a delicious meal simmering on the wood burning cook stove. The kitchen would be cozy on those days. The mysterious house and the tree remain among my fondest memories.

Your second cousin,
Mary Othella Burnette
Van Nuys, California
September 30, 2012

PS: Growing up in Black Mountain, I knew that the first piece of property owned by an African American on the north side off Cragmont Road had been purchased by your Aunt Phoebe, and the property farthest west on the north side of that that road belonged to Cousin Eddie, Aunt Martha and Uncle Hardy Stepp's son. Today, those properties belong to White residents. It won't come in my time, but the day is rapidly approaching when what you and I knew as the Black community will be inhabited by families of other races. A few Black families have moved into areas where no Black people ever lived before. They own property on both sides of what is now Byrd Road. When I was a child, no Black person owned land on the east side of that road or on the east side of what is called   College Street. Today, a Black church stands on the east side of College Street, and for years Black families have lived on the north side of Cragmont Road between Byrd and Brooks Road, but they are surely losing ground in the old Black community. As they say, "You can't stop the river."

PPS: Cousin Elijah, the Germans didn't get us back in the 1940s. But Cousin Edgar Pertiller is gone, and Cousin Eddie Stepp and all of his generation have been gone a long time.

The Burnette Mailbox
(rusted, unused since 1952)
Photo taken by author

APPENDIX A: TERMS AND BELIEFS

A Smithereen of Early 20th Century Black English: Mountain Dialect of South Midland Southern American English and a Few Common Beliefs

Smithereen (n.) was pronounced as smitherin(g). Words and phrases in the following list were common in my community during the 1930s and 40s

A (uh)(vt.) – Used as a verbal prefix, usually before the verb +ing, as in do-ing;

Present tense [action in progress] - What'she (a-)doing[g]? Now he's a-doin[g] his 'rithmetic. Leave him 'lone.

[Action perceived] – He's too dern (darned) dumb to know what he's a-doin[g] an' too all-fired proud to ast for help.

Past tense – He was just a-goin[?] 'round and 'round in circles like somebody half crazy.

Future tense- (planning to do something).

Why ain't you-uns a-goin[?] {Why aren't you all planning to go?}

Well, we wuz a-goin [g], but they never bothered to let us know nuthin til the last minute, so we decided we'd jes set tight.

We figured they jes ast us 'because they was obliged to and we ain't a-aim-in[g] to git all dressed up to go way over there to git snubbed in public.

Me, myself, Ah'm a-stayin[g] right heah by the fyah,

Ah'ight/aw'right. - [All right] Ah'ight/aw'right. I'll take this one, too.

Ah ight' now'aw/right' = all right now— (A warning) That's enough!

Ahowon't — I don't want. Ahown-tat' un. I don't want that one. Awn't t'other one. [I want the other one.]

Ahowanna – I don't want to. He 's going to the post office, but ahowonna go.

Ahm'mo – I'm going to. Ahm'mo go over there and see what he's doing.

Ain'tye/ain'che – Aren't you. Ain'tye going to the store with him?

Al'lus – Always/all the time. He's al'lus got his hand out for a gim'me (give me). He al'lus shows up at mealtime.

Ar'sh tata – Irish potatoes. I love ar'sh tata in my green beans, don't you?

'Assal 'roun(d) – Pronunciation note: Accent is on the first syllable with the second syllable /al/ pronounced as in axel. But the /A/ is a singular sound, like the combination of a long /A/ as in ape and the /a/ as in apple. To fool around, waste time: "You watch. He'll assal 'round for two hours before he makes a move to do any work." [Papa's expression. Don't hear it anymore. But if I said it to another mountaineer, I would be surprised if he didn't understand it.]

Ast (v.,vt.)- ask, asked, asks. Astin'/asking. Did you ast if we could go? He's aw'ways in my face astin' for money.

You astin' me? [How could you possibly expect me to know that?]

Air'y'n –any-a-one, any one of them. And if air'y'n shows up at this door, don'tyu let 'em in. You hear me?

Aw'ways – Always

A'thout (prep.)– Without. She never goes nowhere a'thout having a crowd following along wid'der (with her). Sometimes meaning unless. Won't go nowhere athout she 'all decked out [dressed up].

Wid'out – Without. How'd you 'spect me to git in the house wid'out a key?

Baby-chil' – The youngest child (regardless of age). This is my boy's baby chil'. [My grandmother used this expression to introduce me to strangers.]

Bad-mouthe-in' – slandering. He's aw'ways bad-mouthe-in' somebody.

Be'ence – [Being or beings that] = since. Be'ince you know so much about it already, no need of me tellin' you what little I know.

Biddy/biddies – A baby chicken or baby chickens.

Bi'nes – business.

Big road – usually the nearest road wide enough to accommodate a wagon or an automobile. [In my area of the Black community, Mt. Allen Road was the sand road because of the abundance of crushed isin-glass (mica) at the shoulders where the single lane bent eastward towards Byrd Road. Byrd Road also was an unnamed dirt road, but Cragmont was definitely the "Big Road."]

Bin – Been. He's bin gone. He left a good while ago—a good while before you arrived. He's aw'ready gone.

He's bin gone a good while now. He's been dead a good while, several weeks or years.

Bin – been (has, have or had). I bin to their house before. I bin there lots of times.

Bline – Blind. Yeah, he's bline in one eye and cain't see out the other. [Ridiculing a person who is naïve and lacks perception of what goes on around him.]

Bline. – Blind. Literally, lacking vision, visual or mental.

Bofe – Both. Heck! I cud'da played the song better'n at bline-folded and wid bofe hands tied behine ma back. Heck! I could have played the song better than that [with my eyes] blindfolded and both hands tied behind me.

Bof'ov'em – Both of them. Bof'ov'em together cain't shuck and shell all that corn before sundown, and you know it.

Bus' tout – bust out. To break out suddenly, as in laughter. When she said "Oh, I does," tryin' to be so proper, I jus bus'tout in a big laif.

Cata-whompus – crooked. I showed forty- 'leven times how to sew that seam straight. Now it's all catawhompus. That dress will never hang right.

Cain'tye – Can't you. Cain'tye see I got my hands full? Can't you see that I have my hands full? I can't carry nothin(g).

Chewder [me](vt) – mixed form of chide, to scold and chew (on) to scold and give lengthy reprimand.

Chil'dun/chil'dern – Children.

Chit'lins – Chitterlings – the entrails of the pig or hog, considered a delicacy among many southerners, Black or White, including those living in various parts of the United States.

It is said that in the 1940s, butchers in the North cleaned, packed and gave those organs to their customers free of charge. However, as more Black people moved North and the demand for chitterlings grew, the price tag was added.

Com-'plect-ed – Referring to the color of the skin, not the condition of the skin texture.

Dasent - Dares not - He dasent make a remark like that in front of his parents.

Dain'ja – danger. That girl's in dain'ja of failin' her grades (subjects) in school agin [this year, too].

Dain'jus – dangerous. It's dain'jus to go off to the store and leave a pot on the fire. Cud'da set the house on fire, don'tye know that?

Deef – deaf. That poor old man is bline, deef and dum[b].

Dive – a place of entertainment with a juke box, tables and chairs in a front room, a place for eating and dancing. But the sale of bootleg whiskey and gambling might go on in a back room.

Did'nye – Didn't you. Did'nye know you cain't cook poke salad a'thout lots a oil. Didn't you know you can't cook poke salad without lots of oil? That stuff's poison!

Don'tye - Don't you. Don'tye know any better than that? A three –year-old oughta (ought to) have better sense than that.

Draggin' ye feet – Dragging your feet. Hesitating. Wasting time. If you keep on draggin' ya feet, the sun'll soon be down an' we won't be able to see how to go nowhere.

Gimme = a give me – a hand out, or the request, Give me.
Git-away-from-from – Get away from. Jus' git away-from-from me. Just get away from me. Get out of my face.

Goobas – Peanuts in any form. But raw peanuts, particularly.

Grumbulin' – grumbling. He's back there in the room grumbulin' about his share of the goobas. Thinks one of us got two more'n he did.

Gravel – Grapple. (To dig produce out of the ground.) Now we have to gravel all' em taters from the patch 'bove the branch. Now we have to grapple all of those potatoes from the patch above the branch [stream].

Gwo'an! Go on. Hurry! Gwo'an! Hurry up. What are you poking around for?

Gwo'own' now. (a warning) Go on, now. I'm asking you to leave me alone.

Gyarm – mess. What kind of a gyarm is this? It's not fit for nobody to eat. Every time you try to boil water, you scorch it. [My mother's expression for a product that displeased her.]
How'd – How did. How'd he do that, you reckin? He's not tall enough to reach way up there an' he's got no ladder.
How'd he say he was a-doin'? How did he say he was getting along? [A question regarding one's health or material situation.]
. Is'ze – Is he? He ain't doin' nuthin', is'ze?

Laif – laugh.

Lef' – Left. – He's jus' lef' 'em air to die. He just left 'im there to die – lef' them little chickens out in the hot sun all day with no food or water.
Mess – enough for a meal—usually said of produce, beans, potatoes, fish etc.

Mess – to spoil something, such as a dish you are preparing, and the finished dish itself. That's a mess.
Mess up (v/vt.) – to make a mistake. You just messed up (vi). You messed up (vt) my work.

Messed up (adj.) She's messed up. She's pregnant and may deliver a child out of wedlock.

Munt – Month. Ev'ry munt he comes up short widdiz part of the money. Every month he comes up short with his part of the money.

Mouthe'in (v.)– Quarreling with or arguing. She's aw'ways mouthe-in at her brother.
Talking. back. She's aw'ways mouthe-in back at her mother.

Mouthe (verb) – the habit of talking too much. Or mouth (noun) He's got too much mouth.

Mum'-mul-ing (adjective) – Mumbling. (Complaining) Didn't they crucify my Lord, an'
He never said a mummul-ing word? [Sung by special male or
female groups in the Mills Chapel Baptist Church more than seventy years ago.] Verb.: He just kept on mummuling . I couldn't understand a word he said.

Mummul – to mention. I listened but I didn't say a mummulin' word. I didn't want to get involved. Don't you go mummulin' my name.

Poke or poke salad – a wild herb delicacy, cooked in generous portions of fat or oil believed to prevent poisoning and served as the main vegetable dish. [Usually, it was parboiled and mixed with other greens, wild (lamb's quarter, sheep sorrel etc) or domestic (mustard, turnips, beet tops etc).] Because it was believed to be   poisonous in its natural state, poke was never eaten raw of served in raw salads.

Poke-easy – a slow person who lacks enthusiasm.

Pokin' round – Poking around - Wasting time. What are you pokin' around here for?

Pokin' round – being nosy. She's aw'way pokin' round in my bid'nes. She's always poking her nose in my business.

Pretty much – quite – It was pretty much worn out before I ever got my hands on it. It was pretty much, what tyew (you) might say, worthless.

Put tyeour (your) foot in the big road. Literally Go somewhere. The Big Road led to town and out of town.

Quare (adj) –as in square. Strange behaving. Ignores social manners, won't speak when you pass him on the road. May be translated as "queer," but has nothing to do with sex orientation.

Ridgerunner – a person from a rugged part of the mountains where the roads are so narrow they have space for only one foot at a time. One foot is on the road and the other foot is hanging off the cliff.

Right smart – a good bit/quite a bit – He's got a right smart of taters on that wagon.

This heah- 'heah – This one right here—the one I have in my hand or the one close by. You see this?

This'un heah – This'un heah al'lus helps me git dressed. This one here always helps me when I'm getting dressed. She's better about doing that than other children.

Whain'tye – Why aren't you. Whain'tye over there helping your sister?

Wha'tye – What are you…. Wha'tye going over there for?

Wha'tyewaon? - What do you want? (accepting)

Whatyu'waon? (annoyed) What do you want?

Whatyuwaon now? You're back again. What is it this time?

Nah whadda ye waon? Now what more do you want?

Which'un – Which one? Which'un do you want?

Whown'tye – Why don't you. Whown'tye go with the younger children, to help them carry the boxes? [More of a suggestion that a question.]

Where'dye - Pronounced Where'd-zhee. Where did you. Where'dye go. I bin looking all over for you.

Who'dye - Who did you. Who'dye see over there?

Which'un – Which one. Which'un do you want?
Which'uns – Which ones? Which'uns do you like?

Which'un's - Which one of them is.... Which'un's been botherin' you? (a person) Which one of them is/has been bothering you? (Or a part of your body) Which'un's botherin' you [the most?] Which one is bothering you the most—your right foot or your left?

Ye'ez. [ye=yeah, ez – eez. Yes, he's. Ye'ez helping Papa in the blacksmith shop.

Zat – Is that…? Zat all you gonna do? Zat all you know how to do. Just stand there and look dumb? Zat all of 'em? [Is that all of them?]

COMMON BELIEFS

I do not hold to any of these beliefs, nor do I recommend any of these practices. I include them only as commentary on the culture in which I grew up. Most of these superstitions were common among church members and non-members as well.

If a bird flies into the house accidentally, it's the sign of an impending death.

If a bird gets a few strands of your hair, you will have a headache.

Comment: At nesting time, birds might find strands of hair to secure the twigs of their nests. Consequently, women were careful about disposing of hair left in the comb or hairbrush. A woman of courting age was also careful to keep clippings of her hair out of reach of an undesirable suitor who might want to cast a spell on her.

To get rid of an annoying songbird or hoot owl, turn a shoe upside down.

If you drop the dishrag (dishcloth) accidentally, an unexpected visitor is coming.

If you find the hem of your dress turned upward, kiss it and you will get a new dress.

If you pass a sudden warm gust of air that whirls and picks up sand from the road, it's a ghost. Bless it.

Comment: I've long since forgotten what was to be said to the ghost or haint (haunt.)

If you want to catch a bird, just shake salt on its tail.

Comment: If a bird allows you to get close enough to shake salt on its tail, it is probably so badly injured it could not possibly fly away; so you should easily be able to catch it.

Determination to do something. I'll do that if I don't go blind and the creek don't go dry. Comment: The speaker believes he will be able to accomplish a particular task if his health doesn't change drastically and some highly unlikely event does not occur.

If a dog rolls over on its back, it's measuring somebody's grave.

Want to get your wish? After you have eaten the breast of a chicken, save the wishbone, make a wish and get someone to help you break the bone. If you get the larger part of the bone, you will get your wish.

Break a mirror and seven years of bad luck will follow.

Look at the molting of a locust. If the letter W appears on one of the wings, a period of war will follow; if a P appears, peace will follow (the war will end).

Shoot a snake with your pistol and you might as well get rid of it. You will never be able to hit anything else (a target) with that gun.

Comment: I once heard an expert mountain marksman make this statement.

If you kill a snake, it won't actually die until the sun goes down.

At mealtime, if you happen to get two forks, it means you will have two husbands—will marry two different men in your lifetime.

If you want to get married, never allow anybody to sweep your feet with a broom.

Comment: May be a carry-over from the days of slavery when the enslaved couple publicly stepped over a broom handle as an announcement of their marriage. Was it a bad omen for the business end of the broom to touch the feet of either partner? I do not know.

[After the true emancipation or the surrender of the Confederate army in 1865, slave marriages were considered null and void. The couple wanting to continue in their marriage was then obligated to repeat their vows by civil law. If not, they were free to choose another partner in marriage, or could remain single. This fact is documented in the recorded history of my own family. My Payne/Mills great grandparents chose to remarry; their son George, freeborn of a Cherokee mother, first married to a slave woman, but chose a different wife after that marriage was dissolved.]

A man with muddy shoes won't find a wife.

To get rid of a troublesome visitor, mix salt with black pepper together and sprinkle the mixture on the tracks of your guest to prevent their returning.

Comment: The truth is that any superstitious adult seeing a substance of any kind sprinkled about a walkway or doorstep would be suspicious of the intended purpose and might decide to keep away from that house anyway.

APPENDIX B: FOOT NOTES

1. Black Mountain News, April 23, 2018: "'Catching Babies':
Midwife Mary Stepp Burnette Hayden". Swannanoa Valley Museum & History Center. Submitted by Anne Chesky Smith

2. Slaves of two different plantations, Coleman Stepp and Rosanna Burnette attend and join the predominately White Tabernacle United Methodist church. in 1849 (*A History of Black Mountain*, 1992, Parris, Joyce Justus) Coleman Stepp reportedly died in 1850, and was buried in a cemetery at his church.

Rosanna Burnette (mother of Squire Jones Burnette) was freed in 1865, died decades later, and was laid to rest in the Oak Grove Cemetery at Old Thomas Chapel AME Zion Church. Black Mountain News. April 4, 2019: Article featuring Coleman Stepp's Gravestone Dedication at the Tabernacle United Methodist Church Cemetary -- Fred McCormick, Staff Reporter & Robert Goodson, Church Member.

3. In 1908, my maternal grandfather cautiously reveals Information that could have been given to him only by his Cherokee mother who died in 1892. Unfortunately, his failure to reveal his great grandfather's Native American name and to identify his mother's tribe, as well as their lack of physical connection to the Cherokee community, results in a rejection of his application for benefits. His Deposition is in the front matter of this book.

[1] See Appendix B

[2]

[3]

Printed in Great Britain
by Amazon